Languages of Economic Crises

This book offers a critical engagement with languages that describe, perpetuate, respond to, and resist economic crises. Unlike many volumes on economic crises that offer economistic explanations of their causes or policy suggestions for their resolution, this collection explores the different types of language used to deal with complex economic phenomena. The chapters in this volume examine a range of connections between language and crises: from the metaphors used historically to describe economic crises, to the languages deployed within periods of crises and economic struggle, to the popular responses thereto (including political manifestations and worker-organized enterprises). Also considered are the implications for democratic participation and gender relations, and the lack of language to express economic experience amongst certain groups.

With essays from seven contributors representing five different countries, this collection has global relevance in a time marked by economic volatility and upheaval, and will serve as a valuable resource for those interested in the politics of language, economic discourse, and the epistemological complexities of economic crises.

The chapters in this book were originally published as a special issue of the *Journal of Cultural Economy.*

Sonya Marie Scott teaches in the Department of Social Science at York University, Canada. Her research focuses on economic subjectivity, epistemology, language and economic crises, and the history of economic thought. She is the author of *Architectures of Economic Subjectivity: The Philosophical Foundations of the Subject in the History of Economic Thought* (2013).

Languages of Economic Crises

Edited by
Sonya Marie Scott

Routledge
Taylor & Francis Group
LONDON AND NEW YORK

First published 2022
by Routledge
2 Park Square, Milton Park, Abingdon, Oxon OX14 4RN

and by Routledge
605 Third Avenue, New York, NY 10158

Routledge is an imprint of the Taylor & Francis Group, an informa business

British Library Cataloguing in Publication Data
A catalogue record for this book is available from the British Library

ISBN: 978-1-032-02470-7 (hbk)
ISBN: 978-1-032-02471-4 (pbk)
ISBN: 978-1-003-18348-8 (ebk)

DOI: 10.4324/9781003183488

Typeset in Minion Pro
by Newgen Publishing UK

Publisher's Note
The publisher accepts responsibility for any inconsistencies that may have arisen during the conversion of this book from journal articles to book chapters, namely the inclusion of journal terminology.

Contents

Citation Information vi
Notes on Contributors viii
Foreword: language and crisis in the time of the pandemic ix

Introduction: languages of economic crises – narrating, resisting, speaking otherwise 1
Sonya Marie Scott

1 The metaphors of crises 9
Daniele Besomi

2 Vultures, debt and desire: the vulture metaphor and Argentina's sovereign debt crisis 30
Sonya Marie Scott

3 Confronting Spain's crises: from the language of the plazas to the rise of *Podemos* 49
Jose Luis Carretero Miramar and Christopher Bradd

4 Recuperating and (re)learning the language of *autogestión* in Argentina's *empresas recuperadas* worker cooperatives 69
Marcelo Vieta

5 Making sense of precarity: talking about economic insecurity with millennials in Canada 91
Nancy Worth

6 Language, gender and crisis: an interview with Katherine Gibson 98
Katherine Gibson and Sonya Marie Scott

Index 111

Citation Information

The following chapters were originally published in the *Journal of Cultural Economy*, volume 12, issue 5 (2019). When citing this material, please use the original page numbering for each article, as follows:

Introduction
Languages of economic crises: narrating, resisting, speaking otherwise
Sonya Marie Scott
Journal of Cultural Economy, volume 12, issue 5 (2019), pp. 353–360

Chapter 1
The metaphors of crises
Daniele Besomi
Journal of Cultural Economy, volume 12, issue 5 (2019), pp. 361–381

Chapter 2
Vultures, debt and desire: the vulture metaphor and Argentina's sovereign debt crisis
Sonya Marie Scott
Journal of Cultural Economy, volume 12, issue 5 (2019), pp. 382–400

Chapter 3
Confronting Spain's crises: from the language of the plazas to the rise of Podemos
Jose Luis Carretero Miramar and Christopher Bradd
Journal of Cultural Economy, volume 12, issue 5 (2019), pp. 423–440

Chapter 4
Recuperating and (re)learning the language of autogestión *in Argentina's* empresas recuperadas *worker cooperatives*
Marcelo Vieta
Journal of Cultural Economy, volume 12, issue 5 (2019), pp. 401–422

Chapter 5
Making sense of precarity: talking about economic insecurity with millennials in Canada
Nancy Worth
Journal of Cultural Economy, volume 12, issue 5 (2019), pp. 441–447

Chapter 6

Language, gender and crisis: An interview with Katherine Gibson
Katherine Gibson and Sonya Marie Scott
Journal of Cultural Economy, volume 12, issue 5 (2019), pp. 448–460

Notes on Contributors

Daniele Besomi, Walras-Pareto Centre for the History of Economic and Political Thought, University of Lausanne, Lausanne, Switzerland.

Christopher Bradd, Social and Political Thought, York University, Toronto, Canada.

Jose Luis Carretero Miramar, Escuela Superior de Hostelería y Turismo, Madrid, Spain.

Katherine Gibson, Institute for Culture and Society, Western Sydney University, Penrith, NSW, Australia.

Sonya Marie Scott, Social Science, York University, Toronto, Canada.

Marcelo Vieta, Program in Adult Education and Community Development, Ontario Institute for Studies in Education of the University of Toronto, Toronto, Ontario, Canada.

Nancy Worth, Department of Geography & Environmental Management, University of Waterloo, Waterloo, Canada.

Foreword: language and crisis in the time of the pandemic

As the essays featured in this collection were being finalized in late-2019, we could not have imagined the condition of the world but a year later; a state of affairs which has carried on relentlessly through 2021. Indeed, the global pandemic has now had a resounding impact on all levels in the scale of human relation – from the molecular to the geopolitical. The pandemic might appear to have overshadowed many of our prior concerns, and given rise to a new language and discourse for engaging with economic and social phenomena. Yet most of what we are currently contending with during this pandemic is part of a continuum of economic and social problems that are neither new nor unexpected. The crises explored in this collection are still crises that we face today, even if they have been accelerated or exacerbated by Covid-19.

The pandemic serves as the ground for our foreword not merely because it is what is happening as we write, but also because it illuminates the cracks in the social and economic system already in place. The legacy of neoliberalism and the politics and policies of austerity (including the erosion of social safety nets and public health systems) has had a considerable impact on a great deal of the planet whether in the Global South or North. Combined with exceptional levels of inequality, monolithic alliances of corporate control, and a shift in media, technology and politics, the current moment is both a time of reckoning and a time of great potential.

What has the pandemic revealed about language and crisis? Metaphors have served to bridge gaps in the understanding of why economic crises manifest, what they entail, and what they mean. And now the epistemological struggle to understand crises includes the epidemiological. Historically, as Daniele Besomi shows in this volume, metaphors for crisis have often been meteorological (storms, tornadoes), related to natural disasters (avalanches, earthquakes), to the sea (waves, tsunamis, floods), to mechanics or engineering (pendulum swings, unstable foundations, collapse), or to medical conditions and diagnoses (disease, contagion, fever, cancer, epidemic, viruses). The last set of examples is of particular interest today, as the medical metaphors used to describe financial and other economic crises run up against the epidemiological lexicon that describes the spread of Covid-19 and diffusion of vaccines. Medical language within economic discourse is no longer simply metaphorical, and people who are not experts all over the world have taken a keen interest in the transmissibility of variants, R values, and the credibility of public health measures. Just as economic crises provoke semantic shifts and new terminology with which to understand what are often considered to be highly technical economic problems, the Covid-19 pandemic has likewise created a whole new vocabulary for the general public. Yet we continue to run up against the same problems in the deployment and adoption of this new lexicon – the tensions between expert knowledge and popular knowledge, the politicization of analysis, and the economic imperatives behind public policy set out in response to crisis.

Consider Robert Brenner's commentary on the US's Coronavirus Aid, Relief and Economic Security Act (CARES) of April 2020 which saw an unprecedented transfer of wealth from the public purse to non-financial corporate giants.

> The CARES Act spelled out an elaborate set of formal conditions concerning who qualified for Fed–Treasury largesse and what they could and could not do with the advances they received. But the Act also left the door wide open for Treasury Secretary Steven Mnuchin, who was initially in charge of administering the law, to ignore those conditions over time, thanks to its ambiguity of language, inconsistencies, loopholes and qualifications. In any case, the Fed's assumption of authority over the bailout had the result of limiting if not ending debate over the question, putting the rules to be adopted and how they would be applied effectively out of Congress's reach. (Brenner, 2020)

And now consider the ambiguity in so much of the public health messaging, the 'inconsistencies, loopholes, and qualifications' in messaging from the governments of many liberal market economies of the Global North, and the limited opportunities for public debate over measures designed to control the spread of Covid-19. Where we sit and write now, for example, in Ontario Canada, the term 'lockdown' has continued to drift in meaning. Far from the lockdown of March 2020, during which only essential businesses such as grocery stores and pharmacies remained open, and residents were instructed to self-isolate as much as possible, the lockdown of early April 2021 includes a myriad of activities that were unthinkable a year ago (e.g., shopping in non-essential retail stores, hundreds of thousands of workers continuing to work in industrial and supply chain settings prone to outbreak, no provincial provisions for paid sick leave, and open primary and secondary schools). The motivation for the shift in the meaning of the term lockdown, which one could argue has already become quite hollow, is clearly economic and has little or nothing to do with public health, except perhaps to instil a feeling amongst the population that this third 'wave' of the pandemic is indeed serious. The recent provincial budget entitled *Ontario's Action Plan: Protecting People's Health and Our Economy* (2021) places health before economy in title alone. While acknowledging that 'you can't have a healthy economy without healthy people,' the budget nonetheless continues to perpetuate the idea that public health and the economy exist in tension, encouraging the discourse of economic trade-offs that ultimately prioritizes economic aims – overwhelmingly catering to the conditions necessary for the profit rates of big business – after making limited concessions to social pressures.

Public health discourse varies widely between nation states and even between regions within states, and public attitudes towards the virus, protective measures, and the viability of vaccines differ dramatically as well. In the midst of what some believe to be the fracturing of a shared social reality, there is geopolitical fracturing as well. Many of the metaphors historically used to address viruses and pandemics are etiological, and Covid-19 is no different. Sometimes this refers to the animal from which the virus is believed to originate – bird flu and swine flu are perhaps the most common examples – and sometimes it is geographical. While the Spanish flu is our historical point of comparison, many have tried to peg Covid-19 on the government of China. Former US President Donald Trump perhaps most famously repeated the term 'China virus' (with the occasional 'Wuhan virus') in order to stir up antipathy towards China and bolster his efforts to continue to invoke a trade war between the two nations (Viala-Gaudefroy and Lindaman, 2020).

One could argue that the deployment of the expression 'China virus' was a form of 'performance of position' whereby the virus became part of a politicized and moralized struggle between the United

States and China. This xenophobic strategy had a dramatic effect on the US populace, serving several functions that, while not ideologically coherent, nonetheless fuelled a great deal of contempt for epidemiological science and public health strategies more generally. On the one hand the term renders the virus political instead of medical – a sort of weapon deployed by a strategic enemy. On the other hand, in many nations the association of the virus with communism effectively served to amplify the anti-mask and anti-vaccine arguments espoused by right libertarians. As the pandemic wears on, people of Asian descent in North America and parts of Europe face increasing levels of racial prejudice, often violent. These incidents have reached such a pitch that recently Secretary General of the United Nations António Guterres has expressed his profound concern over violence against Asians and those of Asian descent during the pandemic (United Nations News, 2021).

While conjecture regarding the origin of the virus serves an obvious political function, a form of blame to be directed at others, assigning fault for the spread of the virus is also a common political tactic. The generational dynamics of Covid-19 discourse are complex, but absolutely crucial to understanding the nature of our current crises and the paths forward. Generational experiences indeed vary dramatically in the pandemic. The elderly, in both the Global North and South, are disproportionately likely to die from the disease (O'Driscoll et al., 2021), a fact that has been exacerbated in settings that employ privately owned long-term care homes for the elderly, or in countries with overburdened health care systems. This fact has driven attitudes of extreme social caution in public health policy ('We enact these measures to protect our vulnerable') as well as individualistic self-interest ('Those who are vulnerable can stay home but the rest of us will just keep living our lives'). The individualistic sentiment is echoed by many governments who seek to blame the spread of the virus on 'irresponsible youth' who gather and have parties without concern for their elders or society at large. But this discourse largely serves to deflect responsibility away from public officials as they continue to prioritize the economic needs of corporate capital and supply chains in the face of a public health crisis. These economic needs, of course, require legions of workers to continue to work on the front lines, in close conditions, at greatest risk of contracting and spreading the virus. In North America the fetishization of individual responsibility, dressed up in accusatory language aimed at 'Millennials' or 'Gen Z,' serves to disguise the social policy that puts these millennials and Gen Zers on the front lines of gig economy work and low paid, yet so-called 'essential,' jobs. Those watching government speeches can continue to shake their heads at 'some people' while ignoring the primacy of the economic imperatives at hand.

This leads us to ask: how has the pandemic shaped economic language in terms of power, in terms of resistance? Within this collection one place to start might be with J.K. Gibson-Graham's conception of *capitalocentrism*. The capitalocentrist understanding of the Economy – and along with it the present-day need to 'reopen the Economy' – pits macroeconomic policy against the lives and bodies of citizens. By now it is plain to see that bodies are sacrificed along class, gender, and racial lines. Care work and front-line health care workers are disproportionately women in almost every region of the world (Addati et al., 2018). Those who belong to the working class, featuring a disproportionate amount of racialized women, do the vast majority of the labour required for 'essential services.' This includes labour in grocery stores and pharmacies, labour along all the points in the global supply chain, migrant agricultural labour, and a disproportionate amount of social reproductive labour in the home (Dunaway 2014; Chang 2016; Selwyn, 2019). Race has become a predictor of increased risk of Covid-19 infection because of the aforementioned conditions of 'racialized capitalism' (Pirtle, 2020). Those who are able to work safely from home and avoid the daily risks of contagion nonetheless continue to have the geopolitical delivered to their doors through Amazon packages or online grocery services, all at the hands of the precarious yet essential workers.

All of this leads us back to the question of whether this Economy was ever 'open' to begin with? Whether this capitalocentric vision wasn't always closed to those that today continue to put themselves up against the pandemic out of necessity? Indeed, the all-pervasive language of 'opening the Economy' renders the concept of the Economy more reified and centred than ever. The short-sightedness of lifting public health restrictions when community infection rates are not sufficiently low to ensure adequate control over the spread of the disease reveals the conceptual poverty of the discursive cipher of the Economy. It also reveals the way in which the *temporality of surplus generation* is often frantic, compulsively pushing forward even at the expense of long-term sustainability and the well-being of human communities. While such observations were frequently and easily made pre-pandemic, the primacy of surplus over health has become intensified by the increasing consolidation of corporate capital. In much of the Global North the Economy has been 'stimulated' in such a way as to create, what Grace Blakeley (2020) calls, a 'state capitalist monopoly.'

> The present combination of state-provided liquidity and full-on bailouts mirrors the extraordinary interventions undertaken by states in the Global North to save their finance sectors in 2008 – only this time, the money is being directed towards the entire corporate sector. Moral hazard is a genuine issue – irresponsible lenders and uncreditworthy businesses are being protected by the state – but no one is seriously suggesting that the global economy be allowed to implode. States and central banks are now being forced to engage in the active planning of their entire economies under the imperial coordination of the Federal Reserve. Except that the planning that is taking place is neither democratic nor rational. (p. 31)

Such a response to the pandemic has only led to the further concentration of Big Tech and platform firms (Fernandez et al., 2020), increased the wealth of the corresponding billionaires in heretofore unimaginable ways (Beer, 2021), boosted the profits of already dominant corporations even outside of the tech industry (MacMillan, Whorisky, and O'Connell 2020), and made the possibility of a post-pandemic future a dangerous time for those on the front lines of an impending economic recession.

Who will bear the weight of the new language of crisis? Who will it be directed at and who will it subjugate? Who will bear the burden of austerity once bailouts for corporations and rising debt levels appear to become unacceptable to those planning the economy – those 'central bankers, senior politicians and their advisors in big business and finance'? (Blakeley, p. 35). Some have already attempted to answer these questions in response to the Global Financial Crisis of 2008 (Karamessini and Rubery, 2014), and their work resoundingly points to those whose lives and bodies are already on the line within the essential work of the pandemic economy.

We have already caught glimpses of the 'vulture' strategies of large pharmaceutical corporations developing and distributing Covid-19 vaccines. There is much to be explored in the coming months and years regarding the geopolitical dynamics of the control over the flow of vaccines-as-commodities, and regarding intellectual property rights for life-saving medicines. Recently Pfizer engaged in explicitly vulture-like behaviour when negotiating vaccine contracts with Latin American countries. They demanded, as part of their contracts, that states use sovereign assets in order to protect against liability. 'Latin American countries were asked to put up federal bank reserves, embassy buildings or military bases as a guarantee against the cost of future legal cases stemming from unlikely adverse effects. Under this arrangement, the government rather than the company would shoulder those legal costs' (Al Jazeera, March 2021). Just as vulture funds have frequently attempted to embargo the assets of sovereign nations in litigation strategies used against highly indebted and impoverished nations, large pharmaceutical companies are leveraging their relative power and financial might with predatory conditions upon nations of the Global South. There are also other reported problems with vaccine pricing and accessibility within this geopolitical dynamic. In South Africa, for example, the cost of acquiring vaccines from Oxford's AstraZeneca is more than twice as high as it is in the United Kingdom (*The Guardian*, 2021). The result thus far has been the dissemination of the Russian Sputnik and Chinese Sinovac vaccines throughout the Global South, with limited doses of the European and North American vaccines in play. At this point, the Moderna vaccine, for example, appears to be completely off limits to poor nations. 'Moderna's record stands out because none of its doses are yet earmarked for what the World Bank classifies as low-income nations' (Rauhala, 2021). This is part of what is surely to become an increasingly disturbing pattern of growing inequality between regions that already bear tremendous levels of inequality from centuries of colonial and imperial relations (Bhutto, 2021).

All of these troubling developments and worsening crises are also cause for some degree of hope. Many activists, scholars, and leaders have espoused the idea that this crisis is a different kind of opportunity, and that the 'normal' to which many seek to return was never normal, never a desirable, healthy, or equitable state of affairs. And yet the idea that the pandemic is near an end is far from certain, especially as the Global South finds itself woefully lacking in vaccines and monetary supports. The uncertainties and great length of the pandemic will have an effect on responses to the crises which have been exacerbated by Covid-19, and there is likely a long time ahead before we understand how these dynamics will play out (Watkins, 2020). In the interim, a study of media narratives about responses to the Covid-19 bailout provisions suggests that distributive justice, environmental justice, and anti-capitalist narratives are the most prominent in the Western media (Giuliani, 2020). Of these three, the distributive justice approach appears to be the most widely referenced and supported, leading to the conclusion that, at least in the first trimester of the pandemic, Piketty-style tax reform was gaining popularity amongst those critical of the growing trend towards state capitalist monopoly. Others have suggested that a sort of Green New Deal might be the right combination of economic stimulus and environmental policy to help slow the many crises and catastrophes that have already begun to unfold, or that lie still in wait. The demands of environmental economics, along with those of more explicitly anti-capitalist movements, began well before the pandemic and may yet be mobilized by ever greater necessity and increasing levels of public awareness.

And yet the common sense and mainstream economic discourses that have brought us to this point in history tend to instruct that 'realism' and 'sobriety' are required after periods of social spending and bailout. Blakeley captures this commonplace sentiment of pessimism about the economic future:

> To assume that after a period of largesse – a spending spree, a heavy drinking session – comes a period of atonement – a payback, a hangover – is embedded deep within our common sense understanding of the world. These assumptions are strengthened by the lived experience of modern capitalism. (p. 69)

At what point do these lived economic conditions under the pandemic render the contradictions, inequalities, and injustices too much to bear? Will we see more groundswells of popular uprising, as we did in Spain with the 15M movement, where the brutality of crises is cause for the re-imagination not only of the future but of the narratives of the past? The summer and fall of 2020 offered us a few glimpses – the massive anti-Black racism protests across the United States and the world began challenging not only police brutality but the long legacy of exploitation throughout the world. The Indian farmer's protests which began in late summer of 2020 against corporate-friendly farm laws have been some of the largest that the world has ever seen, levying the massive power of small-scale farmers against state–corporate favouritism. The pandemic has not stopped vital movements for systemic justice, and as inequalities become exacerbated there is reason to believe that global solidarity movements will continue to mobilize and strengthen alliances.

So much of the pandemic eludes visibility. From the potentially deadly microscopic particles of one's own breath, to the package that arrives on a doorstep seemingly out of nowhere, the many and varied scales of human relation all but disappear within languages of economic interest. Does the development of critical language in response to this situation not call for a renewed attention to the many and varied scales of human relation? In the microscopic manipulations of RNA sequences, in the delivery of vaccines and commodities from laboratories, factories, and farms across oceans and continents in a global supply chain – on all of these levels, the material and economic relations of language continue to unfold. They can be seen in the scientific work of virologists and immunologists, in the advice of epidemiologists and public health experts, the plans of economists and politicians, even the responses of popular movements. The discourse of economic trade-offs that has been in play for decades now with respect to environmental policy and climate change, has come to inform the new promise of 'reopening' the Economy. While the pandemic is far from over, and while many have and will continue to suffer the disproportionate burden of this latest of human crises, our current moment nonetheless presents us with an opportunity. Indeed, the crises arising out of the pandemic will leave no option but for a deep and widespread questioning of the discursive power of economists and politicians, together with their capacity for dictating public health policy and the parameters of public opinion.

Christopher Bradd and Sonya Marie Scott
Toronto, April 1st 2021

Works Cited

Addati, Laura et al. 2018. *Care work and care jobs for the future of decent work*. International Labour Organization (ILO) Report. 28 June.

Beer, Tommy. 2021. Report: American Billionaires Have Added More than $1 Trillion In Wealth During Pandemic. *Forbes*, 26 Jan. Available from: www.forbes.com/sites/tommybeer/2021/01/26/report-american-billionaires-have-added-more-than-1-trillion-in-wealth-during-pandemic/?sh=7079db332564.

Bhutto, Fatima. 2021. The world's richest countries are hoarding vaccines. This is morally indefensible. *The Guardian*, 17 Mar. Available from: www.theguardian.com/commentisfree/2021/mar/17/rich-countries-hoarding-vaccines-us-eu-africa.

Blakeley, Grace. 2020. *The Corona Crash*. New York: Verso.

Chang, Grace. 2016. *Disposable Domestics: Immigrant Women Workers in the Global Economy*. Chicago: Haymarket.

Dunaway, Wilma (Ed.). 2014. *Gendered Commodity Chains: Seeing Women's Work and Households in Global Production*. Stanford: Stanford University Press.

Fernandez et al. 2020. *Engineering Digital Monopolies: The Financialisation of Big Tech*. Amsterdam: SOMO (Center for Research on Multinational Corporations).

Giuliani, Elisa. 2020. Piketty, Thunberg, or Marx? Shifting ideologies in the COVID-19 bailout conditionality debate. *Journal of International Business Policy*, 3, 443–450.

Government of Ontario. 2021. *2021 Ontario Budget — Ontario's Action Plan: Protecting People's Health and Our Economy*. Available from: https://budget.ontario.ca/2021/contents.html.

Al Jazeera. 2021. Investigation: Drugmaker 'bullied' Latin American nations. *Aljazeera*. 11 March. Available from: www.aljazeera.com/news/2021/3/11/investigation-pfizer-bullied-latin-american-nations.

Karamessini, Maria and Jill Rubery (Eds.). 2014. *Women and Austerity: The Economic Crisis and the Future for Gender Equality*. New York: Routledge.

MacMillan, Douglas, Peter Whorisky, and Johnathan O'Connell. 2020. America's biggest companies are flourishing during the pandemic and putting thousands of people out of work. *The Washington Post*, 16 Dec. Available from: www.washingtonpost.com/graphics/2020/business/50-biggest-companies-coronavirus-layoffs/

O'Driscoll et al. 2021. Age-specific mortality and immunity patterns of SARS-CoV-2. *Nature* 590, 140–145.

Pirtle, Whitney. 2020. Racial capitalism: A fundamental cause of novel coronavirus (COVID-19) pandemic inequalities in the United States. *Health Education and Behavior*, 47 (4), 504–508.

Rauhala, Emily. 2021. Moderna agreed to 'equitable access' for its coronavirus vaccine, but most of its doses are going to wealthy countries. *The Washington Post*, 13 Feb. Available from: www.washingtonpost.com/world/coronavirus-vaccine-access-poor-countries-moderna/2021/02/12/0586e532-6712-11eb-bf81-c618c88ed605_story.html.

Selwyn, Benjamin. 2019. Poverty chains and global capitalism. *Competition & Change*, 23 (1), 71–97.

United Nations News. 2021. UN chief 'profoundly concerned' over the rise in violence against Asians. 22 Mar. Available from: https://news.un.org/en/story/2021/03/1088002.

Viala-Gaudefroy, Jéroôme and Dana Lindaman. 2020. Donald Trump: les maux et les mots du virus. *The Conversation*, 20 Apr. Available from: https://theconversation.com/donald-trump-les-maux-et-les-mots-du-virus-136530.

Watkins, Susan. 2020. Politics and Pandemics. *New Left Review*, 125, Sept/Oct. Available from: https://newleftreview.org/issues/ii125/articles/susan-watkins-politics-and-pandemics.

INTRODUCTION

Languages of economic crises: narrating, resisting, speaking otherwise

Sonya Marie Scott

Languages of economic crises

There are hundreds of books written specifically about the 2007–2008 Global Financial Crisis. Thousands of articles and op-eds. And even today frequent references are made to the GFC in financial papers as the Federal Reserve seeks to extend the run of the longest bull market in US history. When will the next crisis come? What are its signs and codes? Crisis is now inherent to the mainstream understanding of the economic order, but its nature is often as obscure as it is ubiquitous. In his 2012 essay 'Naming crises: a note on semantics and chronology,' Daniele Besomi cites Ann Fabian's (1989) comment that 'panics produce texts' and explains that

> it has frequently been observed that output of writings on cycles is itself cyclical: economic distress naturally induces professional economists, but also (especially in the nineteenth century, when the profession did not count many practitioners) laypeople, to investigate the causes of the phenomenon and to suggest remedies. (p. 55)

There is no doubt that this nineteenth-century tendency continues. And yet, despite the vast literature on crises, economic analysis, and popular interpretation are still shrouded in a certain veil of mystery – both in terms of the capacity to understand precisely why crises occur and to predict when they will reoccur. This discursive and epistemological uncertainty opens up an important space within which an investigation of language may be particularly fruitful. In this special issue, we do not seek to determine the validity of economistic or technical explanations of crises. Instead, we examine various economic crises and the language(s) they produce. We explore the ways in which various subjects narrate crises, use metaphors to describe crises, arm a language of response and resistance to the perceived causes of crises, and develop languages of rebirth and new dreams of other possible futures. In some instances, this is language that in moments of rupture might sneak through the cracks of what otherwise appears to be a monolithic economic order.

The correlation between language, consciousness, and experience has formed an important dimension of economic history in the era of capitalism. The complexity of contemporary economic crises (such as the GFC) often obscures the ideological component of economic thought, favoring instead technical accounts of financial markets, debt structures, and austerity programs. The need for an account of the logics of debt, austerity, and crisis is a pressing issue as many are attempting to formulate and reformulate languages of resistance and change. Capitalism has borne repeated crises since its emergence in the late eighteenth century, and correspondingly, as various subjects (scholars, journalists, and the interested public) have made efforts to discern the nature of capitalism and its attendant crises, language has been developed and deployed for the task. The epistemological functions of the nascent lexicons of each era have been both descriptive and formative. The connection between language and economic crises is not easily understood as people are often working with language not of their own making. Language often stems from other historical moments or from other classes and interests. 'Sub-prime,' 'bailout,' 'default,' and 'austerity,' however, are distinct neologisms of our particular age. But where do these terms come from? And who might they serve? Marx and Engels have asserted that 'language is as old as consciousness' in order to stress the inextricable relationship between experience and consciousness. With crises, especially as they increase in complexity and extend in global proliferation, we can shift the emphasis and instead suggest that consciousness can only be as new as the language with which it operates.

In 1839, French historian Agustin Thierry argued that we do not have a language to adequately narrate political and economic developments as they occur:

> As new interests are born, they are forced to explain themselves in the idiom of those who have disappeared, and as such they are poorly understood; current relations are disfigured beneath the expression of destroyed relations, and they trick the eye, or even escape it. (p. 305, my translation)

And yet over the last decade, we have seen the explicit development of a new popular lexicon of economic crisis – including a new language of debt and austerity. How do varying interests deploy, absorb, and operate within these new discursive registers? And how are they limited by the inadequacies of past expressions, past conceptualization of the economic problem?

In 1973, French theorist Jean Pierre Faye wrote *La Critique du Langage et son Économie*. In this work, Faye engages in a critique of what he calls 'narrative economy,' which, he argues, 'necessarily includes a sociology of language and a semantics of history as constitutive disciplines' (1976, p. 69). The sociology of language is an empirical science which examines the connection between language and class, especially in utterances of class struggle and war. In contrast, the semantics of history is a theoretical orientation which 'should determine the relations between the levels connecting the production of meaning with the "ideological syntax," with the political prosody, of discourses' (Faye 1976, p. 69). Responding to May 1968, and deeply entrenched within the debates of the French philosophical left of the 1970s, Faye is ultimately concerned with narrating the dialectics of economic relations, or in reference to Lenin against Althusser, 'what is *true* in happenings' (p. 71).

Today, after the first major global crisis of the twenty-first century, we are no longer embedded in the same circumstances or debates, and the revolutionary urgency of post 1968 France seems historically distant. But the urgency of the recurrent crises of the twenty-first century demands a narration of the economic both in empirical and theoretical registers. Rather than proffering accounts and analyses of the 2007–2008 GFC as a US-centered financial event, this issue instead approaches *crises* as a broader and ongoing global phenomenon, one which reveals equilibrium and stability to be, if not entirely fictional manifestations of mainstream economic thought, at least epiphenomenal in nature. With papers stemming from an international colloquium entitled *Languages of Economic Crises*, hosted in March 2016 at York University (Toronto, Canada), this issue takes an interdisciplinary approach to the way in which language narrates, constitutes, and resists crisis in its many manifestations. For just as 'crisis' expresses more than market crashes and panic in the financial core, language itself extends beyond the growing lexicon of terms used to explain or categorize the financial technicalities and social consequences of crisis.

This issue opens up to explore languages of debt, languages of austerity, and languages of popular resistance. Language gives an account of crisis and narrates possible futures, both austere and otherwise. Yet many feel disenfranchised from economic debate because they are excluded by the technical language of economics, a language which tends to employ high-level mathematics or the complex terminology of academic texts. Given these exclusionary functions of economic language, it is particularly pressing in periods of crisis that language be examined in its connection to current economic relationships and struggles.

While there has been extensive scholarship of the GFC, often inducing amongst academics what Bryan *et al.* (2012) termed 'crisis fatigue' and 'finance overload,' there is far less current scholarship on the relationship between language and economic crises. Certainly many have followed in the tradition of Norman Fairclough (1989, 2010), engaging in critical discourse analysis in order to explore the relationship between the structure of capitalism and language itself. And while there is indeed work on the history of economic crisis as a concept and its significance for economics (Kindleberger 2005, Lawson 2009, Besomi 2012, Shaikh 2016) or on the use of language as business rhetoric during times of crisis (Armenic *et al.* 2007, López and Llopis 2010, Tourish and Hargie 2012), this issue offers a contribution on language in the narration of crises from below and from above. It explores the question of language as response to crisis and, in necessary connection, explores the ways in which language sometimes serves to constitute crises. This includes the debate about causes, solutions, and broader socio-economic goals that so often become the topic of public debate in the wake of volatile economic moments. It also includes the voice of dissent and protest, so notable in recent popular and institutional movements against austerity and debt in Spain, Portugal, and Greece as a response to the Eurozone crisis, where we see the creation of new languages of resistance grounded in thinking the economy otherwise. The primary themes woven throughout this issue are the narration of crisis, resistance to crisis, and speaking otherwise.

Narrating crises

How do we *give an account* of what is so complex, so contested, so difficult to understand? The essays in this issue that address the question of narration all do so by explicitly grappling with the general social absence of an adequate language to deal with crisis; with the difficulties in finding language to describe systemic economic phenomena (Besomi); global economic relations (Scott); and lived economic experience (Worth). In the context of narrating crises, metaphors are a particularly rich topic of investigation, as they reveal the abstraction necessary to make sense of complicated happenings. Some view metaphors as 'deviant' forms of meaning, asserting that they break with the accepted and literal chain of signification. In this way metaphors may need 'to be explained in terms of "normal" or "literal" uses of language, and [...] their main function is to provide an alternative linguistic mechanism for expressing ideas' (Ortony 1993, p. 4). This conceptualization of metaphor can be especially powerful when exploring the varying responses to economic crises, and when encountering voices from below who are often competing with a dominant, official, and purportedly literal narrative about what both the economy and its crises signify.

In Daniele Besomi's essay 'The Metaphors of Crisis,' he shares his research on the use of crisis metaphors in the history of economic thought. The metaphors he addresses reveal the great breadth and scope of meaning that has been ascribed both to the economic crisis itself and to the economic system which underlies it. Besomi aims to explore metaphors not only as a point of interest in and of themselves, but as a way to uncover the ideological and methodological assumptions behind the conceptualization of the nature of the economic system in the first place. Besomi begins his research with the nineteenth century and explains that

> during most of the 1800s theories of crises were formulated by laypeople instead of professional economists, in natural language, with a conceptual apparatus often lacking precision. In these conditions, the usage of metaphors can reveal the underlying premises and interpretive framework on which specific theoretical approaches are built.

But for Besomi, in order to understand the use of metaphors that describe crisis, it does not suffice to simply classify the metaphors by type, as this alone does not reveal the complexity of their meaning. Instead, we must focus on 'how precisely the metaphor is used to transfer meaning to the object or phenomenon to which it refers.' For example, in the early part of the nineteenth century, the economic storm often represented a singular and accidental crisis, something not inherent to the economic system itself but an outside, unexpected, and destructive force. Later in the nineteenth century, and even into contemporary usage, the idea of the storm becomes more cyclical – a part of a recurrent set of crises that constitute the natural cycle of the system itself. In this way, crises might even be considered as necessary and normal corrections to the economic whole:

> In the early usage of this metaphor, the purifying of the atmosphere was seen as a silver lining, then it was realized that this was a systematic accompaniment of crises, later it was seen as a necessity (thereby giving crises a

positive role to fulfill), and eventually the storm was even seen as seeding and actively promoting the recovery process.

Thus metaphors like storms, 'the pendulum' and 'earthquakes' are all used to describe crises, both by laypeople who may be using the metaphors imprecisely or by contemporary economists who may use the metaphors in the thick of technical language. Within each group of metaphors, however, it is imperative that a careful 'analysis of metaphorical transfers can help in recognizing hidden assumptions or postulates.'

The construction of and engagement with social problems are also inherently issues of narration. For example, Schön (1993) emphasizes the dual process of 'naming and framing' that helps to set the field of inquiry for social theory:

> Each story constructs its view of social reality through a complementary process of naming and framing. Things are selected for attention and named in such a way as to fit the frame constructed for the situation. Together, the two processes construct a problem out of the vague and indeterminate reality which John Dewey (1938) called the problematic situation. They carry out the essential problem-setting functions. They select for attention a few salient features and relations from what would otherwise be an overwhelmingly complex reality. They give these elements a coherent organization, and they describe what is wrong with the present situation in such a way as to set the direction for its future transformation. (pp. 146–147)

Naming and framing were particularly relevant to Argentina's response to a debt crisis which began after its massive economic crisis of 2001, wherein foreign private equity firms who had purchased distressed Argentine bonds, were suing the nation for full value plus interest in US courts. While many from the global north and mainstream press described these hedge funds as 'bondholders' or 'investors,' the naming of the litigious investors as 'vulture funds' fundamentally changed the narrative about the nature of Argentine debt and global debt relations more generally, reframing the characterization of the relationship between sovereign nations and financial capital. In my essay 'Vultures, debt and desire: the vulture metaphor and Argentina's sovereign debt crisis,' I trace the history of the vulture metaphor from its roots in Elizabethan England where it references a power-laden debt-relationship in Shakespeare's *Venus and Adonis*, to contemporary finance where it references a speculative strategy of litigation. A long legal history of dispossession by litigation links the two periods, and vulture fund cases such as *Elliot Associates v. The Republic of Peru* (1998) make reference to instances of this predatory practice in the Elizabethan era.

The reframing inherent to the contemporary use of the vulture metaphor is part of a concerted political strategy to combat the speculative predation from investment funds in the global north. I argue that

> it is not merely a matter of rhetorical artifice to invoke the vulture image, but rather integral to the struggle against the vulture strategy in legal and economic arenas. With its use, contract and debt-relationships that in legal or economic framings appear to be neutral and grounded in rational institutions, are exposed as power relations filled with intention, opportunism and deceit.

What is often understood to be the impartiality of the terms of contract law, implying regular lender-debtor relationships, is revealed instead to be a morally charged power relation. The reframing of legal disputes with the provocative vulture metaphor is part of what I term a *performance of position* – 'the public presentation of certain legal and economic postulates which define the parameters of subjective identities and relations.' This performance seeks to alter the frame both of the legal charges and of the broader ethical debate about whether sovereign nations should be open to speculative suit by opportunistic investors. It also questions how global debt relationships operate, and how the seemingly neutral cover of contract law is in fact a construction of a very specific legal subjectivity, one which conforms very well to the modern corporation and investment capital.

Nancy Worth, in her commentary piece 'Making sense of precarity: talking about economic insecurity with millennials in Canada,' deals with generational perspectives on crisis and economic identity, focusing on the difficulties experienced by millennials (those born in the early 1980s until the mid-1990s) to articulate their own feelings of anxiety in the face of economic crisis. Worth explains that 'While there are many effective metrics for quantifying economic precarity, talking to young people about their experiences in the labour and housing markets reveals a gap in explanatory language around living in/through crisis.' More specifically, although Canadian millennials

> could *state the facts* about how hard it is to get a good job or afford decent housing, the experience of this pervasive *sense of insecurity* is much harder to put into words. For many, a generalized sense of precariousness invades everyday life, even when work and housing are relatively secure. Thinking through this sense of anxiety, that the future might not be any better than the present and that young people might not be as well off as their parents, leads to a generational understanding of economic crisis – and for a group of young adults who came of age during the downturn of 2008–9, considering why they can't talk about precarity is revealing. (Worth, p. 441–447)

Worth set out to explore the narratives that were available to the millennials that she interviewed. She found that the very unremarkability and normalcy of precarious work and living situations contributed to difficulties in describing crises. Narratives of flexibility – that flip side of precarity favored in the language of employers and those espousing the efficiencies of casualized and contract labor (Appay 2010) – were also part of an internalized identity that Worth describes as the 'millennial me.' Finally, the very realities of crises themselves make temporal considerations, such as talking about the future, difficult. Radical uncertainty, itself a consequence of the crises of capitalism, makes hedging or short term thinking more common for millennials. 'When you no longer think in long-term plans (or even hopes), precarity becomes hidden by just-in-time decision-making and an increasingly popular language about flexibility and responsiveness to change.' Indeed, as Chandler and Reid (2016) have argued, the narrative of individual *resilience* has become ubiquitous in social policy and planning, pedagogy, and even social theory. Resilience has become one of the most heralded subjective traits in our neoliberal era, urging us to be responsive to a world over whose economic disorder we have no control, and preparing us to survive no matter the catastrophes and crises headed in our direction. Narratives about the nature of what we are to be resilient against, or how this expectation of flexibility and resilience might shape our experience are, as Worth suggests, the more elusive (yet important) part of the story.

Resisting crises and speaking otherwise

In her book on *Langauge and neoliberalism* (2015), Marnie Holborow explores the tenuous relationship between neoliberal ideology and social consciousness.

> Despite the apparent weight and overwhelming diffusion of neoliberal ideology, social consciousness is never smooth and singular; it is fractured and contradictory. A verbal and ideological rupture is most evident in the emergence of new collectively articulated language of *trickle down economics*, or *the need for austerity*, deepening social deprivation and greater social inequality can give rise to alternative representations. One such representation was the verbal labeling of the '*the one percent*' for the top wealthy few who were profiting from this crisis, a designation which rapidly caught on around the world. It struck a blow against neoliberal common sense and became what one might call 'good sense.' (p. 6)

The crisis in the financial core was what sparked the linguistic rupture of 'the one percent.' And fascinatingly this happened on Wall Street, in the core, precisely where it was *not supposed to happen*. Where market liberalism and years of neoliberal reform were thought to have brought a stable prosperity, and where capital had concentrated to such an extent as to hide the deepening levels of consumer debt, the increased bubble in asset prices, and the gross inequality in income that had not been rivaled in the US since the period immediately preceding the Great Depression of the 1930s (Shaikh 2016). The failures of the neoliberal experiments in the peripheries, however, were felt even more intensively, and two essays in this issue bring us language of resistance that emerged as a direct result of devastating neoliberal crises in peripheral regions. The first, by Vieta, deals with Argentina after the failed neoliberal strategies of the 1990s and the default of 2001, while the second, by Carretero Miramar and Bradd, deals with Spain's economic crisis of 2010 at the subsequent crisis of political legitimacy that followed through mass social movements and new political parties.

In both cases, the intensity of the alienation produced by the crises was great due to their relative position in relation to the forces of global capital – in relation to the Global North for Argentina, and in relation to the Northern powers of the European Union for Spain. The vulnerability to poverty and social upheaval for great proportions of the population caused political disarray with mass protests in the hundreds of thousands filling central squares in Buenos Aires and Madrid. Both of these essays, however, focus on the generative function of crises, and deal with the creativity of workers and members of social movements, their new forms of language, and the development of collective dreams. The languages that resist the effects of crises so often aim to speak the present and future otherwise. This is not to put languages of resistance into a necessary state of dependence upon the occurrence of crises in the first place (neither a silver lining, nor a historical necessity), but rather to see crises as potential ruptures with the dominant logic of neoliberal global capital, opening up spaces for a new *sentido común* (common sense) and new collective action.

Marcelo Vieta's essay 'Recuperating and (re)learning the language of *autogestión* in Argentina's *empresas recuperadas* worker cooperatives' explores the radical potential of worker cooperatives to resist not only the crises of capitalism, but to resist 'capitalocentrism' itself. In many ways, the crisis of neoliberalism in Argentina, which came to a resounding head in December of 2001 with what was at the time the largest sovereign default in global history, is what sparked a great wave of resistance that characterizes ERTs (worker-recuperated enterprises). It has also inspired these same movements not to become beholden to what J.K. Gibson-Graham has described as 'capitalocentrism' – 'the idea that all economic activity is measured against the norm of capitalism or capitalist economic practice.' ERTs were born out of the organization of workers who reclaimed factories, workshops, and other places of employment that had formerly been organized through capitalist relations of production, but whose owners had gone bankrupt or abandoned them. Vieta explains that the shift in consciousness engendered within the ERT movement is both profound and complex,

> in the process of recuperating workplaces and converting them to worker cooperatives, ERT protagonists have been seized by a two-fold praxis of *rebellion* – in a subversive refusal of status-quo social relations of production – and *prefiguration* – in a foreshadowing of another way of organizing work and economic life beyond the dominative logics of existing property-based capitalist relations.

The rebellion and prefiguration of ERTs can be found in what Vieta terms the recuperation of productive life. This includes (1) the self-valorization of living labor; (2) cooperation in the labor process; and (3) the socialization of surpluses and wealth. All of these goals require a massive process of re-learning, that is, returning to ideals of a radical past in the Argentine and Latin American labor movement, and relearning the language of self-management (*autogestión*). Self-management ultimately implies a productive life without bosses and capitalist property relations, and it is learned in the very struggle to reclaim the factories and places of work.

Vieta describes an expansive and collaborative process of learning that emerges out of the ruins of crisis. He discusses the 'transformative nature of learning in social movements, in workplaces, and especially during moments of crisis where people must work together to overcome shared difficulties.' While ERTs are often modest endeavors (small or mid-sized operations) filled with ordinary working people, the language of *autogestión* – learned through practice and struggle – is a radical and powerful intervention in a post-crisis landscape where neoliberal forces seek to regain control of property and policy alike.

In 'Confronting Spain's Crises: From the Language of the Plazas to the Rise of *Podemos*,' Carretero Miramar and Bradd address the many activist and popular responses to the 2010 financial crisis in Spain. They argue that it was not only the crisis of European neoliberal austerity that had led to the discontent in Spain of 2011 – evidenced by a mass protest movement called 15-M, whose protagonists were aptly named '*los indignados*' (the indignant) – but rather a much broader crisis of political legitimacy which dated back to the transition from the Francoist dictatorship to democracy in the late 1970s. Of many of the public collective enunciations that emerged from the plazas during 15-M movement, the cry '*dormíamos, despertamos*' (we slept, we awoke), perhaps best encapsulates the resistance that took hold of a massive portion of the Spanish population in 2011. Carretero Miramar and Bradd argue that 'the financial crisis of 2010 ignited a retroactive re-signification of Spain's history, its understanding of democracy and its relationship to past authoritarianism.' The awakening that was expressed in the plazas sought a new political and economic landscape, no longer beholden to the bipartisan pact of the Transition from dictatorship to democracy, nor to the neoliberal adjustments which had been necessary to enter the European Union. Politics was up for grabs in Spain, and the so-called institutional assault led by *Podemos* ('We Can') – a political party that many have described as a movement-party emerging from the 15-M protests – represented an attempt to re-articulate Spanish political life outside of the left-right dichotomy and the corruption of the old order.

Carretero Miramar and Bradd trace out a dual set of crises in Spain by engaging with the work and words of activists – many of whom were responsible for the development of new forms of language capable of challenging both the economic and political corruptions of the Spanish state. Much of the language of 15-M activists can rightfully be termed the language of the plazas, as it was within the public squares in moments of mass protest that it was developed. 'By exploring the *language of the plazas* [...] within the context of Spain's economic and political crises, we attend also to subsequent legislative responses, including the rise of the *Podemos* party and the new municipalism of several major centers.' Ultimately, Carretero Miramar and Bradd argue that new and radical movement-parties such as *Podemos* run up against a genuine problem of language:

> The question of political legitimacy in Spain ultimately became a question of how to bring popular language from below (which we see in the collective enunciations of 15-M) to a language capable of engaging with institutions and the state. So the problem becomes: how to speak within an institution without becoming one? How does a movement-party resist speaking from above?

These complex issues of language are what make Spain's post-2010 experience a particularly rich and dynamic case study. It reveals the development of and challenges to new social movements in their concerted resistance to the neoliberal order.

Finally, in 'Language Gender and crisis: an interview with Katherine Gibson,' we discuss the possibility of speaking and thinking the economy otherwise. Otherwise often implies an 'outside' of the frame of crisis, even an outside to the frame of 'the economy' itself. Gibson goes beyond some of the challenges made to this notion of 'the economy' from *The End of Capitalism (As We Knew It)* (1996), and also addresses the seemingly all-encompassing nature of the financial economy. Indeed, in the first section of the interview we learn that,

> just as a feminist exploration of phallocentric narrative practices reveals the use of the masculine as the standard by which to measure all else, a linguistic analysis of capitalocentrism allows us to see the way in which the financial economy is posited as the 'real' economy, with alternatives and other formulations being conceptualized as subordinate. The analysis of economic crises, therefore, is particularly interesting, as it runs the risk of being recuperated by a capitalocentric analysis which shows that crisis is simply an aberration of the dominant, stable and organic economy. Thus the language of crisis – if it folds into one coherent crisis narrative – has the potential to de-mobilize those concerned with economic justice, or to feed into authoritarian reactions or the logic of austerity.

Gibson reveals that while crises might serve as a point of rupture where we might extricate ourselves from the totalizing language of economic explanation, a more pressing and likely danger is that crises instead consume us, instigating fear, allowing for abuse of power and incitement of right-wing populism or authoritarianism, and sparking the desire to return to normal, to recover, to recuperate the system at hand.

The second portion of the interview takes J.K. Gibson-Graham's language politics (1996, 2006) and situates it within the context of the 2013 text *Take Back the Economy*. Gibson explains that in their content and style that she and her coauthors moved from the critical stance most commonly associated with academic scholarship, and instead began to foster a 'reparative stance.' A reparative stance 'is more curious, more open, more exploratory.' In a popular text like *Take Back the Economy*, the idea was to write a book that not only everyone could read, but also that 'would reframe things like work and business and finance and property as something that you actually had a relationship with, but that this relationship could be brought back to something quite simple, like how do we actually survive well?' There are many theoretical and critical framings that may underlie much of the book's content, but these feminist and ecological underpinnings often go unmentioned. In part, this is because the language of the text would no longer be accessible as part of a pragmatic document, and in part, it was because, as Gibson explains, 'we wanted to create a new common sense.' Indeed, in all three of these contributions to the special issue that deal with speaking otherwise, there is a serious focus on reclaiming 'common sense.' In many ways, this represents one of the most radical potentialities of a language from below and one of the most hopeful ways to construct an economy otherwise.

Disclosure statement

No potential conflict of interest was reported by the author.

References

Appay, B., 2010. Precarization and flexibility in the labour process: a question of legitimacy and a major challenge for democracy. *In*: C. Thornley, S. Jeffrys, and B. Appay, eds. *Globalization and precarious forms of production and employment: challenges for workers and unions.* Cheltenham: Edward Elgar, 23–39.

Armenic, C., Craig, R., and Tourish, D., 2007. The transformational leader as *pedagogue, physician, architect, commander*, and *saint.* Five root metaphors in Jack Welch's letters to stockholders of general electric. *Human Relations*, 60 (12), 1839–1872.

Besomi, D., ed., 2012. *Crises and cycles in economic dictionaries and encyclopaedias.* New York: Routledge.

Bryan, D., *et al.*, 2012. An important failure: knowledge limits and the financial crisis. *Economy and Society*, 41 (3), 299–315.

Chandler, D. and Reid, J., 2016. *The neoliberal subject: resilience, adaptation and vulnerability.* London: Rowman & Littlefield International.

Fabian, A., 1989. Speculation on distress: the popular discourse of the panics of 1837 and 1857. *Yale Journal of Criticism*, 3, 127–142.

Fairclough, N., 1989. *Discourse and power.* New York: Longman.

Fairclough, N., 2010. *Critical discourse analysis: the critical study of language.* 2nd ed. New York: Routledge.

Faye, J.P., 1976. The critique of language and its economy. *Economy and Society*, 5 (1), 52–73.

Gibson-Graham, J.K., 1996. *End of capitalism (as we knew it).* New York: Wiley.

Gibson-Graham, J.K., 2006. *A postcapitalist politics.* Minneapolis: University of Minnesota Press.

Gibson-Graham, J.K., Cameron, J., and Healy, S., 2013. *Take back the economy.* Minneapolis: University of Minnesota Press.

Holborow, M., 2015. *Language and neoliberalism.* New York: Routledge.

Kindleberger, C., 2005. *Manias, panics and crashes: a history of financial crises.* New York: Palgrave Macmillan.

Lawson, T., 2009. The current economic crisis: its nature and the course of academic economics. *Cambridge Journal of Economics*, 33, 759–777.

Lopez, A. and Llopis, M., 2010. Metaphorical pattern analysis in financial texts: framing the crisis in positive or negative metaphorical terms. *Journal of Pragmatics*, 42, 3300–3313.

Ortony, A. 1993. Metaphor, language and thought. *In*: A. Ortony, ed. *Metaphor and thought*, 2nd ed. Cambridge: Cambridge University Press, 1–16.

Schön, D.A. 1993. Generative metaphor: a perspective on problem-setting in social policy. *In*: A. Ortony, ed. *Metaphor and thought*, 2nd ed. Cambridge: Cambridge University Press, 137–163.

Shaikh, A., 2016. *Capitalism: competition, conflict, crisis.* New York: Oxford University Press.

Thierry, A., 1839. *Lettres sur l'histoire du France, pour servir d'introduction a l'étude de cette histoire. Dix Ans D'Etudes Historiques.* 8th ed. Brussels: Bruxelles et Liége.

Tourish, D. and Hargie, O., 2012. Metaphors of failure and failure of metaphors: a critical study of root metaphors used by bankers in explaining the banking crisis. *Organization Studies*, 33 (8), 1045–1069.

The metaphors of crises

Daniele Besomi

ABSTRACT

Metaphors, analogies, and other figures of speech are ubiquitous, and far from being mere ornaments they have heuristic, illustrative, analytical, methodological, or epistemological roles in scientific discourse. The present paper offers the prolegomena to a metaphorology of economic crises and business cycles, from the perspective of an historian of economic thought.

The paper traces a general historical outline of the usage of metaphors applied to these phenomena, and offers a characterization of the metaphorical transfer of features from the source domain to the target domain. It shows, by referring to storm and pendulum metaphors, how the selective transfer to crises and cycles of some properties rather than others contributes to define different, even incompatible, interpretation of the role of these phenomena in the working of the economic system. The study of the actual usage of metaphors (as opposed to a cataloguing of source domains supposed to provide a unique view of the target) is therefore important to throw light the tacit presuppositions on which the understanding of crises is based.

In 1844, discussing *National distress: its causes and remedies*, Samuel Laing described 'the alternations of hot and cold fits of commercial depression and excitement, to which the country has been, for many years past, periodically subject' (Laing 1844, p. vi). He was not talking of simple accidental oscillations in the state of trade, but in using the terminology associated at the time with recurrent fevers (such as malaria), he stressed at once their gravity, violence, the approximate regularity in their reappearing, and their being constituent parts of the same phenomenon.

Similar characterizations of economic crises and their features by means of metaphors were quite common in the nineteenth century. It was in the early 1800s that crises first appeared in their modern form and triggered the early discussions on their nature. The usage of such figures of speech, however, is still common in the literature, both professional and (more frequently) addressed to the broader public. Far from being a mere textual embellishment, metaphors and other figures of speech have been long since recognized as important components of scientific discourse, where they are applied with different purposes – be it pedagogical (they convey meaning by explaining something new by means of something with which the reader is more familiar), heuristic (by understanding an object by means of a comparison with another, or the transference of a selected set of properties from an object to another), rhetorical (by persuading the reader by reference to a better established science), analytical (by modeling an object in terms of another), or epistemological (by transferring to one process the kind of explanations governing another one). To take up Hoffman's conveniently concise list, scientific metaphors have been shown to serve a remarkable variety of functions:

> (1) To suggest new hypotheses, hypothetical concepts, entities, relations, events, or observation terms,
> (2) To predict and describe new phenomena or cause-effect relations,
> (3) To give meaning to new theoretical concepts for unobservable or unobserved events,
> (4) To suggest new laws or principles,
> (5) To suggest new models [or] refinements of old ones,
> (6) To suggest new research methods or ideas for experiments or hypothesis tests,
> (7) To suggest choices between alternative hypotheses or theories, often a choice between more and less fruitful metaphors,
> (8) To suggest new methods for analyzing data,
> (9) To contrast theories or theoretical approaches,
> (10) To provide scientific explanations in the form of metaphoric redescriptions,
> (11) To suggest alterations or refinements in a theory,
> (12) To suggest new theories, theoretical systems, or worldviews. In a sense, metaphors, images, and models are embryonic theories in that they can lead to the generation of mathematical or other formalisms which other theorists then can use, perhaps without explicit reference to the initial images or models. (Hoffman 1985, pp. 332–333)

Metaphors (let me, for the sake of brevity, use this term, when unambiguous, to encompass all forms of transfers from one domain to another via figures of speech[1]) are thus frequently powerful ingredients of the cognitive process, be it in the phase of its creation or its transmission. As is forcefully stressed by metaphor scholars in various disciplines (from philosophy of science to linguistics), in most if not all fields of knowledge, metaphors enter at a very deep level in the understanding of problems and their subsequent conceptualization. For this reason the analysis of metaphors enables researchers to disclose the most fundamental principles of scientific theories. The metaphor is not only conducive to concept formation, but provides the guiding thread to the interpretation of the world (Blumenberg 1997, p. 88).

This paper introduces an ongoing research project aiming at examining whether and how metaphors can help characterize basic understanding of crises and their place in the working of the economic system, with particular emphasis on the theories developed in the nineteenth century. The rationale of this inquiry is that during most of the 1800s theories of crises were formulated by laypeople rather than by professional economists,[2] in natural language, with a conceptual apparatus often lacking precision. In these conditions, the usage of metaphors can reveal the underlying premises and interpretative framework on which specific theoretical approaches are built, thereby enabling one to answer the questions, 'What *are* crises and business cycles?' and 'What role do they play in the unfolding of the economic system's dynamics?'. In the twentieth century, with the formalization of economics and business cycle theories, the usage of figurative language has not disappeared, although metaphors and similes have become rarer in the technical literature while more elaborate analogies have appeared, used to detail the specific working of a mechanism or to provide the formalism for economic models of business cycles. Metaphors remain a powerful heuristic tool in contemporary discoursive texts on crises. In the recent literature on crises, the usage of metaphorical transfers also enables the reader to bring to light the assumptions and points of view hidden behind the technicalities of models.

The paper is organized as follows. In the first section, I outline the usage of metaphor through the course of time, in both the general and professional literatures. In the second section, I briefly discuss how the metaphorical transfer is structured, placing the emphasis on the features of the source domain that are selectively assigned to the target domain, showing how a phenomenon can be characterized by means of different metaphors and, conversely, how the same trope can convey different meanings depending on the properties that are attributed to the phenomenon to be explained. In the two sections after that, I provide examples of this multiple significance derived from a single image by discussing how two metaphors widely used in the literature on crises and business cycles were each used to support, or even to construct, the multiple distinct interpretations of the phenomenon that have emerged in the history of this subject in economics. Subsequently (in the fifth section), I briefly place these contrasting interpretation of the phenomenon in the light of the developments of the theories of crises and cycles. Finally, I draw some conclusions.

Timeline of metaphorical usage

One might expect that as economics becomes more and more formalized, the presence of metaphors in the literature would dwindle. One can try to evaluate the evolution of the usage of certain metaphors in time in the general literature by means of Ngrams, by Google Labs (http://books.google.com/ngrams), an instrument that depicts graphically the relative frequency in time of the occurrence of selected strings of words in a sample amounting to about the 4% of the books in the Google books collection. The search box only allows for a limited number of characters, which permit one to simultaneously illustrate the frequency of usage of twelve relatively common metaphorical expressions in connection with crises. The normalized frequency of occurrence of the expressions 'wave of depression', 'speculative fever', 'casino economy', 'financial contagion', 'economic disease', 'financial madness', 'fever of speculation', 'financial storm', 'vortex of ruin', 'commercial earthquake', 'financial meltdown', and 'financial explosion' in the corpus of English language[3], from 1800 (when these expression begin to become significant) to 2008, the last year included in the sample, can be seen at https://goo.gl/MfA7oe.[4] The Ngram shows that some metaphors were only used in the early stages of the debate on crises (as for instance 'vortex of ruin', scarcely used after 1890), others emerged at a later date (e.g. 'financial meltdown', 'casino economy' and 'financial contagion'), others are found throughout most of the period in consideration ('financial storm', 'fever of speculation'), others only occur at some points ('commercial earthquake', 'financial madness' or 'financial explosion').

One can also depict the overall usage of these metaphors (http://goo.gl/pRvZuc), by adding together the normalized frequencies of the same set of metaphorical expressions to give a clear idea of their development in time. The graph shows that these metaphors for crises started appearing when crises became a frequently discussed subject, after the panic of 1825. Their usage steadily increased till the peak in the 1930s, then decreased till the mid-1990s, to increase again sharply with the financial crises at the turn of the century. The financial crisis of 2007–08 is not captured by these data. This does not contradict the conjecture that the formalization of economics was accompanied by a less frequent usage of metaphors (these metaphors, at least), but does not provide full evidence either. At the end of the millennium, with the return of financial crises culminated in the subprime crisis of 2007–08, the literature on the subject had a new spike (which can be verified by producing N-grams of expressions relating to economic, financial, monetary, and currency crises), and the usage of metaphors grew with it.

These diagrams relating to the general literature have a counterpart in the scientific literature. JSTOR, in its Data for Research section (dfr.jstor.org), produces graphs with the absolute and relative frequency of expressions within a corpus. Figure 1 charts the relative frequency in the corpus of the 'business and economics' subjects group of the occurrence of any of a list of 64 metaphorical expressions, including the 12 represented in the N-grams mentioned above[5]. JSTOR records 6631 articles containing one or more of these expressions out of a corpus of 1.14 million articles.

The JSTOR graph seems to corroborate, up to the end of the twentieth century, the conjecture that a growingly technical literature does without the simple metaphorical expressions that have been searched: metaphors were very frequent up to 1870, with significant peaks in correspondence of or around the occurrence of crises or panics (1836, 1847, 1858); then the frequency of occurrence declined and remained low for over a century (again with peaks at the time of crises: 1893, 1920, 1930s), to increase slowly at first up the early 1990s and sharply first with the crises at the end of

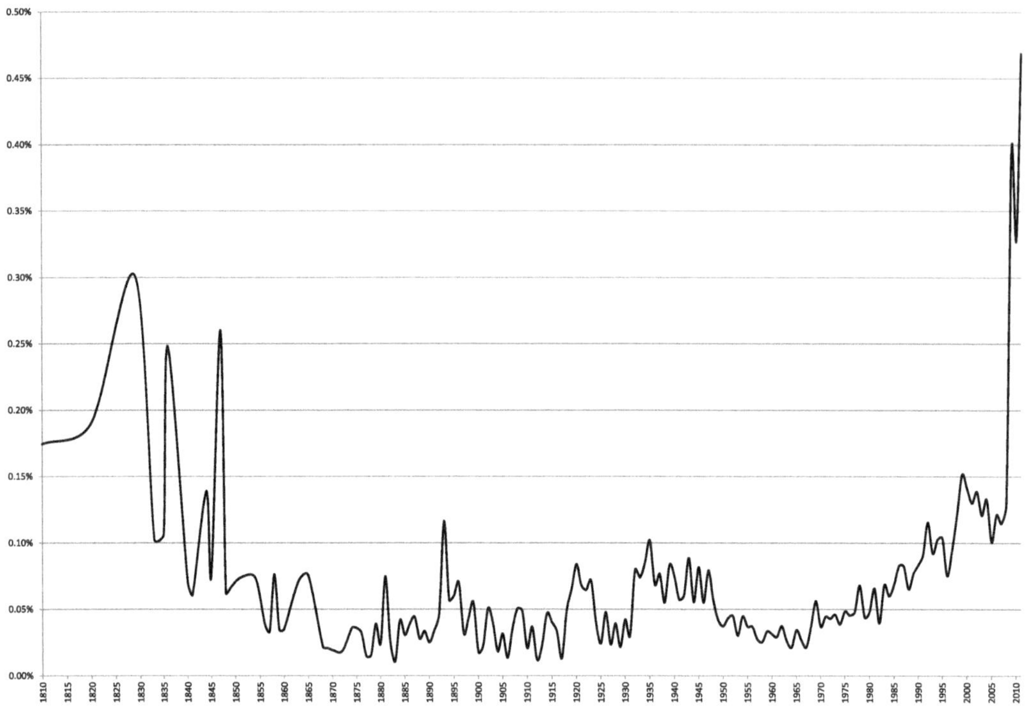

Figure 1. Relative frequency of the occurrence of any of 64 metaphorical expressions in the JSTOR corpus of business and economics articles (dfr.jstor.org).

the century and especially after 2007–08, when metaphorical usage was almost twice as frequent than it was in the first half of the nineteenth century.

This is counterintuitive: the economic literature is no less technical than it was 20 years ago, yet writers feel an increasing need to use metaphors to express their ideas on crises. Surely the increase in the very recent literature is higher in the 'economics and business' subject than in the economics discipline alone (the relative frequency of metaphors in economics (discipline) is aboult half the size of 'economics and business' (subject) with respect to their respective corpuses in 2011), and the spike in the usage of metaphors is partly due to the increase in the share of literature devoted to crises (again, this can be ascertained by searching with the same tool the occurrence of expressions for crises[6]). Yet this remains the case if we focus on texts on crises in the discipline of economics. In the JSTOR collection, of the 163,891 items that contain any of the terms related to crises or cycles, 3702 (just under 2%) also contain at least one of the metaphors.[7] It is possible to calculate the share of items on crises that contain at least one metaphor. Figure 2 illustrates that since the end of the nineteenth century metaphors occurred in about 2–3% of the crises articles, with a tendency to decrease and to fluctuate widely, up to the interwar years; thereafter they dropped to a stable 1% and remained at that level until the late 1970s; then they started to increase, reaching again about 3% with the crises at the turn of the century, to spike to almost 7% in correspondence of the subprime crisis and its aftermath. This is intriguing: to be able to conceptualize the new crisis, economists cannot merely rely on their sophisticated analytical tools and mathematical language but seem to have resorted to metaphors and figurative language.

The recent revival of usage of metaphors can be exemplified by means of a list of titles of books written in the aftermath of the crises of the early twenty-first century, where the metaphors appear in a very prominent position: *The Wall Street Takeover and the Next Financial Meltdown* (Johnson and Kwak 2010), *Corporate Aftershock: The Public Policy Lessons from the Collapse of Enron* (Culp and Niskanen 2003), *Casino Capitalism* (Sinn 2010), *Digital Phoenix: Why the Information Economy*

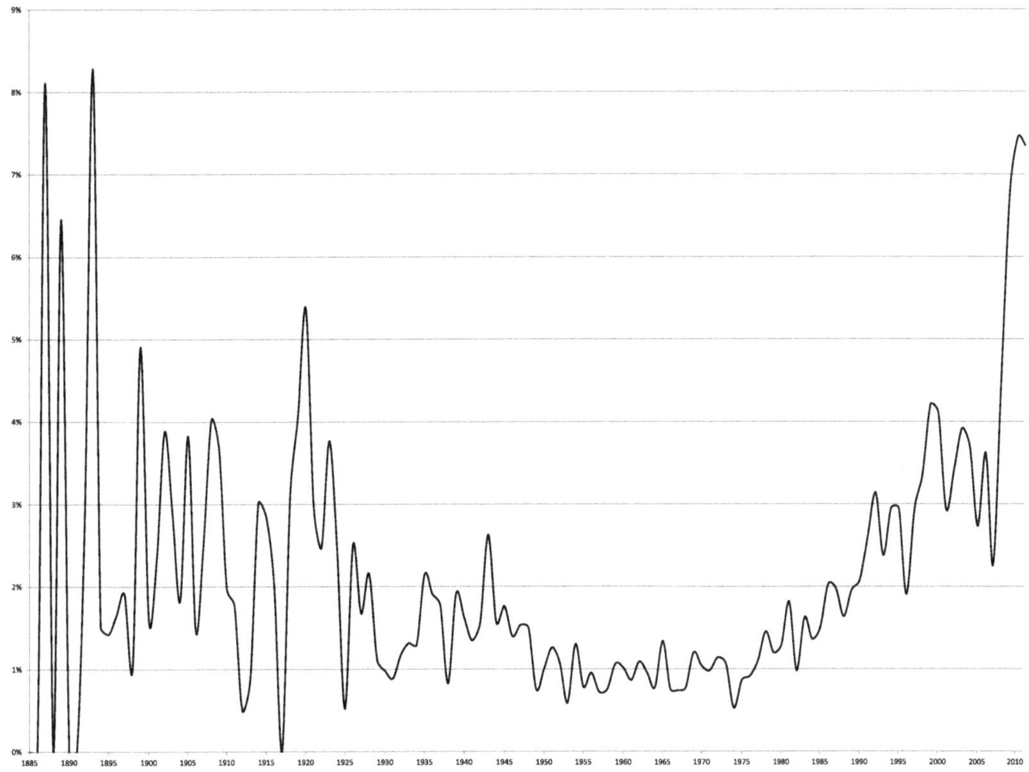

Figure 2. The percentage of writings in the economics discipline texts stored in JSTOR that contain at least one of the words denoting crises or cycles and one of the metaphors giving rise to the diagram in Figure 1.

Collapsed and How It Will Rise Again (Abramson 2005), *The Subprime Virus* (Engel and McCoy 2011), *Financial Alchemy in Crisis* (Nesvetailova 2010), *Financial Contagion; The Viral Threat to the Wealth of Nations* (Kolb [2011]), *Panic: The Story of Modern Financial Insanity* (Lewis 2009), *The Panic of 1907: Lessons Learned from the Market's Perfect Storm* (Bruner and Carr 2007). Similar metaphors occur in the technical literature: for instance, *Econlit* lists 173 items containing the word 'meltdown' in the title (mostly qualified by terms such as financial, mortgage, or economic), and we have financial viruses, financial and economic storms, contagion, epidemic and pandemic, speculation fevers, domino effects, and many others.

Naturally, some of the metaphors have changed in time due to the evolving cultural and scientific references: for instance, cholera and pestilences have been substituted by viruses; meltdowns are processes relating to the core of nuclear reactors and the term only came into use in the 1950s (*OED*); 'chain reaction' is a term dating from the 1920s (*OED*). Table 1 collects by way of comparison some of the metaphorical references as first used in the nineteenth century and as evolved in recent times, grouped by source domain or by the action they represent.

The structure of metaphorical transfers

The resurgence of a large number of varied metaphors for crises in the early twenty-first century has stimulated research into their usage, in particular by means of systematic classification of metaphors in certain corpora of texts, often comparing different languages or selecting the references to different countries. For instance, López and Llopis (2010) analysed a corpus of English and Spanish financial articles on the 2007–08 financial crisis from *The Economist* and *El Economista* to show how the choice of different tropes enabled the magazines to frame the crisis in diffferent ways, serving

Table 1. Metaphorical references in the 19th and twenty-first century.

source domain, action	19th C.	21st C.
storm	financial/commercial storm/tempest/hurricane/ tornado/cyclone	financial storm, hurricane, perfect storm
melting	credit melts like snow (rare)	financial/economic meltdown
natural disasters	commercial/financial earthquake, avalanches,	apocalypse, cataclysm, shockwaves, aftershocks, seismic
contagion	pestilence, cholera, epidemics, infection	financial contagion; viruses; infection
disease	speculation fever, cancer, disease	economic/financial disease
mental health	manias, madness	manias, hysteria, fear, distress
gambling	gambling speculation	casino economy
war		defence, battle, struggle, …
turbulence		economic/financial turbulence
vortex	vortex, maelstrom	maelstrom
sea metaphors	waves, tides, tidal waves	tsunami, floods
pendulum	pendulum, see-saw	pendulum (rare)
[diffusion]	wildfires, *trainée de poudre*	domino effect, chain reaction
buildings	unstable foundations, building too high, rotten structure	collapse

different political interests; the authors counted a number of metaphors belonging to different categories (the great chain of being, metaphors describing paths, of the kind 'actions are events') and examined the distribution of their occurrence. Bickes *et al.* (2014) examine how the media shaped public opinion in Germany with respect to Greece and the Eurocrisis by examining and quantifying the metaphors used by *Der Spiegel*, *Time* and *The Economist*, again classifying the tropes by domains of origin: natural disasters, disease and contagion, victims and rescuers, faulty devices. Arrese and Vara-Miguel (2015) examine the metaphorical expressions used in the European sovereign debt crisis, and worked out a list of the metaphorical sources discussed in the secondary literature on metaphors during the 2008 crisis (p. 5).

The logic behind these papers is explained as follows by Bickes *et al.*:

> Lakoff and Johnson's well-known Conceptual Metaphor Theory (1980) suggests that metaphors are not just poetic features of language, but that they form, structure, and influence human thought. Metaphor is thus central to all processes of perception and 'plays a central role in defining our everyday realities' (Lakoff and Johnson 1980, p. 3). Mostly relevant for our purposes of analysis is the *Structural Metaphor* since it structures abstract concepts with the help of concrete and easily accessible *source domains*. In other words, the structure of the concrete *source domain* is used to shape the vague *target domain*. It hence simplifies its understanding, highlights or hides certain aspects of the *target domain*, and has a big impact on how the abstract concept is conceived. Different *source domains* go along with different perspectives. (Bickes *et al.* 2014, p. 428)

The last sentence suggests that it is the source of the metaphor – the domain from which the metaphor is originally drawn – which shapes the object to which the metaphor is applied. The authors thus draw a number of implications from each family of metaphors, as for instance those concerning metaphors belonging to the category of natural disasters:

> The media metaphorically construct a reality in which the crisis has gained momentum and seems to have become independent. The crisis is referred to as a "natural disaster" and therefore seems beyond individual responsibility. This metaphor makes the crisis seem like a natural development and denies the responsibility of banks, financial markets, speculators, politicians, and governments. The media still avoid naming the responsible social actors and construct a reality in which the single currency suffers from a stroke of fate. In the course of this argument and the interpretation of this metaphor, Greece is no longer blamed for having triggered the crisis. As a *natural disaster* cannot be defeated by humans, the metaphor also implies a certain powerlessness of the social actors involved. The metaphor makes all political attempts to stop the crisis seem insignificant.
>
> Moreover, the metaphor lays emphasis on the unpredictability of the crisis. The future of the euro does not only depend on the success of a savings policy, but is to a great extent influenced by European banks, the stock market, investors, and speculators. These factors can hardly be controlled. Since a *natural disaster* can hit everyone, even financially secure nations are in danger. (Bickes *et al.* 2014, p. 435)

In spite of its seeming rather reasonable, this approach misses the subtle but all important nuances involved in both the theories of crises (note the unavoidable plural) and the nature of metaphors. This needs elaborating further.

Fascinating as it might be, classifying the use of figurative language by family of metaphors is not really helpful. If we want to understand how the metaphor contributes to the discussion of the object it is meant to describe, what matters is not so much to what discipline or common phenomena the original image belongs, but how precisely the metaphor is used to transfer meaning to the object or phenomenon to which it refers.

Broadly speaking, a metaphor is 'a figure of speech in which a name or descriptive word or phrase is transferred to an object or action different from, but analogous to, that to which it is literally applicable; an instance of this, a metaphorical expression', while an analogy is 'a comparison made between one thing and another for the purpose of explanation or clarification' (*OED*). Both the metaphorical transfer and the analogical comparison involve three terms. The object to which the metaphor or analogy originally refers is called the *source*. The *target* is the object to which the comparison is applied. It is never claimed that the target is isomorphic to the source (otherwise they would be one and the same thing[8]): the transfer is, implicitly or explicitly, selective. Only *some* properties of the source (the *tertium comparationis*) are transferred or compared to the target. And it is precisely this selective process that makes the study of metaphors useful for interpreting the meaning of the text where metaphors are used.

Let us consider an example. An anonymous contributor to an American newspaper in the late nineteenth century wished

> that the process of natural selection through bankruptcy shall go on till the weak concerns are all weeded out. The feeble and unpromising kitten of the litter should be decently drowned and the strong ones left to thrive (Anon 1884, p. 7).

The multiple sources of the comparison consist in the process of natural selection, the weeding out of bad weeds, and human selection by means of drowning the feeble kitten. The target is bankruptcy, and the *tertium comparationis* consists in the elimination of weak individuals, the preservation of strong ones, and giving the latter better conditions. The logical scheme is depicted in Figure 3.

Sometimes, as in the example above, writers explicitly declare which features of the source are transferred to the target; other times they do not. *Analogies* are usually explicit, especially when used to illustrate the working of some mechanism. For instance, when Tugan-Baranowsky likened the working of the accumulation of loanable funds to the operation of a steam engine he drew a detailed comparison of each stage of the cyclical movement of the piston:

> The operation of the whole mechanism can be compared with the steam engine. The accumulation of free money plays the role of the steam in the cylinder; when the pressure of the steam on the piston reaches a certain fixed norm, the resistance of the piston is overcome, the piston moves, reaches the end of the cylinder, a free way out opens for the steam and the piston returns to its former place. In the same way accumulated free money capital, having reached certain proportions, makes its way into industry, moves it, is spent and industry again returns to its former state. It is natural that under such conditions crises must recur periodically. Capitalist industry must continuously traverse the same cycle of development. (Tugan-Baranowsky 1901, Engl. transl. pp. 796–797)

Metaphors, on the contrary, sometimes omit the *tertium comparationis*: this makes them semantically richer than concepts, and therein lies their heuristic power. For instance, when an article in a daily paper described the 'periodical panics which are the earthquakes of the commercial world' (Anon 1864), the writer did not specify which aspects of panics resemble earthquakes. He surely had some characteristics in mind (possibly the destructiveness of quakes, or their sudden and unforeseeable character), but by not specifying what he was thinking of, he left the elaboration to the reader's imagination along a path he suggested. The reader, however, may choose different features than those the writer had in mind, possibly arriving at a completely different undestanding of the object

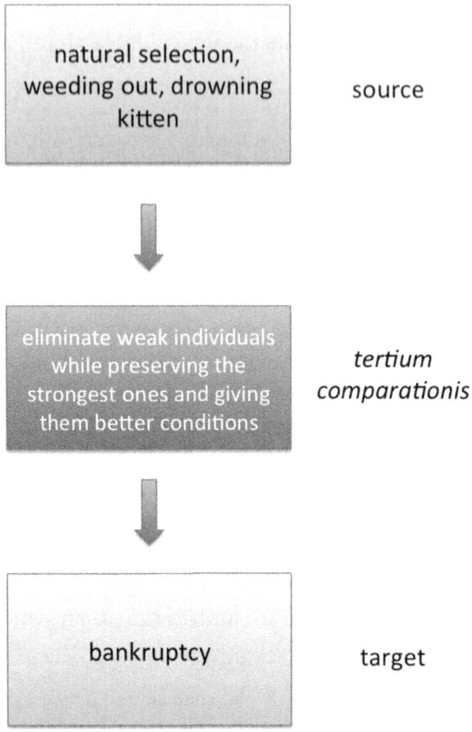

Figure 3. The structure of a metaphorical transfer.

under examination. Indeed, often the *same* metaphor was used by different writers to present completely different (even contradictory) views of the same subject.

The example of kitten selection and bankruptcy illustrates at least two features of the metaphorical usage. We have already seen that it is selective: bankruptcies are *not* an instance of natural selection (metaphors are not literally true), but they share *some* features with natural selection, while other properties are irrelevant or inapplicable (for instance, the natural selection process operates on random mutations through several generations of individuals and therefore takes a very long time). A second feature is that each property can be shared by different sources: the elimination of weak individuals can take place either by natural or human selection. The choice of the source, then, is also selective. A third feature, not illustrated in the example, is that the target may be characterized by multiple properties: besides the ones illustrated in the example, bankruptcies are painful and distressing, generate loss of resources, are chained to each other, and so on; in this example, the author of the article has thus chosen to stress the strengthening role of bankruptcies over their bringing misery.

In their actual usage, metaphors are therefore linked to each other in a tangled web rather than being neatly pigeon-holed according to their source, as in the (still oversimplifying) scheme represented in Figure 4.

The relationships illustrated in the figure reproduce the structure of actual metaphors found in the literature. The movement of a pendulum subject to friction tends to a position of rest, and has therefore been used to describe the stability of equilibrium. But the same pendulum, coupled with exogenous shocks, was also invoked to account for irregular but persistent business fluctuations. A frictionless pendulum, or a pendulum energized by an escapement mechanism, shows persistent and periodical fluctuations, which have been used to describe rhythmic business cycles. Periodicity (at least approximate), however, is also an attribute of tides and comets, which have therefore also

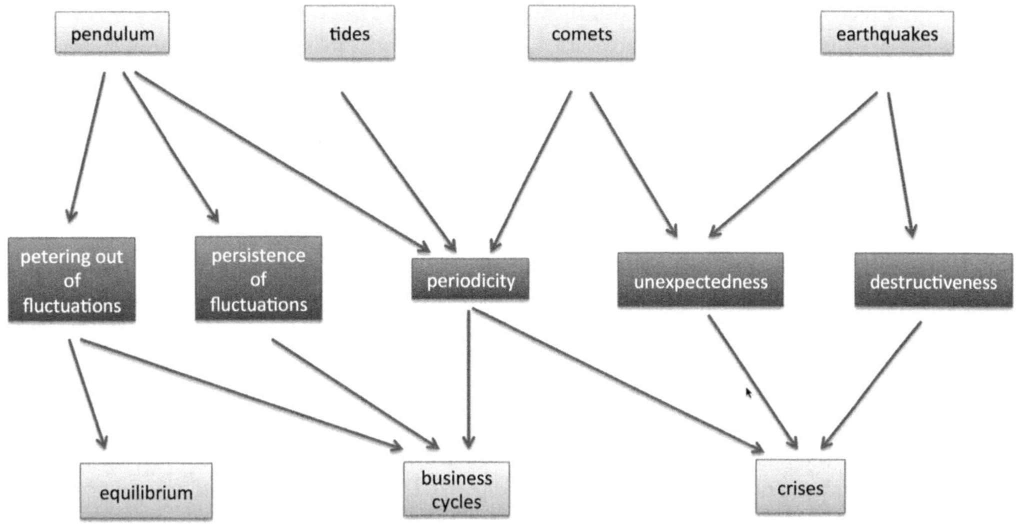

Figure 4. Scheme of part of the network of metaphorical relationships originating from a few sources and transferring different properties to different targets.

invoked in the description of cycles and fluctuations and in the recurrence of crises. But comets can also materialize unanticipatedly, and as such they were considered as terrifying and ominous signs up to the middle of the nineteenth century, and were accordingly used to characterize the unexpectedness of crises. This is a feature shared by earthquakes, which have thus been used in the same way also adding destructiveness to the description.

Some of these properties are unrelated: there is no need, for instance, that something unexpected is also destructive. The various properties invoked contribute thereby to the characterization of the target. It may happen, however, that some properties are conflicting: fluctuations cannot be at once persistent or dampened, and a phenomenon cannot at the same time be recognized as periodical and be unexpected. Using one or another of the properties of the pendulum and the comets, respectively, involves in reality referring to different objects: the pendulum with friction *vs.* the frictionless pendulum, and periodical *vs.* hyperbolic comets. Such contrasting characterizations of the source metaphor either is used to describe different targets or, more interestingly still, reveals different, even contradictory, theories concerning the same target.

This is precisely the space where metaphorology becomes revealing of the deepest level of understanding of the target. While precise and detailed analogies often carry a high explanatory or illustrative power, broader metaphors – when made precise by an explicit or at least recognizable choice of the properties transferred from the source to the target – bring to light a very basic characaterization of a phenomenon. This especially applies when the source is an everyday phenomenon, understood by all readers: for instance, weather metaphors (discussed in detail in the following section) refer to phenomena that are familiar to everybody, and the selective process of the features to be transferred to the target and those to be left out is clearly voluntary and not driven by the intrinsic difficulty in understanding the technicalities concerning the source, as opposed for instance to the mode of operation of a virus.

In the next two sections, we shall consider two examples of how the selection of different properties of the same source transmitted to the same target characterize that target in completely different ways.

Economic storms: one metaphor, two different notions of crises

The first example of a trope used to describe two different and mutually incompatible interpretations of crises concerns a metaphor frequently used for these phenomena from the early nineteenth century to the recent literature on the subprime crash: the crisis as an economic storm.[9] When nineteenth-century writers compared crises to storms, they characterized crises in two completely different ways. One is based on the view that crises are an anomalous disturbance to the normal working of the economic system, as a destructive disruption of the ordinary course of business. Let me call this 'the crisis approach', in the singular, to emphasize that crises do not have a systematic but an accidental nature; this view was prevalent in the early part of the nineteenth century. The other perspective characterizes crises as the recurrent outbreak of the tension that accumulates in the system during its normal course; in this perspective, the crisis has a useful function, as it eliminates this tension and enables the economic system to restart afresh. I call this 'the recurrent crises approach', with the emphasis on the periodical rebuilding of the conditions determining a crisis. These views reflect different and mutually exclusive understandings of the working of the economic system. The 'crisis approach' implies that the economic system is capable of self-adjusting, unless it is disturbed by a major or persistent external perturbation – be it a famine, a war, or a piece of legislation that impedes the smooth functioning of the mechanisms of exchange; as soon as the disturbance is absorbed or removed, business returns to its normal flow. The 'recurrent crises approach' sees instead the economic system as incorporating some destabilizing factors that eventually cause an excess in some respect (in particular of production with respect to consumption or of credit relative to traders' capital), which the crisis will have to eliminate. In the 'crisis approach', then, the crisis *is the disease* (another metaphor that was often employed in the nineteenth century: see Besomi 2011), while in the 'recurring crises' approach it *is the consequence of, and the remedy to, a preliminary disease.*

The use of the storm metaphor by the writers in the 'crisis approach' attributes to crises a selected group of properties of storms that characterize 'economic tempests' in a very precise way. Some writers stressed that crises are aberrations with respect to some (generally unspecified) 'normal' state of the system, characterized by the flow of business running uninterrupted. 'Normal' being not only a statistical norm but also (and especially) a theoretical one, such anomalies were bound to be only temporary. Like a tempest, crises are universally destructive: failures and bankruptcies (unemployment was rarely mentioned!) cause misery and distress to everyone, no matter how solid and time-honoured were the banks, commercial houses, and manufactures involved. Finally, crises were described as sudden and unexpected, and were therefore surprising, because they were not rooted in any of the economic system's normal features. A few examples are cited in Table 2.

Table 2. The usage of the storm metaphor by writers in the 'crisis approach'.

tertium comparationis	example
anomalous and temporary	crises as 'thunderstorms temporarily perturbing the good weather of industrial horizons, after which – notwithstanding some devastation – business resumes its usual course' (Blanqui 1836, p. 257).
destructive	'There was a fair show of outward wealth and a false security, which continued until the unfortunate speculator was roused from his golden dreams by the commercial storm, and by a scene of ruin which was without a parallel in the history of commerce. The alarm began in Great Britain, where credit had been carried to a great excess' (Buchanan 1842, p. 475).
universal	'House after house, of high commercial repute, succumbed to the panic, and several heavy banking firms were added to the list of failures. … The avalanche of discredit swept down merchants, bankers, moneyed corporations, and manufacturing companies, without distinction. Old houses, of accumulated capital, which had withstood the violence of all former panics, were prostrated in a day; and when they believed themselves to be perfectly safe against misfortune. The bank suspension of New York and New England, in the middle of October, was the climax of this commercial hurricane. Such is the outline of the most extraordinary, violent, and destructive financial panic ever experienced in this country' (Gibbons 1858, p. 346).
sudden and unexpected	'This financial cyclone came upon us suddenly, and, to a certain extent, unexpectedly, as a storm from an unclouded sky. It came in the midst of what appeared to be a time of unparalleled prosperity in all branches of business. Trade was active, manufacturing establishments were working to their full capacity, agriculture was broadening its acres, railroads were extending their lines, and substantial progress was apparent in every direction. Suddenly every interest was threatened with disaster for the want of money, which could not be obtained: deposits were rapidly withdrawn from the banks, and urgent applications for loans were of necessity refused or but partially responded to' (Anon 1887).

Writers in the 'recurring crises' tradition also referred to the weather image, but in a completely different way. Rather than being surprised at storms, they saw them gathering; instead of treating them as anomalies, they understood them as the result of excessive electricity (or humidity, or other kinds of impurity) having accumulated in the air, which they subsequently cleared. Interestingly, in the early usage of the metaphor, the purifying of the atmosphere was seen as a silver lining, then it was realized that this was a systematic accompanyment of crises, later it was seen as a necessity (thereby giving crises a positive role to fulfill), and eventually the storm was even seen as seeding and actively promoting the recovery process. In this view, the crisis is prepared by the impurities present during the prosperous phase (excesses of credit and speculation, or overproduction) and cumulatively rises the tension within the economic system; the crisis is the moment when this tension is released by means of a selective (rather than universal) elimination of the overspeculating and overindebted firms, so that the economic system is free to restart again unencumbered (for some time, at least) by imbalances (see Table 3).

The storm metaphor is naturally not sufficient to give a full characterization of the crisis and the recurrent crises approach, and other metaphors were called to fill in the gap. On the other hand, storms are not the only possible source for the properties we have just examined, and other images have actually been used in their place. Storms, for instance, are not very suitable for accounting for the periodicity of crises, and the writers wishing to emphasize this feature had to resort to other metaphors such as comets, tides or waves, while the storm's destructiveness, suddenness and unpredictability could be substituted by earthquakes and other natural disasters. Table 4 illustrates the most common metaphors and their usage in the 'crisis' and 'recurring crises' approaches (for further discussion see the section after the next).

The pendulum of commerce: one metaphor for different notions of oscillatory movements

The second example of a metaphor suitable to multiple usages is that of the pendulum. Here I focus only on those concerning crises and cycles. The first and oldest reference was in the context of what I call the 'fluctuations approach', fairly frequent as an alternative to the 'crisis' approach in the 1820s to the 1840s and resurrected in the 1980s: a point of view that recognizes that trade is subject to continuous oscillations, due to the constant changes in the conditions of both supply and demand. Although the system tends to move back to equilibrium after each disturbance, the resulting movement is oscillatory, without any intrinsic regularity or internal mechanism. The early proponents of this approach recognized that occasionally such fluctuations around and towards equilibrium can give rise to major crises, if they are amplified by institutional constraints (e.g. banking policy or tariffs) or if by chance the fluctuations originated by a number of small disturbances accumulate into a large wave. The second perspective relying on the pendulum understands the dynamics of the economic system as a cycle, driven by an internal mechanism in which each phase (prosperity, crisis, depression, recovery) causes the following one in a closed causal circle, the oscillations of which are persistent and approximately regular. Apart from a few instances in the 1840s and 1860s, this 'cycle approach' (as I will call it) gained popularity at the end of the nineteenth century and became dominant in the interwar years. A third view on the movement of the economy that relied on the pendulum can be called 'complex dynamics approach'. It emerged in the 1980s, when the mathematical shortcomings of the 'cycle perspective' became apparent and the introduction of nonlinear dynamics, instead of the more simple linear equations used earlier, started to give rise to aperiodical movement nonetheless based on the system's endogenous relationships.

These approaches again reflect different understandings of how the economic system works (and, together with the 'crisis' and the 'recurring crises' approaches, they exhaust the range of perspectives actually taken by commentators since the outset of modern economic crises[10]). The 'fluctuations approach' considers equilibrium as stable and blames temporary disequilibria on exogenous events or political or institutional constraints; this view is similar to the 'crisis approach', except that the

Table 3. The usage of the storm metaphor by writers in the 'recurring crises approach'.

tertium comparationis	example
storms can be seen 'gathering'	'By the middle of November [1825], the shadow of the approaching storm was upon us. It was yet to burst – but the gloom was palpable' (Joplin 1837, p. 67). 'The signs of the coming financial storm are steadily growing more ominous. The comparative dullness of business, the downward tendency of prices, the increasing number of failures, and the uneasiness manifested in nearly every department of trade, are sure harbingers of a general financial crash. Every shrewed observer has been convinced, for a long time that a monetary crisis is inevitable, and that its coming is only a question of time. The financial atmosphere has been closely watched' (cited in Anon 1866).
cumulation of impurities (causality); instability	'Mutual indebtedness always exists as an unknown quantity, and a state of excessive engagements may unexpectedly be disclosed. When business is in such a condition, some cause, in itself trivial, often serves to alter the entire aspect of affairs. With the air barely above dew point, the sky may be perfectly clear, but in an instant, by some unlooked- for cold cross-current, it becomes covered with dense black clouds ; so with excessive obligations pending, the apparently clear commercial atmosphere in a few days, even hours, is agitated with storms, the rate forced to panic point, ruining many who entered into engagements heedless of the warning, plain though inarticulate, usually afforded by a persistent drop of the industrial weather glass, in other words by a continuous outflow of bullion from the coffers of the Bank of England'. (Laing 1867, p. 237).
clearing the atmosphere	'By "purifying the commercial atmosphere," I certainly mean the removal, by failure, of insolvent commercial houses – a pressure for money tends to expose the weakness and cause the stoppage of such houses. This effect is salutary and such was its effect with us. Not a single failure took place where the parties were not *deeply insolvent*' (Anon (Boston Merchant) 1823, p. 358).
silver lining	'The storm has now expended itself, and has begun rapidly to abate; the clouds are breaking up the heavy pall which for a time seemed to enshroud the whole heavens in a portentous darkness, and their black masses are already beginning to roll away; the atmosphere has been purified of the evil elements with which it had gradually become surcharged' (Anon 1837, p. 109).
regular accompaniment of crises	'In the natural world, a tempest frequently is of material benefit, by clearing the atmosphere, and distributing the elementary phenomena, which, when congregated, might produce disease in the animal creation, or throw blight upon the vegetable productions with which the teeming soil fructifies, and by which life is sustained. In like manner, in the world of business, a strong convulsion such as we have lately witnessed, and the effects of which, even yet, agitate our commercial system, may not be without its use. Great as have been, and are, the evils which the 'panic' has brought in its train, they may be even more than counterbalanced by great advantages, if principles of action be introduced of a more healthy nature than those which have guided, or rather *misguided*, us for the last thirty years' (Begbie 1848, p. 5).
necessity	'This remarkable reaction [the revulsion of 1857] was as necessary as a thunder-storm in a mephitic and unhealthy tropical atmosphere. It purified the commercial and financial elements, and tended to restore vitality and health, alike conducive to regular trade, sound progress, and permanent prosperity' (Evans 1859, p. 121)
irrigating and fertilizing the soil	'Crises should be compared to a terrible thunderstorm, with lightning and thunder and torrential rain, during which people are killed, storage warehouses burned down, meadows in bloom flooded, with devastating losses to livestock and crops – but which in the end sends to the region a fertilizing rain. Crises generate monstruous losses, which destroy many institutions, ruin lives, not a few of which are driven to suicide by desperation! The impact is felt deeply by all classes of the population, and yet it must be said: when overspeculation – comparable to a thoroughbred racer with the bit between his teeth – has ignored all the cautionary warnings, exceeded all limits and brought the catastrophe, the latter must be considered as a healing process of purification and an equilibrating process, which separates the pure metal from the slag and brings the feverish state of markets to the normal condition of health' (Wirth 1890)

latter treats crises as anomalies with respect to a normal state while the fluctuations perspective takes for granted that the economic system persistently oscillates, albeit erratically, around an equilibrium. The 'cycle approach' treats as 'normal' not the equilibrium, but the cycle. Some writers in this tradition consider equilibrium to be unstable and attribute the turning points to some constraints (endogenously determined by the system's dynamic, or semi-exogenous, such as the evolution of technology, population, and resources) that would prevent the system from exploding; others take

Table 4. Some common metaphors and their usage in the 'crisis' and 'recurring crises' approaches in the nineteenth century.

source domain	crisis approach	recurrent crises approach
earthquakes	sudden, unpredictable, destructive	releasing of tension, wiping out weak firms
avalanches	destructive	result from unstable pile-up of snow
contagion, epidemics		spreads the disease (speculation is contagious) and the consequences
illness	crisis is the disease	predisposition costututed by excesses, crisis as elimination of excesses and impurities (the disease is in the prosperity); recurring fevers (periodicity)
mental illness		mania of speculation
natural selection, weeding out		crises as elimination of the weak and excessively speculative firms
rot		collapses (previous lack of solidity)
buildings		instability of too tall or not wide enough buildings; ground not solid enough
house of cards		instability
comets	unexpected and scary	periodic, predictable
tides	destructive	periodic, predictable
waves		periodic, superposable
vortex		drags everything with it
explosion	destruction	preliminary preparation of explosive material, instability, elimination of weak firms
gambling		constitution of excesses, individul responsibility of gambler

equilibrium to be stable, but incorporate in their models some energizers that keep the system in motion. In the 'complex dynamics' perspective, the normal state of the system is a *strange attractor*, namely, a complex non-periodical motion determined by the system's own dynamics; while its appearance is erratic, its structure is deterministic (as distinct from the movement described in the 'fluctuations' perspective), even if very strongly affected by small changes in intitial conditions.

The writers in the 'fluctuations approach' evoked the pendulum to stress that the economy is never at a state of rest but invariably oscillates, so that states of 'unnatural' prosperity or depression are never persistent but must reverse into their opposite, precisely because of the tendency of the pendulum to regain its equilibrium state: any disturbance sets up a force acting in the opposite direction with equal strength. The reversal is therefore approximately symmetrical, so that movement up one arc of the pendulum following a stimulus (e.g. the imposition of tariffs) will eventually determine a reaction of almost the same magnitude in the opposite direction. Remarkably, most examples of usage in these senses (see Table 5) show an awareness of the causal relationships involving the reversal of the movement.

While writers in the 'fluctuations approach' refer to the actual pendulum, the real oscillating object subject to small friction, writers in the 'cycle approach' have in mind other kinds of pendulums: the idealized, frictionless pendulum, capable of forever oscillating with constant amplitude and period; or the mathematical pendulum, defined by an equation; or a pendulum subject to friction energized by external shocks which, superposed to the oscillating structure of the pendulum, force its swings to a persistent quasi-rhythmical path; or, finally, the pendulum clock with an escapement mechanism, with a constant external source of energy (a weight or a spring) transmitted to the bob with the timing dictated by the structure of the pendulum itself. In all cases, the emphasis is on the persistence of fluctuations and on the rhythmical nature of the economy (see Table 6).

The variety of pendulums used to model the same phenomenon in the twentieth century originates in their mathematical properties. This is a development that began in the 1930s. The ideal, frictionless pendulum is a mathematical abstraction describing an unattainable limit case, valid only for a specific set of values of the system's parameters. As there is no a priori reason to assume that economic systems should hold precisely those values, writers had to find a different formulation. Some retained the couching of the problem in terms of linear functional equations; these can only give four kinds of results, besides the infinitely improbable constant oscillations case: exponential growth or decay, either gradually or combined with a sine curve. None of these describes a cycle,

Table 5. The pendulum metaphor in the 'fluctuations approach'.

tertium comparationis	example
oscillations	The general prosperity of the entire country is unnatural. It is the swing of the pendulum up to the highest degree of the arc of profitable commerce. Four years ago, the pendulum swung the other way up the other branch of commercial depression. For seventy years the pendulum has swung between adversity and prosperity (Anon 1899).
necessarily reverses its direction of movement	An excessive quantity of gold in the country engenders speculation, an abuse of credit, fitful prosperity, and high prices; those high prices produce a large amount of imports, which in turn causes an export of gold: this leads to hoarding and speculation in money, destruction of credit, and its natural consequences, panic, stagnation, and distress; thus one extreme begets another in proportion as the pendulum sways one way it is sure to oscillate the other (Liverpool Currency Reform Association 1849, p. 3).
symmetry	We see how kind the Debt and the paper money have been to each other, with what anxious solicitude they have kept each other's side, how mutually and how lovingly they have assisted each other; the Debt first causing the paper money, then the paper money causing the Debt! This is a true kind of accommodation bill system, each amount requiring a large amount to cover the expenses, and not unlike the impulsive and repulsive motions in a pendulum, the farther you swing it one way, the farther it will return the other (Anon (Birmingham manufacturer) 1832, p. 16)
movement tends towards equilibrium, but passes beyond it.	Whenever the pendulum of price (if I may use the expression,) has, either by the operation or the natural course or events, or by the unwise and unskilful tampering of government, been thrown far into one extreme of the arc, it will, in its effort to regain its natural position, go almost so far into the opposite extreme; and the vibrations will frequently last through a long period of time (Dew 1835, pp. 68–69).
fluctuations take time	he who watches the vibrations in the great pendulum of commerce, will discover that a round of fifteen or twenty years, rectifies all variations and brings all seeming anomalies under the sway of permanent and steady law (Anon 1856)

unless either a dampened sine curve is energized by external shocks (Yule 1927, Frisch 1933) or an exploding curve is constrained upwards and downwards by some boundaries (Hicks 1950). The alternative road was to abandon the assumption of linearity and model the economy as a clock with escapement (Goodwin 1951), the behavior of which is a limit cycle – that is, a cycle towards which all trajectories tend, even if the system is disturbed.

The cyclical view described by Goodwin turned out to be an exceptional case as the linear one with constant amplitude. Goodwin himself later called attention to the fact that, generally speaking, non-linear functional equations give rise to complex dynamics: deterministic but irregular movements, strongly dependent upon initial conditions in such a way that no matter how close two points are, path passing through them would sooner or later considerably diverge. This describes a different view of the cycle: fluctuations are still determined by the structure of the economic system, but are not regular. The irregularity reminds of the view of the 'fluctuations' approach, but in the complex dynamics perspective (Table 7)

The pendulum image is thus so rich in features that a selection can give rise to different interpretation of oscillation in economic variables: fluctuations determined by exogenous events and by the system's effort to return to equilibrium; cycles determined by the economic system's internal dynamics, possibly energized by exogenous impulses; or chaotic but deterministic movements. As in the case of the storm, this is not a matter of emphasis but of intrinsically different ways of understanding the working of a capitalist economy and the role played by cycles in it.

Contrasting worldviews

The examples of the storm and of the pendulum illustrate how the selection of different properties from the source can render fundamentally different understandings of the working of the economic system and the role economic crises play in it. The main contrast is aptly summarized by Keynes:

Table 6. pendulums and cycles.

tertium comparationis	example
oscillations persist symmetry full causal circle	'each trader stretches his capital, his credit, his skill, and his industry to produce the utmost possible quantity of goods, under the idea, that the more he manufactures and sells, the more profit he will reap. But as all his neighbors are animated by the same spirit, *they* manufacture as much as possible also; and none of them knows certainly how much the other traders in his own line are producing, or how much of the commodity in which he deals the public will really want, pay for, and consume, within any specific time. The consequence is, that a superfluity of goods is produced; the market is glutted; prices fall ruinously low, – and all the manufacturers who have proceeded on credit, or who have limited capital, become bankrupt, and the effects of their rash speculations fall on their creditors. They are, however, excluded from trade for a season – the other manufacturers restrict their operations, – the operatives are thrown idle, or their wages are greatly reduced; – the surplus commodities are at length consumed, demand revives, prices rise, and the rush toward production again takes place; and thus in all trades the pendulum oscillates, generation after generation, first toward prosperity, then to the equal balance, then toward adversity – back again to equality, and once more to prosperity' (Combe 1840, p. 218)
regularity in timing and amplitude (vs. disturbances)	'If I were to choose a physical analogue it would be not the swing of a clock pendulum but the swaying of the trees or their branches. If, in the woods, we pull a twig and let it snap back, we set up a swaying movement back and forth. That is a real cycle, but if there is no further disturbance, the swaying soon ceases and the twig becomes motionless again. In actual experience, however, twigs or tree-tops seldom oscillates regularly, even temporarily. They register, instead, chiefly the variations in wind velocity. A steady wind may keep the tree for weeks at a time, leaning almost continuously in one direction and its natural tendency to swing back is thereby defeated or blurred. Its degree of bending simply varies with the wind. That is, the inherent pendulum tendency is ever being smothered. In the net resultant motion there is no perceptible trace left of real recurrences and no would-be forecaster would attempt to base his estimate of the future behavior of a tree-top on a statistical average period of recorded swayings taken in gusts of wind'. (Fisher 1925, p. 192)
pendulum-like equations	'the economic question that forces itself upon us here is: is it possible to understand the phenomena that play a role in the business cycle, as velocities of the same variables of which integrals also occur? If this is the case, then we would have, besides the already indicated schemes, one with a new character. One in which not one or another a priori fixed time interval, either a lag or a life-span, would determine the period, but one in which an oscillation is caused only by nearly direct affective relations between the variables. Such an oscillation is well-known under the name of harmonic oscillation, that occurs with pendulums, swings, elastic swingings, etc'. Tinbergen 1933 (typescript in Dutch, cited in Boumans 1992, p. 73).
damped fluctuations sustained by exogenous shocks	'If we observe at short equal intervals of time the departures of a simple harmonic pendulum from its position of rest, errors of observation will cause superposed fluctuations [...]. But by improvement of apparatus and automatic methods of recording, let us say, errors of observation are practically eliminated. The recording apparatus is left to itself, and unfortunately boys get into the room and start pelting the pendulum with peas, sometimes from one side and sometimes from the other. The motion is now affected, not by superposedfl uctuationsb ut by true disturbances, and the effect on the graph will be of an entirely different kind. The graph will remain surprisingly smooth, but amplitude and phase will vary continually' (Yule 1927, p. 268).
robust constant amplitude cycle	'Mention should also be made of the fact that there exists an alternative way out of the dilemma [that linear equations 'either explode or die away with the consequent disappearance of the cycle or the society'] – that of an impulse-excited mechanism. There are two basically different classes of such mechanisms to be dis-tinguished. (a) – There are the synchronized systems of which the most familiar is the ordinary pendulum clock. Here the pendulum executes damped motion, but its own motion is used to time regular shocks so that it settles down to a steady routine in which the energy which is dissipated in friction during each cycle is exactly replaced. The wider system, including the feedback mechanism (the escapement) for delivering the shocks, is a particular type of nonlinear oscillator since it is autonomous and maintains a uniform cycle independently of initial conditions. (b) Significantly different is a system subject to random shocks'. (Goodwin 1951, p. 2).
cycles and growth	[an energized pendulum] 'will give a picture of the *oscillations* but not of the secular or perhaps supersecular tendency of evolutions. This tendency seems to us to be irreversible because we have not yet lived long enough to see the decline. It is not difficult to complete the instrument in such a way that it will express also this

(*Continued*)

Table 6. Continued.

tertium comparationis	example
	secular or supersecular movement. We may, for instance, imagine that the pivot to which the pendulum is suspended is not fixed but slides in a crack in the wall, the crack ascending towards the right. This being so, the whole instrument will move by jumps, and each jump will carry it to a higher position than before. We only have to feed the instrument by a [constant source of energy]. The impulsion [...] will maintain the oscillations, and these oscillations will constitute the jumps which carry the instrument steadily to higher levels. Thus there will be an intimate connection between the oscillations and the irreversible evolution'. (Frisch 1933, pp. 34–35).

Table 7. Pendulum and chaotic dynamics.

tertium comparationis	example
complex, irregular but deterministic motion	compound pendulums (Frisch, as discussed by Louçã 2007, pp. 166–170).

> On the one side are those who believe that the existing economic system is, in the long-run, a self-adjusting system, though with creaks and groans and jerks, and interrupted by time lags, outside interference and mistakes. [...] These authorities do not, of course, believe that the system is automatically or immediately self-adjusting. But they do believe that it has an inherent tendency towards self-adjustment, if it is not interfered with and if the action of change is not too rapid. On the other side of the gulf are those who reject the idea that the existing economic system is, in any significant sense, self-adjusting. They believe that the failure of effective demand to reach the full potentialities of supply, in spite of human psychological demand being immensely far from satisfied for the vast majority of individuals, is due to much more fundamental causes. (Keynes 1934, pp. 486–87)

The two main positions, however, admit different articulations. Among those maintaining that the economic system is capable of self-adjustment, some understood crises as the consequence of exogenous disturbances to an otherwise smooth process of production and exchanges (the crisis approach, as held for instance by J.-B. Say); others admitted that the system is by its very nature oscillatory, permanently trying to accomodate itself to the discontinuities that routinely affect trade in the face of changing market conditions but rarely subject to major fluctuations, unless random shocks accidentally accumulate into a major crisis or some systematic friction prevents adjustments to take place (the fluctuations perspective; e.g. Lord Overstone).

Among those who believe instead that the economic system does not tend towards a state of equilibrium, some emphasize that there are intrinsic tensions cumulating during prosperity which necessitates a sudden and violent recomposition (the recurrent crises approach, adopted by such different writers as Clément Juglar and Marx), while others emphasize that equilibrium is by its nature unstable but movement around it is deterministic and constrained by thresholds that prevent the system from exploding (the chaotic dynamics approach, as exemplified by Richard Goodwin). The cycle approach has room for both believers in and deniers of the system's capacity of self-adjusting: the former emphasize maladjustments, lags, and frictions that prevent equilibrium from being reached and maintained (e.g. Albert Aftalion), the latter emphasize the forces cumulatively pushing the system away from equilibrium until the movement is checked by exogenous or endogenous constraints. Both, however, maintain that the system behaves rhythmically, oscillating around equilibrium, either because it is attracted to it or because it is constantly pushed away (Roy Harrod, for instance).[11]

These five views exhaust the list of the approaches that have been historically taken on the subject of crises and equilibrium, and perhaps include all the logically possible views on the topic. However, not all writers were fully aware of their positioning within this range or cared to discuss it. A few writers in the 'recurring crises' approach were explicitly distancing themselves from the 'crisis' approach, even mocking the competing perspectives for attributing crises that were increasingly recognized as being similar to each other to different causes (for instance Juglar, James Anthony

Lawson, and Jevons); again, some early writers in the 'cycles approach' stressed the distance of their view from those of the writers who emphasized crises rather than placing these events in the framework of the rhythmical alternance, and mutual causation, of four phases of a complete cycle (Aftalion, Wesley Mitchell).

With the exception of chaotic dynamics which only emerged in the 1980s, these approaches were born in the nineteenth century. At that time, most writers advanced their explanations of crises without placing them in a broader theoretical perspective – also because most of these authors were not theorists but bankers, merchants, journalists, politicians, or social reformers. The metaphors they used, however, sometimes help to reveal the view on the role of crises in the working of the economic system to which they implicitly subscribed.

Let us go back to Table 4 for examples contrasting the 'crisis' and 'recurring crises' approaches. In the 'crisis' perspective, the normal state of the economy (in both the statistical and normative sense of the term) is characterized by a condition where consumption meets production and exchanges take place without being disrupted. The crisis is caused by whatever disrupts this process: either a natural phenomenon, or a 'political disease' (Say) consisting in government interference with the operation of markets. It has an external origin, it is destructive, is is sudden and unexpected, it affects everybody in the same way. Any image from other disciplines or life experience is suitable to represent this view, and indeed many were used, in particular diseases, earthquakes, storms, avalanches, tidal waves. Most of these images, however, could be used in a different way by transferring other properties. Consider earthquakes: they could be seen as universally damaging, thereby fitting the 'crisis' view, but – when more was learned about the nature of earthquakes – they suggested the release of tension slowly accumulated in the earth's crust, and could be used to point out that *not all* buildings fall under their violence, but only the weak ones. The perspective is turned on its head: the problem is no longer the earquake, but the increasing tension in the earth's crust; the quake is only its inevitable consequence. So is the crisis: it results (so went the most popular explanation) from excessive speculation and facile credit, which are the real problem. The occurrence of the crisis only eliminates the fragile commercial houses, namely, those that had most imprudently exposed themselves to excessive debt.

Examples concerning the business cycle are less frequent. Apart from the pendulum, waves were sometimes cited in the early literature (shortly after the middle of the nineteenth century) when the notion of cycle was struggling to differentiate itself from that of recurring crises. Both these approaches recognized that crises are periodical, but while recurring crises emphasized the increasing tension and its subsequent violent relaxation without closing the causal circle by connecting the liquidation of the crisis and the next prosperous phase, the cycle view emphasized the movement as a whole. Towards the end of the century, the very specific analogies evoked by the early business cycle researchers referred to recognizably cyclical mechanisms, such as the piston of a steam engine (Tugan-Baranowski 1901), the Old Faithful geysers (Jones 1900), or the thermic inertia of a coal stove (Aftalion 1913), which made the nature of this perspective fully unequivocal.

Conclusion

The examples of the storm, the pendulum, the earthquake, and others briefly quoted above illustrate how the specific usage of the same metaphorical source produces rather different descriptions of the target depending on the set of properties that are transferred to it. Here lies at once the power and the danger of metaphors: similarity in one respect may be suggestive of other resemblances, which can be of heuristic value[12] or turn out to be totally deceptive depending on whether or not the transfer is pertinent.

For the historian of ideas this ambivalence is of great interest, for often the set of properties that are (or are not) transferred refers to matters at the core of one's beliefs, in many cases at a pre-analytical level. In particular, the usage of metaphors and analogies by writers discussing economic crises contributes to revealing their broad understanding of the role of these phenomena in the working of the economic system. When in the development of the argument this deep heuristic level is not always made explicit, perhaps due to the lack of linguistic precision (as often happened in the nineteenth century), or when it is couched in technicalities (as usually happens in the contemporary literature), the analysis of metaphorical transfers can help in recognizing hidden assumptions or postulates. For instance, the metaphor of bankruptcies selecting the fittest enterprises, as in the example of the kitten cited above, reveals at once that crises perform a useful function and that the ideal state of the system was poorly characterized. The survival of the fittest was interpreted in the tautological sense that the fittest is the one who survives, and accordingly the 'normal' state of the economy was understood as the one resulting from non-bankrupt firms rather than being characterized in terms of the conditions guaranteeing a smooth flow of trade and industry.

As the writer who uses metaphors should be careful to transfer only pertinent properties, so the historian of ideas should never forget that the metaphorical transfer is selective. Focusing only on source and target omits what is really important, the *tertium comparationis* characterizing *what* is transferred from source to target. The description of crises as 'tradequakes' (Kinnear 1847, pp. i–ii) is a brilliant piece of rhetorics for its expressiveness and economy of words, but does not mean much unless one understands in what, precisely, crises resemble earthquakes for that writer. Metaphor analysis can help to reveal the broad views and hidden premises on which different approaches on crises are based, provided, however, that it can identify the actual triplets defined by each writer's usage of metaphors, and map the triplets that emerge from a corpus of texts, looking for any patterns emerging and evolving in time, across languages and national traditions. It will be a rather tangled and messy web of relationships; my bet, however, is that it will be worth trying to unravel it.

Notes

1. This practice is followed routinely by the journal *Metaphor and the social world*, acknowledging that the border line between metaphors and other types of figurative language is often blurred and inviting researchers to extend the domain of inquiry into different types of tropes in so far as they are relevant to the process of interaction of thought and language (Cameron and Low 2011).
2. As Schumpeter observed, 'not much to their credit, the scientific leaders of the profession were not conspicuous' among the participants in the debates on crises: 1954, p. 742.
3. Although it is possible to distinguish between British and American English, the results (as cursorily checked in the associated list of literature that Ngrams provides together with the diagrams) do not seem to be fully consistent, probably due to the imprecisions in the bibliographic database of Google Books.
4. The figure cannot be reproduced here due to poor resolution, but the reader is invited to explore with these and other expressions cited below in the text. In particular, the figure omits some more frequently-appearing metaphorical expressions in order not to squeeze down the other lines in the graphic, making it illegible: 'credit crunch', 'economic collapse', 'financial collapse', 'economic breakdown', and 'wave of prosperity'. 'Smoothing' (a moving average of data on both sides of each year) has been set to 3 to better evidence the trend. The normalized frequency is calculated as the number of occurrences of each expression divided by the total number of words in the sample for each year.
5. The metaphorical expressions are: wave of depression, speculative fever, casino economy, financial contagion, financial madness, fever of speculation, financial storm, vortex of ruin, commercial earthquake, financial meltdown, financial explosion, credit crunch, economic collapse, financial collapse, economic breakdown, wave of prosperity, financial contagion, mania of speculation, speculation mania, ebb and flow of trade, commercial tide, tide of prosperity, financial earthquake, commercial earthquake, financial tempest, commercial storm, trade storm, financial whirlwind, trade storms, economic storm, economic tempest, financial hurricane, financial cyclone, commercial tempest, trade tempest, financial flurry, financial tornado, economic cyclone, financial explosion, commercial explosion, speculative contagion, financial contagion, financial disease, financial madness, financial insanity, commercial madness, financial struggle, financial struggles, financial storms, commercial struggle, trade struggle, economic meltdown, commercial disease, economic disease, malady of trade, financial disease, pendulum of commerce, pendulum of trade, trade pendulum, commercial pendulum, vortex of speculation, vortex of debt, vortex of bankruptcies, vortex of bankruptcy.
6. The expressions searched were any of the following: crisis, crises, business cycle, business cycles, trade cycle, trade cycles, recession, recessions, panic, panics, depression, depressions, stagnation, fluctuations, distress, gluts, glut.

7. An additional 489 items contain the metaphor but none of the words describing crises.
8. I am pretty sure that I owe this observation to René Thom, but I have not been able to retrieve the exact source.
9. For a more detailed discussion, see Besomi 2014.
10. I conjecture these five approaches also exhaust the possible list of logically conceivable distinct interpretations of the role of crises within the economic system. I am not, however, capable of proving it.
11. For a more detailed discussion of these approaches, see Besomi 2010, section 4.
12. See Klamer and Leonard 1994, p. 30.

Disclosure statement

No potential conflict of interest was reported by the author.

Funding

This work was supported by the Swiss National Science Foundation [project number 100018_169900].

References

Abramson, B., 2005. *Digital phoenix: why the information economy collapsed and how it will rise again*. Cambridge, MA: MIT Press.

Aftalion, A., 1913. *Les crises périodiques de surproduction*. Paris: Marcel Rivière.

Anonymous (Boston Merchant). 1823. Rate of exchange. &c. *Niles' Weekly Register*, 23 (595), 18 February, 356–358.

Anonymous (Birmingham manufacturer)., 1832. *A few plain remarks on the currency question, with reference to trade, taxation, and reform: containing also, strictures on the plan of the council, for restoring the prosperity of the country*. Birmingham: Barlow.

Anonymous., 1837. The moral of the crisis. *The United States Magazine and Democratic Review*, 1, October, 108–122.

Anonymous., 1856. Premiums for 1856: the year 1855 a remarkable year. Heard book controversies. *Ohio Farmer* 5 (2), 12 January, 6.

Anonymous., 1864. Commercial. *Liverpool Mercury*, issue 4964. Jan 6.

Anonymous., 1866. A panic. *Keowee Courier*. Jun 2, p. 2.

Anonymous., 1884. The business situation. *Omaha Daily Bee*. Dec 25, p. [7].

Anonymous., 1887. The financial question. *St. Paul Daily Globe*. Dec 25, Christmas Number, p. 28.

Anonymous., 1899. A commercial reaction. *The Hawaiian Gazette*. Oct 31, p. 4.

Arrese, A. and Vara-Miguel, A., 2015. A comparative study of metaphors in press reporting of the Euro crisis. *Discourse & Society*, 27 (2), 1–23.

Begbie, M.B., 1848. *Partnership 'en commandite', or, partnership with limited liabilities (according to the commercial practice of the continent of Europe, and the United States of America) for the employment of capital, the circulation of wages, and the revival of our home and colonial trade*. London: E. Wilson.

Besomi, D., 2010. 'Periodic crises': Clément Juglar between theories of crises and theories of business cycles. *Research in the History of Economic Thought and Methodology*, 28A, 169–283.

Besomi, D., 2011. Disease of the body politick. A metaphor for crises in the history of nineteenth century economics. *Journal of the History of Economic Thought*, 33 (1), March, 67–118.

Besomi, D., 2014. Tempests of the business world: weather metaphors for crises in the nineteenth century. *In*: R. Baranzini and F. Allisson, eds. *Economics and other branches – in the shade of the oak tree*. Essays in Honour of Pascal Bridel. London: Pickering & Chatto, 291–308.

Bickes, H., Otten, T., and Weymann, L.C., 2014. The financial crisis in the German and English press: metaphorical structures in the media coverage on Greece, Spain and Italy. *Discourse & Society*, 25 (4), 424–445.

Blanqui, J.A., 1836. Crise commerciale. *In*: *Encyclopédie des gents du monde*. Paris: Librairie de Treuttel et Würtz, vol. VII, 257–259.

Blumenberg, H., 1997. *Shipwreck with spectator. paradigm of a metaphor for existence*. Cambridge: MIT Press.
Boumans, M., 1992. *A case of limited physics transfer: Jan Tinbergen's resources for re-shaping economics*. Amsterdam: Thesis publisher.
Bruner, R.F. and Carr, S.D., 2007. *The panic of 1907: lessons learned from the market's perfect storm*. Hoboken, NJ: John Wiley & Sons.
Buchanan, D.[initialled F.], 1842. United States of America. *In*: *Encyclopaedia Britannica*. Edinburgh: A. Bell and C. Macfarquhar, 7th ed., vol. 21, 450–481.
Cameron, L. and Low, G., 2011. Metaphor and the social world. Introduction to the first issue. *Metaphor and the Social World*, 1 (1), 1–5.
Combe, G., 1840. *Lectures on moral philosophy: delivered before the 'Edinburgh Philosophical Society,' and reported for the 'Edinburgh Chronicle'*. 2nd ed. Boston, MA: Marsh, Capen & Lyon.
Culp, C.L. and Niskanen, W.A., 2003. *Corporate aftershock. The public policy lessons from the collapse of Enron and other major corporations*. Hoboken, NJ: J. Wiley.
Dew, T.R, 1835. On price—the causes and effects of the fluctuations considered, and the principles maintained applied to the present rage for speculation. *The Farmer's Register*, 3 (2), June, 65–72.
Engel, K.C. and McCoy, P.A., 2011. *The subprime virus: reckless credit, regulatory failure, and next steps*. Oxford: Oxford University Press.
Evans, D.M., 1859. *The history of commercial crisis, 1857–58 and the stock exchange panic of 1859*. London: Groombridge.
Fisher, I., 1925. Our unstable dollar and the so-called business cycle. *Journal of the American Statistical Association* 20, 150, June, 179–202.
Frisch, R., 1933. Propagation problems and impulse problems in dynamic economics. *In*: *Economic essays in honour of Gustav Cassel*. London: Allen & Unwin, 171–205.
Gibbons, J.G., 1858. *The banks of New York, their dealers, the clearing house, and the panic of 1857. With a financial chart*. New York: Appleton.
Goodwin, R.M., 1951. The non-linear accelerator and the persistence of business cycles. *Econometrica* 19 (1), January, 1–17.
Hicks, J.R., 1950. *A contribution to the theory of the trade cycle*. Oxford: Clarendon Press.
Hoffman, R.R., 1985. Some implications of metaphor for philosophy and psychology of science'. *In*: W. Paprotté and R. Dirven, eds. *The ubiquity of metaphor. Metaphor in language and thought*. Amsterdam: John Benjamins, 327–380.
Johnson, S. and Kwak, J., 2010. *13 bankers. The wall street takeover and the next financial meltdown*. New York: Pantheon Books.
Jones, E.D., 1900. *Economic crises*. New York: Macmillan.
Joplin, T., 1837. *An examination of the report of the joint stock bank committee: ... to which is added an account of the late pressure in the money market, and embarrassment of the Northern and Central Bank of England*. 3rd ed. London: J. Ridgway and sons.
Keynes, J.M., 1934. "Poverty in plenty: Is the economic system self-adjusting?", *The Listener*, 21 November 1934. *In*: *The collected writings of John Maynard Keynes*. London: Macmillan, vol. XIII, 485–492.
Kinnear, J.G., 1847. *The crisis and the currency: with a comparison between the English and Scottish systems of banking*. 2nd ed. London: Murray.
Klamer, A. and Leonard, T.C., 1994. So what's and economic metaphor? *In*: P. Mirowski, ed. *Natural images in economic thought*. 'Market reads in tooth and claw'. Cambridge: Cambridge University Press, 20–51.
Kolb, R.W., 2011. *Financial contagion: the viral threat to the wealth of nations*. Hoboken, NJ: Wiley.
Laing, J., 1867. *The theory of business*. London: Longmans, Green & Co.
Laing, S., 1844. *National distress: its causes and remedies*. London: Longman, Brown, Green, and Longmans.
Lakoff, G. and Johnson, M., 1980. *Metaphors we live by*. Chicago: The University of Chicago Press.
Lewis, M., ed., 2009. *Panic: the story of modern financial insanity*, London: Penguin.
Liverpool Currency Reform Association., 1849. *Suggestions for a new system of currency by which monetary panics will be rendered impossible: submitted to the trading community of Liverpool, by a committee of gentlemen who believe that the permanent prosperity of the country depends upon a proper settlement of the money question*. Liverpool: Lace and Addison.
López, A.M.R. and Llopis, M.A.O., 2010. Metaphorical pattern analysis in financial texts: Framing the crisis in positive or negative metaphorical terms. *Journal of Pragmatics*, 42 (12), 3300–3313.
Louçã, F., 2007. *Ten years of high econometrics. A short history of the generation that reinvented economics*. London: Routledge.
Michel, J.-B., *et al*., 2011. Quantitative analysis of culture using millions of digitized books. *Science*, 331, 176–182.
Nesvetailova, A., 2010. *Financial alchemy in crisis: the great liquidity illusion*. London: Pluto Press.
Schumpeter, J.A., 1954. *History of economic analysis*. London: Allen & Unwin.
Sinn, H.-W., 2010. *Casino capitalism: how the financial crisis came about and what needs to be done now*. Oxford: Oxford University Press.

Tugan-Baranowsky, M.I., 1901. Studien zur Theorie und Geschichte der Handelskrisen in England. Jena: Fischer (2nd German edition; Russian original 1894; partial English translation of the 4th edition, 1914, as periodic industrial crises: a history of British crises. *Annals of the Ukranian Academy of Arts and Sciences in the United States*, 3 (3), 1954, 745–802.

Wirth, M., 1890. *Geschichte der Handelskrisen*. 3rd ed. Frankfurt a.m.: Sauerländer.

Yule, G.U., 1927. On a method of investigating periodicity in disturbed series, with special reference to Wolfer's sunspot numbers. *Philosophical Transactions of the Royal Society of London, Series A*, 226, 267–298.

Vultures, debt and desire: the vulture metaphor and Argentina's sovereign debt crisis

Sonya Marie Scott

ABSTRACT

This paper explores the development of the vulture metaphor in relation to economic ideas, focusing on its reference to vulture funds in post-2001 Argentina. It traces the metaphorical connection between 'vultures' and the extraction of debt back to Elizabethan England, to Shakespeare's poem *Venus and Adonis* (1593). In the same period, we also see English law's earliest cases of the predatory purchasing of land titles in order to dispossess the poor. Contemporary cases involving sovereign nations defending against vulture funds have cited case law in the Elizabethan context in order to invoke a moral claim against speculation in distressed sovereign debt. The moral charge of the vulture metaphor – laden with connotations of greed, desire and manipulation – contrasts with legal arguments about repayment based on the rationality of contract law which demands repayment of debt and presumes equality of party. I explore this tension in both historical and contemporary litigation, ultimately focusing upon the performance of position taken by vulture funds, on one side, and the Argentine government on the other, in the 'case of the century' – *NML Capital v. the Republic of Argentina*.

Introduction

Vultures are striking creatures. They are scavenging birds of prey that kill the weak or wounded, feed on dead carcasses and rotting flesh, gorge themselves until they bulge. Because they have extremely corrosive stomach acid, vultures can eat rotten flesh laden with disease that would be toxic to other animals. The world of contemporary finance appears, in contrast, to be clean, rational and calculated. And yet certain arms of contemporary finance bear their own relation to scavenging predatory activity, such as debt markets and the securitization of sovereign debt. Within this highly lucrative, volatile, and crisis-inducing arm of global finance, the now infamous 'vulture funds' are usually characterized as private equity firms (or hedge funds) who buy distressed sovereign debt on secondary markets at low cost, with the intention to litigate later for full value of the bonds plus interest. These funds rely upon economic misfortune and crisis in order to later make a substantial profit. Litigation has successfully yielded high returns from debtor nations of the Global South such as Peru, Bolivia, Zimbabwe, the Congo, and Argentina.

A vast scholarship exists on the operation of these funds globally, and on the many efforts to thwart or stop this type of litigation altogether. Legal scholars have examined the issue from the perspective of bond contracts and debt litigation (Blackman and Mukhi 2010, Muse-Fisher 2014, Samples 2014, Kolb 2015, Billiet 2016, Rossi 2016, Carletti *et al.* 2017, Schumacher *et al.* 2018), foreign sovereign immunity laws (Pereyra 2014, Weidemaier 2014, Halverson Cross 2015), and the doctrine of odious debt (Michalowki 2007, Sookun 2010). Political economists, in turn, have explored the conditions that have given rise to the debt crises and opened up the terrain for vulture funds to operate (Fridman 2010, Hernandez Vigueras 2015, Cantamutto and Ozarow 2016, Ugarteche 2016). Finally others have explored the effects of vulture funds in the financial sphere, exploring what it means for markets, the movement of global capital, and speculative returns (Schultze and Lewis 2012). While each of these approaches inevitably informs my work, in this paper I engage in an interdisciplinary and heterodox project. Here I explore the vulture's metaphorical and performative value as an image mobilized ideologically. I trace the development of the vulture metaphor itself, from its economic meaning in connection to a debt-relationship in Elizabethan England to a speculative strategy in contemporary finance. The vulture image serves a powerful function in economic terms. I will show that it is not merely a matter of rhetorical artifice to invoke the vulture image, but rather integral to the struggle against the vulture strategy in legal and economic arenas. With its use, contract and debt-relationships that in legal or economic framings appear to be neutral and grounded in rational institutions, are exposed as power relations filled with intention, opportunism and deceit. Thus the use of the vulture metaphor is part of what I term a *performance of position* which claws back at the legally codified yet depoliticized subjective relations of contract and property. For this reason, perhaps the biggest and most notorious sovereign debt litigation to date – *NML Capital v. The Republic of Argentina* – will be the focus of my analysis of the manifestation of the contemporary vulture figure. This case reveals not only the legal and economic nuances of vulture activity, but also the importance of engaging in a cultural analysis of an economic phenomenon. Indeed, the battle lines of *NML Capital v. The Republic of Argentina* were often drawn well outside of the courtroom and bond markets, invoking a larger cultural and political struggle against the incursions of a very unique form of financial capital.

What follows is an examination of both the use of the vulture metaphor in historical context, as well as an exploration of the economic and legal contexts that give rise to vulture activity in the first place. The legal tradition itself provides the conceptual linkage from Elizabethan England to contemporary sovereign debt litigation, as vultures are marked both by the selection of an asset in distress, and by the intention to later litigate. For vultures accumulation by dispossession requires litigation. Legal history shows both how vultures have tended to operate, and how the law has served to sanction or prohibit such activities depending on the period of economic history (and location) in question.

In order to work through legal and economic history at the same time as the metaphorical and discursive value of the vulture metaphor is fleshed out, this essay is organized into four primary sections. The first section traces the history of a landmark case in vulture fund litigation – *Elliot Associates v. The Republic of Peru* – through the legal offences of champerty and maintenance as they appear in medieval and early modern England. The economic and legal history of champerty and maintenance, the legal offences which apply to the strategy of dispossession by litigation, is the contextual ground of the first use of the vulture metaphor in Shakespeare's poem *Venus and Adonis* (1593). Shakespeare's use of the vulture metaphor in relation to the extraction of debt shows more than a certain type of extortionate behavior. It also reveals the nature of subjects who use their position of power in order to satisfy their desires. This particular power relationship pertains to economic practices of the time, and also illuminates the implications of the metaphor in later legal and economic usage. Thus in the nineteenth century in the US, several courts found these offences to be legally obsolete as power and class dynamics were substantively different than those of early modern England. Indeed, this obsolescence was perceived to hold until vulture litigation began in earnest in the 1990s and champerty and maintenance made an appearance in a sovereign nation's defense in *Elliot Associates v. The Republic of Peru*, where a hedge fund successfully litigated for full bond repayments from a sovereign nation. The second section explores the neoliberal turn that made cases such as *Elliot v. Peru* possible, examining the confluence of geopolitical factors such as changing global debt-relationships, neoliberal economic experimentation in South American military dictatorships, changing foreign sovereign immunity laws in the United States, and new attitudes towards global capital and debt in the International Monetary Fund. The third section tracks the re-emergence of the vulture metaphor to describe extraction of debt and the practice of dispossession by litigation, primarily with reference to the venture capitalism of Wall Street in the 1980s and 90s and with respect to the behavior of vulture funds. These modern vultures are rendered all the more significant when the source of the distressed debt that they target is determined to be 'odious,' that is, incurred by illegitimate or unconstitutional regimes such as the Argentine military dictatorship of 1976-1983. The final section uses what many Argentine commentators have termed 'the case of the century,' or *NML Capital v. The Republic of Argentina*, in order to show how the vulture metaphor plays a leading role in the ideological performance of position. Here we look at the attempt by the Argentine government to transform what the hedge fund presented as merely a matter of contract over the terms of bond repayment, into a charged moral and ethical debate over the power of speculative capital and the sovereignty of nations. Legal arguments about repayment based on the rationality of contract law which presumes equality of party contrast with the moral charge – laden with connotations of manipulation and premeditation – of the vulture metaphor.

Dispossession by litigation and the extraction of debt

One of the most cited modern cases brought against a sovereign nation by a vulture fund is *Elliot Associates L.P. v. Republic of Peru* (1998). In this case Elliot Management, a private investment firm established by Paul Singer,[1] successfully sued Peru over unpaid bonds which the firm had refused to renegotiate (unlike the vast majority of the bondholders, who accepted renegotiated terms) and then compelled the Peruvian Central Bank to pay despite the new terms of the renegotiated bonds (the importance of which will be addressed later). The lineage from this case back to Elizabethan England relies on a few key cases such as *Slyright v. Page* (1587), *Gerarde v. Worsely* (1579) and *Patridge v. Strange* (1552), all of which were cited by Peru in their defense as they claimed that Elliot Management was actively engaging in the practice of champerty 'in purchasing the debt in violation of Section 489 of the New York Judiciary Law' (*Elliott Associates, LP v. Republic of Peru*, 12 F. Supp. 2d 328, 1998).

Champerty in fact goes back yet further than the Elizabethan cases cited by the Peruvian defense, and we can trace its origins to medieval England. During the reign of Edward I (1274–1307) champerty was understood to be a type of maintenance (i.e. support) for those parties litigating with the purpose of deriving some of the profit or advantage that might come from the suit (Winfield 1912). In contemporary terms, 'the law of champerty deals with an aggravated form of maintenance, i.e. maintenance and a right to obtain a share of the proceeds of a lawsuit. This definition applies in the UK and aims to stop solicitors "trafficking" in litigation' (Sookun 2010, p. 32). But in Richard II's reign (1327–1377) statutes explicitly prohibit maintenance by great officers, minor officers, or others who might have had the power to support litigation for their own pecuniary gain. There is ample evidence of dispossession by litigation by those wanting to share the profits of such activity:

> Cap. 9 recites complaints that many people, great and small, having a good title to lands or goods are delayed in actions for their recovery because the defendants convey such property to lords or other great men, and the plaintiffs are thus frightened from pursuing their claims. (Richard II, c.4, cited Winfield 1912, p. 152)

Remedies against champerty and maintenance tended to fail, for those who were entreated to uphold such laws were often the very same powerful men who were violating them in the first place. Winfield explains that

> the offences of conspiracy and maintenance had a fatal attraction for all alike who held high office. At one moment the King, his Council, and Parliament are giving remedies against these offences. At the next, he and they are committing them. The judges, sheriffs and the Justices of the Peace, the clergy were no better. (p. 154)

So by the sixteenth century, these practices were entrenched amongst the elite. The practice of evicting those who possessed lands by buying up the titles and then litigating, using wealth and influence to sway the courts' decisions, was a significant enough problem that in 1540 legislation was passed against the purchase of pretended titles with intent to then sue for eviction without having first possessed the land.[2] Of course this law was abused as well, as it did not require genuine possession, only a visit of an hour by the litigating party. Nonetheless, an attempt was made to curb the behavior whereby the rich could claim title to lands possessed by the poor and through litigation dispossess them of their land. The rule of maintenance was also useful in this context, as it prohibited leading a party into legal action without any justifiable cause.

While in Elizabethan England the practice of dispossession by litigation was well established, the vulture metaphor was not yet commonly used in relation to economic practices. The first known connection between the vulture metaphor and the collection of debt can be found in Shakespeare's *Venus and Adonis* (1593), a poem which retells a scene from Ovid's *Metamorphoses*. The economic metaphorical register throughout the poem reveals the subtleties of a power struggle between two individuals of competing wills and differing positions of strength. What is perhaps more interesting yet is that during the same period that we see Shakespeare employ the vulture metaphor in relation to lust, greed and manipulation of a weaker party, we also see the aforementioned legal changes in English law. His work can be read as a reflection upon the time and place that he was living, and upon the abuse of power that was rampant in feudal society. Through his allegorical tale Shakespeare inevitably takes us into some of the political and economic debates of the Elizabethan era, including jurisprudence relating to the questions of maintenance and champerty.

Shakepeare's *Venus and Adonis* is notable for many reasons, and it is generally considered to be his most sexually explicit work. It was well received at the time of writing, and, according to literary scholars, many of its contemporary readers allegorically associated the character of Venus with Queen Elizabeth (Duncan-Jones 1993). In this version of Ovid's tale Venus is older and far more sexually experienced than Adonis. Ignoring his pleas for solitude, she lusts after him with a voracious appetite. Adonis is not interested in her advances, nor in love generally, believing it to lead to jealousies and other debilitating afflictions. Instead his interest lies in hunting for wild boar and caring for his horse. He believes himself to be too young to be tied down, and throughout the poem tries to escape her grasp. Ultimately Adonis gets his wish and escapes her, only to be killed by the very boar he so desired to hunt, leaving Venus disconsolate and alone.

The theme of lust is crucial to the economic language used in Shakespeare's poem. The relationship of unrequited love between Venus (older, experienced, relentless) and Adonis (young, beautiful, wary) is established in decisively economic and legal terms. Themes of exchange, debt, price and interest are used metaphorically to depict the demands made by a woman who is more powerful than the object of her desire. The economic register is introduced to the poem when Venus attempts to lure Adonis into her arms with the promise of gain through interest: 'Give me a kiss, I'll give it thee again/And one for interest, if thou wilt have twain' (209–210).[3] Adonis, however, is indifferent to this particular incentive. Indeed, the transaction works against his desire to be free and unconstrained, able to hunt without further obligation.

Throughout the poem, embodied sexual pleasure is portrayed almost exclusively as a form of exchange, yet it is neither mutual nor voluntary. Instead lust requires debt as a bonding agent, an insidious point of contact and contract. In broad strokes Shakespeare shows the difference between love and lust: 'love surfeits not, lust like a glutton dies / Love is all truth, lust full of forged lies' (803–804). Unlike love which may cause *unintended* sorrow, lust brings *intentional* ruin upon the reluctant party, as it is fundamentally opportunistic, seeking weakness or moments of hesitation. For example, when Venus hears Adonis' vehement discourse against love, she faints, falling unconscious to the ground. Adonis' attempt to revive her leads him to kiss her, and with this small concession she feigns greater injury yet. Seizing upon the moment and his sense of guilt, Venus quickly establishes a debt contract:

Pure lips, sweet seal in soft lips imprinted
What bargains may I make, still to be sealing?
To sell myself I can be well contented
So thou wilt buy and pay and use good dealing
Which purchase, if thou make, for fear of slips
Set thy seal-manual on my wax-red lips. (511–516)

Venus' body becomes the site of contract, and Adonis, incautious, guilty, and ever hoping to leave, abides her wishes. But this contract bears interest, and Venus appears to hope that Adonis will not pay, as his lapse would set a process of accumulation into motion: 'say, for non-payment that the debt should double, / is twenty hundred kisses such a trouble?' (521–522). Adonis attempts to respond in non-economic terms, bringing moral questions to his defense, claiming that he is too young for such an encounter and that he is neither ready nor mature enough. We witness here in the first use of the economic vulture metaphor the introduction of an accompanying moral register – making a shift in language away from mere contract or technicality to a defense against the extractive logic itself. This shift in language and register will be integral to the *performance of position* taken up by Argentina in its legal and political defense against its modern day Venus, NML Capital.

When Venus and Adonis finally part 'the honey fee of parting tender'd is' (538), leading us to believe that this transaction may indeed be coming to a conclusion. Instead, however, Venus reveals the true nature of lust. Lust hopes to entrap, and possess fully, regardless of the feelings or wellbeing of the other party. Further, lust is never satisfied, just as a large debt that bears interest can never be fully paid by a poorer party. Thus as Adonis pays his parting kiss, Shakespeare shows us the insatiable nature of the lust, 'whose precious taste her thirsty lips well knew/whereupon they surfeit, yet complain on drouth' (543–544). The vulture moment is thus at hand, as Shakespeare likens Venus to a predator feasting on her prey:

Now quick desire hath caught the yielding prey
And glutton like she feeds but never filleth
Her lips are conquerors, his lips obey
Paying what ransom the insultor willeth
Whose vulture thought doth pitch the price so high
That she will draw his lips rich treasure dry. (547–552)

As Adonis obliges Venus we see her greedily feed, with her vulture thought revealing the manipulation which allows her to continue to draw from Adonis' treasure despite the risk to his being. Her vulture thought shows the use of position – relationally she is more powerful than the younger, inexperienced and naïve Adonis – to her advantage in order to satisfy her lust, which is metaphorically likened to an insatiable quest for riches.

While medieval and early modern England saw considerable jurisprudence working to curtail champerty and maintenance, the same could not be said for the modern era. Indeed, in the nineteenth century, a new discussion of the validity of laws against champerty and maintenance took place in the United States. In the reasoning for *John Wright v. William Meek* (1851), the court, instead of moving to curtail the practice, discussed the historical importance of champerty in order to later argue that the economic conditions and class relations of the contemporary U.S. made it largely obsolete. The doctrine of champerty serves the function

> to repress the practices of many who, when they thought they had title or right to any land, for the furtherance of their pretended right, conveyed their interest, or some part thereof, to great persons, and with their countenance did oppress the possessors. (*Western Law Journal* 1851, p. 546)

Thus reference to *Slyright v. Page* was rejected as precedent in *John Wright v. William Meek et al*, because, the court reasoned, the class structure and capacity for abuse of position was not substantively similar in the United States of the nineteenth century. The doctrine of champerty was thus perceived to be largely obsolete as there were no barons or lords with such stature and political influence. In 1892 the Supreme Court of Oregon echoed this same reasoning (Albany Law Journal 1892, pp. 29–30).

In recent years some have warned of the dangers of declaring the doctrines of maintenance and champerty obsolete. In Australia, under the auspices of the *New South Wales Law Reform Commission* (1994), the reasoning behind the abolishment of maintenance and champerty as part of Australian law was found to be legitimate because maintenance is 'an obscure and dubious offence, of which we have found no reported instance' (p.8). However, as the investigative commission noted, the abolition of maintenance and champerty has unexpected modern consequences, including the inability of the court to address speculative lawsuits. The Commission's report concludes,

> It is clear [...] that one consequence of abolition is the proliferation of litigation support by third parties. This increase in litigation support has manifested itself, for example, in public interest litigation, speculation in law suits, and the credit hire cases. (p. 26)

Thus from Elizabethan vultures, maintainers, and champetors we come to *Elliot Associates L.P. v. Republic of Peru*, where once again these abusive medieval practices such as the purchase of title with *intention* of litigation, are relevant in disputes over the non-payment of sovereign debt. While Peru used the very principle of champerty in its defense against Elliot Management, and were initially successful, upon appeal the court overturned the ruling disallowing claims of champerty in defense against vulture litigation. The decision was based on the argument that the intent of the private investment firm is first and foremost to receive payment in full. Should that fail, as merely a secondary option, the funds will litigate for full repayment. The Court's initial admission of the champerty claim by Peru was crucial both in terms of the understanding of the relative positions of power of vulture funds and sovereign nations, and in terms of the legal tolerance for the vulture strategy of bond purchases with the intention of litigation. Had the court upheld the initial ruling in favor of Peru, the precedent in jurisprudence would have been incredibly important for vulture fund cases to follow. Instead, explain Blackman and Mukhi (2010):

> In a game-changing decision, the Second Circuit reversed the district court, holding that if the suer's intent in purchasing the discounted debt was to be paid in full or *otherwise* to sue, such intent did not meet champerty's intent requirement. The Court of Appeals found Elliott's intent to sue on the debt was 'contingent' even though 'Elliott knew Peru would not, under the circumstances, pay in full.' The Second Circuit's narrow reading of the champerty defense was accepted by other courts, as by the D.C. District Court in *Turkmani v. Republic of Bolivia*, and saved the business of speculating in defaulted sovereign debt from what would otherwise have been a major setback. (Blackman and Mukhi 2010)

With this precedent in mind, we can turn to the political and economic circumstances that have led this new breed of vultures to tarry with old legal conventions and heavily indebted sovereign nations. We will see in *NML Capital v. The Republic of Argentina* that while the Peru case meant that champerty did not hold in Argentina's defense, the vulture metaphor could be used in popular discourse and in the political arena to establish the moral validity of the contemporary struggle against vulture litigation, in much the same way that the objection to champerty and maintenance was based upon the moral objection to the abuse of position against the poor as a strategy of accumulation. Ultimately the vulture metaphor becomes an important tool for sovereign nations pushing back against dispossession against litigation.

The neoliberal turn: a new stage for vultures

Despite some continuity in the practice of dispossession by litigation throughout the centuries following the reign of Edward I, the vulture metaphor does not reappear in the West in connection to the abuse of a position of debt or distress until the late 1970s and early 1980s. During this period we find a confluence of changes relating to debt relations globally. The new financial period then dawning in the Global North is accompanied by an increase in indebtedness in the Global South. This of course is well documented and well known (Bianchi 1985, Griffith-Jones 1988, Roddick 1988, Cohen 2015). With respect to the resurgence of the vulture metaphor in Latin America and in Argentina in particular, certain ideological and material shifts in this period are nonetheless worthy of note. The early shift in Latin America to what we now know as neoliberalism was epitomized in strategic terms by the work of the Chicago School. The market solution to nationalized industry was first tried in Pinochet's Chile under the guidance of Milton Friedman and other Chicago School economists (Valdés 1995, Kogut and Macpherson, 2008). The privatization of pensions, state industries and public firms and the commensurate potential to free up considerable amounts of capital for financial markets held great appeal, and in several senses both Chile (with a well-entrenched and US-backed right-wing dictatorship) and Argentina (with its newly formed military dictatorship) were ideal spaces for neoliberal experimentation.[4]

And with this experimentation came a lot of ideological work both in terms of public policy and public attitudes towards markets and economic individualism. A significant part of the ideological work necessary for the 'modernization' (i.e. marketization) of the Argentine economy during the period of the 1976–1983 dictatorship involved a shift in economic subjectivity[5] (Fridman 2010, Cohen 2015). The normalization of individualized debt-relationships (albeit on a small scale compared with counterparts in the Global North) and formalized market structures for investment required the dissemination of knowledge and a rupture with prior customary and informal means of investment, credit-seeking and lending. Previously familiar and interpersonal relations of market knowledge became formalized through government-sponsored education campaigns aimed at creating a new generation of conscientious consumers (Martinez de Hoz 1981, 1991) and through the publication of financial tables, inflation rates and prices in the newly emergent financial press, including the financial newspaper *Ámbito Financiero* which gained political influence throughout the dictatorship (Ruiz 2005, Fridman 2010).

Of course changes in legal and macroeconomic policies were also crucial to the neoliberal shift, and in the US-Argentina relationship we can trace out various key moments. Likely the most relevant to later vulture activity is the 1976 legal reform of the Foreign Sovereign Immunity Act (FSIA) in the United States. Victor Abel Pereyra (2014) contextualizes this shift in Foreign Sovereign Immunity Law:

> in the context of sovereign debt litigation, the FSIA enshrined that foreign governments were not immune from suit if they had previously waived their immunity in a contract and provided successful litigants a limited avenue of enforcement against sovereign assets used for a commercial activity. (p. 5)

Moreover,

> a shift […] occurred in the wake of the 1976 enactment of the Foreign Sovereign Immunities Act (FSIA) in the United States. The statute seemingly acted as a trigger. Before enactment, virtually no country's bonds included terms designed to facilitate legal enforcement; afterwards, virtually all did. (Weidemaier 2014, p. 71)

These legal shifts in sovereign immunity legislation correspond to the increase in sovereign debt that had been growing in the 1970s, though scholars have noted that a substantive increase in litigation against sovereign debtors did not take hold until the early 2000s (Halverson Cross 2015, Schumacher *et al.* 2018). Corresponding to internal US policy, there was also a shift in the International Monetary Fund's approach to economic stabilization as evidenced in the 1976 reforms to the fund, along with the IMF's 1979 'Policy Guidelines' (Boughton 2000, Ugarteche 2016). The policy guidelines in particular reflect

> the basis for the introduction of contemporary economic ideas to central banks and to the governments of debtor nations. This was the moment of triumph for the Mont Pelerin Society, founded in 1947 by von Hayek, von Mises and Lippmann, among others, and a moment of triumph for their 'libertarian' ideas which were shared by Milton Friedman and Alan Greenspan, president of the Federal Reserve between 1987 and 2007. (Ugarteche 2016, p. 71)

Finally, our survey of the geopolitical context is rounded out by the fact that Argentina began to accumulate significant debt under the military dictatorship, both from external lenders and due to fraudulent internal policies. During his tenure as Secretary of the Economy (1976–1983), Martinez de Hoz was responsible for a complex debt strategy involving finance, publically owned enterprises and privately held companies. Sabine Michalowki (2007) explains that Martinez de Hoz's strategy in fact rendered a significant portion of private business-related debt public, and provided lucrative opportunities for those in finance to export the interest they had gained from loans as a form of capital flight (Michalowski, pp. 8–9), for publically owned enterprises to take up large loans in pesos while the US dollars funding these loans stayed with the central bank (p. 10), and for privately held companies to dump their debt into a consolidated state debt. By the end of the military dictatorship, therefore, debt had been incurred in order to support the pecuniary interests of the financial and economic elite who were supportive of the dictatorship, as well as state projects in infrastructure, educational reform, reputational work such as the hosting of the 1978 World Cup, and its repressive function including the disappearance, detention and torture of approximately 30,000 Argentine citizens.

The estimate of Argentina's debt as of the end of the dictatorship in 1983 is 48 billion dollars, and this continued to grow throughout the 1990s with the full endorsement of the IMF (by whom Argentina was labeled a model-debtor) and with the ill-fated neoliberal policies of president Carlos Menem (1989–1999). Hernandez Vigueras (2015) explains that 'the military dictatorship, who first chose the US as the jurisdiction in which to resolve the conflicts relating to the external debt' (pp. 99-100, my translation) also set into play a legacy of economic conditioning for future generations. While this geopolitical contextualization is but a cursory glance at the shifts effected relevant to US-Argentine relations in the late 1970s and early 1980s, it does help us to identify the confluence of factors under the military dictatorship which contributed to Argentina's debt crises of 2001 and 2014, and sets the stage for the emergence of the new vultures – those seeking sovereign debt in crisis in order to extract surplus through litigation. An analysis of the shifts effected during the military dictatorship is helpful not only in terms of understanding changes in economic subjectivity attempted throughout the body politic, but also will help us make sense of the moral claims against sovereign debt incurred under dictatorships, and the use of the moralistic language of vulture in order to describe the private equity hedge funds seeking its repayment.

Modern vultures and odious debts

In the early reappearance of the term vulture, economic use appears to be restricted to the United States, and to Wall Street and speculative capitalists in particular. As the use of the term increases alongside the varieties of speculative capitalism in the 1980s, it is applied more generally either to venture capitalists purchasing assets in companies who were underperforming, or to the investment in debts in failing companies that nonetheless had tangible assets. In the latter case, corporate law – with the general principle of the priority rule (Hansmann and Kraakman, 2004) – ensures that a corporation that becomes insolvent must first cede its assets to its creditors, who would thus be the first to recuperate their investment in the case of bankruptcy. This type of behavior is marked by a clear intention to buy precisely when distress is detected. The risk of bankruptcy is not a risk at all for vulture capitalism. Rather, it is precisely at the point of an already anticipated ruin that profit can be extracted, so long as the debt is sufficiently distressed as to be offered at low cost.

One of the very first references to contemporary vulture capitalists in the printed press comes from the *Washington Post* in 1978, where a financial column explains to its readers: 'In some circles, venture capitalists are unaffectionately referred to as "vulture capitalists"' (1 October 1978, pp. 2–3). References to vultures throughout the 1980s and 1990s are almost exclusively within the business press, either as depreciative comment on unscrupulous business activity, or, in some cases, as a sure bet for investment. The latter can be seen clearly in *BusinessWeek* where the analysts argue that in terms of investing, 'One of the best bets for now could be the 'vulture funds' that are snapping up debt of disconnected telecoms' (Braham 2001, p. 162). In this case, we begin to see the clear link between vultures and crises. As the dot.com bubble burst in the late 90s and early 2000s, and as companies with tangible computing and technical assets went under, the capacity to buy up distressed debt from telecoms and then to sell their tangible assets at a profit, was utterly tantalizing. The connection between crisis and the purchase of distressed debt in this fashion can also be seen in the Great Depression of the 1930s US, where this type of vulture activity was instead termed predatory capitalism. Indeed, predatory capitalism was the preferred term for this type of anticipatory investment in debt, until it gradually became joined by the term vulture capitalism from the 1970s through to the 1990s.[6]

In general, the use of the term vulture funds predicts that they are viewed negatively in most contemporary academic scholarship, as these funds describe private equity firms who through their hedge funds buy up the distressed bonds of sovereign nations once they are available on secondary markets at reduced rates, i.e. once they attain the status of junk. The vulture funds buy specifically with the intention of suing for the full original value of the bond – often standing to make 200–300% returns on their original purchase. Just as Venus did not merely intend to extract the value of the perceived debt owed to her by Adonis, but whose vulture thoughts were not abated, vulture funds seek not their original investment plus interest, but rather the full value of the bond issued, prior to its junk valuation, plus interest. There is extensive contemporary legal scholarship that has described the work of vulture funds particularly with respect to the unsustainability of their actions against sovereign nations.[7]

It is useful to note, in the context of the vulture acquisition of junk bonds, that sovereign debt renegotiation tends to be the norm and preference within the international community of lenders. Sovereign debt renegotiation allows nations in default or in deep crises the capacity to remain functional within, and open to, global capital flows. Debt renegotiation is fully entrenched within the logic of global capital as it allows for conditionalities – now all too familiar under contemporary austerity regimes – to be placed on debtor nations, keeps the country's market open, and keeps the nation viable (yet subordinate) in global markets all while salvaging a portion of the bond payments. While in most cases sovereign nations are able to renegotiate their bond payments with the majority of bondholders, vulture funds operate as 'holdout creditors' who refuse to accept anything but the full value of the bond as originally issued. In some cases holdout creditors represent 10% or less of the total creditors, but are able, through litigation over terms of contract, to thwart repayment to the majority of creditors as they seek full payment including all amassed interest. For this reason, in some jurisdictions such as in the UK, Collective Action Clauses (CACs) have come into effect, imposing the terms of the renegotiated debt on all creditors so long as a substantial majority has approved it. This thus theoretically prevents vulture funds from acting as holdout creditors and stalling the recovery of sovereign nations attempting to emerge from deep crises or defaults (Muse-Fisher 2014, Samples 2014, Kolb 2015, Megliani 2015, Carletti *et al.* 2017).

Certain legal scholars, on the other hand, help take the question of vulture funds and the treatment of sovereign debt further by adding a layer of analysis and engaging with the legitimacy of many sovereign debts by invoking the question of odious debts, or debts incurred under dictatorships or non-democratic regimes, often for the purpose of financing repressive activities or military budgets. This is particularly pertinent to the question of vulture funds, because it calls into question the analytical treatment of debt as a fundamentally neutral contractual issue, rather than an ethically charged, unequal and historically located credit relationship. Michalowski (2007) argues that the current economic reality of the Argentine state cannot be divorced from the economic policy of the dictatorship during the late 1970s and early 1980s:

> the debt policies of a military regime that governed without any democratic participation or control decisively shaped the future of the country, as it not only left it with an unsustainable debt, but through this indebtedness has moreover influenced and conditioned the economic, financial and social policies of the democratic government ever since. (p. 31)

Given the combination of systemic corruption that we have already discussed in the case of Martinez de Hoz's conversion of privately held debt into state debt, with the many debts incurred by the dictatorship in order to carry out violent repression and what some term political genocide, the term odious debt has earned a place in the long legacy of Argentina's sovereign debt. Michalowski argues that at the core of the debate about the nature and repayment of debt incurred by former dictatorships is marred by differences in linguistic registers and in the nature of argumentation. Specifically, she claims that

> the reality and the ideological and political visions of the anti-debt campaigners, on one side, and of creditors trying to get the developing world to repay its debt, on the other, are so far removed from each other that the arguments raised on each side hardly connect. (pp. 2–3)

Thus in order to reconcile the moral indignation which propels those opposed to odious debt with the financial and recuperative aims of international capital, specifically speculative purchasers of distressed debt, legal scholars demand a more robust framework through which to understand contract. In such a manner, the claims of creditors can be brought into the same arena as the claims of those concerned with the legitimacy of the debt owed. Notwithstanding these voices, the ongoing work of vulture funds and their legal and political representatives is to reduce the discourse of debt to a matter of contract and the parties of contract to the present day. As we will see, doing so requires a particular framing of sovereign debt crises, which remains a significant site of epistemological and ideological struggle.

Understanding crises: contracts v. vultures

During his tenure as the US Secretary of the Treasury, Henry Paulson commented before the 2007 House Committee on Financial Services that, 'we use moral solutions. But the vulture funds have the rule of law on their side' (cited Muse-Fisher 2014, p. 1671). Indeed, since purchasing distressed Argentine bonds on secondary markets, both private equity firm NML Capital and its parent company Elliot Management have brought numerous claims against the Republic of Argentina, all in the effort to extract the full value of bonds purchased at deep discount. Since 2003 the U.S. Second Circuit Court of Southern New York has seen numerous claims relating to the country's repayment obligations, to the discovery of Argentine assets in the United States (with the future aim of embargoing said assets), and to the relationship between holdout bondholders such as Elliot and NML, and the vast majority of bondholders who instead accepted renegotiated loans (exchange bondholders).

The immediate historical backdrop to the vulture fund suits brought against Argentina is found in the 2001 Argentine default, where the country was unable to service its 132 billion dollar debt, at that point the single largest default in world history. The crisis that ensued was particularly devastating, and poverty grew to unprecedented levels. In a 2003 World Bank Policy Research Paper economist William Cline argued that most economists could agree that the Argentine crisis was the result of the 'combination of several influences that, like a "perfect storm," brought about what might be called the 3D collapse: default, devaluation, and depression' (2003, p. 10). In 2003 Nestor Kirchner was elected president and despite the fact that the country owed a debt of over 120% of its actual GDP (Cohen 2015), a slow plan of recovery started to take shape, evidenced by steady improvements in GDP growth for the duration of his presidency (2003–2007). Critical to the economic recovery strategy was a renegotiation of the country's debt, and through a massive swap in 2005, the majority of bondholders agreed to a significant write-down (Cantamutto and Ozarow 2016). In 2010 another swap took place, and at this point almost 93% of all bondholders had agreed to a valuation worth about 30% of the original debt (Doyran 2014). The remainder of the holdout creditors were primarily vulture funds, who had never intended to agree to any renegotiation (despite the fact that it would have nonetheless been profitable for them to do so, as they had bought the debt so cheaply) but instead had intended to litigate for full value through U.S. courts.

From 2005 until 2014 these hearings continued, with the most important and publically noted proceedings taking place in 2012 and 2014 in the Southern District of New York, under the purview of Judge Thomas Griesa. While in 2012 the court denied NML's attempt to discover Argentine assets within the US, ultimately the courts sided with the holdout creditors in 2014 by temporarily freezing the funds used for regularly scheduled payments to the exchange bondholders, and denying Argentina's appeals against NML and Elliot Management. Subsequent to the election of government of President Mauricio Macri in 2015, the vulture funds have been paid in full, financed by loans arranged through creditors on Wall Street. In what *The Washington Post* described as a 'handsome and historic payoff' (Merle 2016), the Argentine government signed off on what economists Joseph Stiglitz and Martin Guzman (2016) described as 'something close to the terms that Judge Griesa set. NML Capital will receive about half of the total agreement – $2.28 billion for its investment of about $177 million, a total return of 1,180 percent' (Stiglitz and Guzman 2016, p. 25). Argentina was also obliged to pay the legal fees of the vulture funds.

Because securitized debt and debt restructuring tend to be difficult for the general public to follow and for the press to depict in an appealing manner,[8] what I term the *performance of position* became critical as an ideological and political complement to the legal struggle between NML Capital and Argentina. The performance of position involves the public presentation of certain legal and economic postulates which define the parameters of subjective identities and relations. The performance of position arises in spaces of perceived epistemological uncertainty and necessarily requires a very specific positing of subjectivity and of the subjective relationship between parties. The constraints of the legal defense available to sovereign nations being sued by vulture funds, notably the upper hand held by the private equity firms in contests of contract law, and the non-admissibility of the champerty defense, made the deployment of a specific from of language and the clear signaling of moral position utterly essential to Argentina's legal strategy. The funds also responded to this signaling as their credibility was clearly at stake. Given that *NML Capital v. The Republic o. Argentina* was both incredibly politicized and incredibly publicized the importance of understanding the ways in which the rhetorical framings of position were deployed cannot be overstated. Each side in this particular dispute engaged in differing strategies with differing degrees of success.

NML Capital and other vulture funds, or the more favorably termed 'holdout creditors' were able to engage in this performance within the legal system in which a legal subjectivity confined to the rules of contract law could be asserted. They were also able to represent themselves in publicity put out by lobby groups and think tanks funded by those controlling the interested private equity funds. Finally, they had excellent coverage in the international press and in the center-right Argentine media[9] who tended to accept the position of US capital as both the most accessible and most objective.

The Argentine government positioned itself in several different ways as well. These included official government statements made in court, speeches and press releases made by the President and the Finance minister, and by government representatives to the United Nations. There were also numerous extra-governmental agents who contributed to Argentina's positioning including the sympathetic media,[10] a significant left intelligentsia, trade unions and popular supporters, international experts who supported Argentina's debt renegotiation, and international bodies such as the United Nations.

Within the various sites of subjective performance, very specific linguistic representations of subjects and relationships emerged. From NML's position, holdout creditors were presented as individuals, creditors, investors, taxpayers, parties to contract, and legal subjects appealing to the dictates of contract law. From this position Argentina, in contrast, was represented as a 'bad actor,' who was negligent, immature, petulant, with a long history of debt and poor behavior, and a legal subject both stubbornly refusing the dictates of contract law, at the same time as it perpetuated falsehoods about holdout creditors and the process of debt repayment. The debt itself is presented as ahistorical and acontextual, merely a fact over which a contract was drawn, though in a few instances the debt is presented as just another case in a long history of a bad international debtor. This particular performance of position, therefore, is based in a methodological individualism that locates ethics and moral rectitude squarely within the confines of contract law and the contract relationship.

Under both the presidency of Nestor Kirchner (2003–2007) and, far more so, the presidency of his wife and successor Cristina Fernández de Kirchner (2007–2015), the performance of position looks dramatically different. NML Capital is not portrayed as a holdout creditor but instead as a vulture fund, or, in Spanish, often just *buitre*, or 'vulture.' The difference here was to push back against the position of NML and to demonstrate that they were not *normal* creditors, nor was this a normal contractual relationship. The character of the private equity funds is moralized in and through the name vulture itself. In striking similarity to Shakespeare's Venus, the character of the vulture fund is predatory upon weakness, opportunistic with *intent* to litigate, with a voracious desire for profit through interest. From this perspective it is not simply a vulture behavior, but in the very nature of these private equity funds, to seek opportunities for extortion. In contrast the nation, Argentina, is presented as responsible and willing to diligently repay the 93% of exchange bondholders. It is also vulnerable to imperialist threat, as hostage to an extortionate situation, and as principled and firm in its resistance the vultures acting against the norms of restructuring preferred by global capital. Debt in this relationship is understood systemically, and while not often associated with the odious debt we have already explored, it is often traced to the reckless neoliberalism of President Carlos Menem in the 1990s, and to the legacy of North-South economic relations.

We can trace these two performed positions through three episodes in particular in order to glean the way in which each vies for legitimacy both the eyes of their constituencies and with respect to the legal apparatus of the New York Circuit Court, the United Nations, and the Argentine government. The three episodes include: (1) the publicity around the 2012 ruling; (2) the attempts to embargo Argentine assets, and; (3) the publicity around the 2014 ruling and Argentina's pseudo-default.

Publicity around the 2012 Griesa ruling

The framing of parties as individuals is requisite of contract law, and with respect to *NML Capital v. the Republic of Argentina*, we can see even as early as 2012 how the conservative Argentine press was sympathetic to the holdout bondholders and portrayed them as individual investors – or, in this particular instance, as 'creditors.' Burgueno (2014) cites an interview by Martin Kaninguiscr in *La Nación* with Robert Shapiro, a spokesperson from the lobby group *American Task Force Argentina* (ATFA),[11] wherein NML and Elliot are portrayed as creditors. Among many of the references to the funds as creditors, Shapiro says 'Let's call for Argentina to accept negotiations in good faith with the creditors who have not yet been paid' (cited Burgueño, p. 155, my translation). The use of the term 'creditor' to describe vulture funds implies not only that these funds are portrayed as 'individuals' who are party to a contract, but also that the funds have the status of 'investors' rather than scavenging opportunists (as the vulture metaphor implies), or speculators operating on behalf of high net worth individuals who manage private equity funds that specifically make their gains through litigation.

This creditor characterization of NML and Elliot reveals the discursive weight of contract, credit and debt. The neutral register used to describe the funds as creditors invokes the correlate burden of responsibility on their debtors. This ultimately aims to equate a subject's submission to legal demands (or maintenance and champerty, as we have seen in earlier jurisprudence) with its responsibility and maturity on the world stage. In this particular instance the language of creditorship neutralizes and depoliticizes the overtly power-laden relationship in order to appear fair and objective, and more importantly to coerce payment according to an ethical order in which those who comply with the terms set by the creditor are perceived to be mature subjects and full participants in the legal order, while those who do not comply are perceived to be deviant, immature and rightfully excluded. Reflecting upon the 2012 ruling in 2014, *The Economist* ran an editorial which described the inherently stubborn and adolescent Argentine character with respect to the treatment of creditors and law on the international stage: 'the exercise of a kind of teenage narcissism in which it is fine to break rules you don't like, in the belief that you will get away with it' (Bello 2014). This is of particular curiosity when weighted against the norm of sovereign debt renegotiation, or the many morally based arguments against the repayment of odious debt.

This characterization has precedent in the very first resolved case involving holdout creditors in post-2001 Argentina, namely *Abaclat and Others v. Argentine Republic* (2007). Legal scholar John Billiet (2016) explains the careful framing of vulture fund activity as that of 'holdout creditors' and as the expression of individual contract rights in the context of international investment arbitration. This is an important case because of the status that holdout creditors were granted as investors. Its power of precedent was somewhat mitigated, however, by the fact that the majority found in favor of *Abaclat and Others* on the basis of a breach in the bilateral investment treaty between Italy and Argentina, rather than on the grounds of the validity of holdout creditorship (usually argued through the legal principle of *pari passu*, or 'in equal step,' which implies the equal treatment of all creditors) or expectation of full returns on bonds purchased on secondary markets.

Attempts to embargo Argentine assets (2005–2012)

'To embargo goods is fundamental to the vulture strategy' (Burgueño 2014, p. 106). As part of the claim brought by NML Capital against Argentina came the strategy of embargo. In total, between 2005 and 2012, NML Capital attempted to embargo 28 Argentine assets across the United States, Europe and Ghana. The assets included the Argentine Central Bank's reserves in Switzerland, the historically significant residence of Argentine liberator General José de San Martín located in Boulogne Sur Mer (France), and most symbolically the Argentine naval frigate *Libertad* which was held in port by the Ghanaian government at the behest of NML Capital. The strategy of embargo can be considered part of a recuperative economic strategy on the part of a creditor seeking repayment from an uncooperative debtor. Indeed the subject of NML's appeal in 2012 was precisely the discovery of Argentina's assets within the US. In 2010, summarized the court, NML served subpoenas in order 'to gain an understanding of Argentina's financial circulatory system' (695 F .3d 201 2012) and locate its assets, and the movements thereof, worldwide. The goal of this strategy of discovery is to use this rather clinical understanding of the 'financial circulatory system' in order to recuperate missing bond payments through legally accessible Argentine assets housed outside of its borders.

Some argue, however, that this economic viewpoint does not correspond with the intent behind attempts to embargo:

> In reality, vulture funds know at the end of the day jurisprudence will conclude that state assets located in another state cannot be embargoed. That is not overly relevant, however, as the strategy at hand aims elsewhere. The vulture fund, with these legal actions, is seeking to publically humiliate the debtor state for a period, obliging the debtor state, in the eyes of the international press, to defend its honor and sovereignty in front of another country's courts to liberate whatever asset is being embargoed. (Burgueño 2014, p. 107)

The frigate *Libertad* was a symbolically loaded example of this strategy, both because of the timing of the embargo and its impact on patriotic sentiment. Only two years after the bicentennial celebrations of Argentine independence (2010), which were instrumental for the Kirchner government as part of a long ideological positioning against mayor of Buenos Aires and presidential aspirant Mauricio Macri, the leverage of the *Libertad* in many ways allowed a patriotic anti-vulture narrative to take on popular resonance. Indeed, while both the terms 'los holdouts' and 'los buitres' were used in the media, the vultures, or *buitres*, predominated even pro-vulture media outlets. During the fall of 2012 President Cristina Kirchner gave a speech from the Bicentennial Museum that reiterated the Argentine state's refusal to be shamed internationally into paying the vulture funds, and refuted national critics who were beginning to buy into the Argentina as bad-actor narrative (Burgueño 2014, p. 127).

Hector Timmerman, who served as Argentine Minister of Foreign Affairs from 2010–2015, argued in front of the United Nations, and ultimately won their support, by first personifying the ongoing court cases with the identification of Paul Singer as owner of the funds, and then by equating the behavior of vulture funds with piracy:

> Never has a vulture fund managed to expropriate a property of the government of Argentina, and we are not going to permit that vulture funds, who are today the Pirates of the twenty first century, in any way try to do what the pirates of the seventeenth or eighteenth century did. (cited Burgueño 2014, p. 129)

This appeal held moral and ethical sway, and as a result in the fall of 2015 the United Nations adopted the 'Basic Principles of Sovereign Debt Restructuring Processes' resolution. Two of the key themes throughout the resolution are the sovereignty of nations to restructure debt, and the validity of foreign sovereign immunity in the courts of other nations. It also upholds the basic tenets of CACs in order to prevent further vulture activity. Notably, however, the US, the UK and Germany voted against the resolution.

In some of the many legal proceedings that took place in the run up to this particularly showy international embargo dispute over the frigate *Libertad*, NML Capital and Elliot Management made serious attempts to subpoena and lay claim to Argentina's foreign assets, particularly those located in the US. The legal argumentation is of course always contract-based and neutral, referring to the particularities of the case insofar as they relate to the Foreign Sovereign Immunity Act (FSIA). It is important to note that these legal proceedings against sovereign nations are more complex than those for corporations in periods of insolvency. Bankruptcy and Chapter 11 provisions are well codified, and generally aim to prevent the absolute collapse of large business entities because of the economic and political impact of their demise. In the case of sovereign nations, however, bankruptcy is not an option, nor do they benefit from the codification of the terms of debt renegotiation so clearly. A different attitude is thus taken, and the nation, unlike the ailing corporation, is often characterized as wrongdoer. For example, José A Cabranes, the Court of Appeal Second Circuit Judge who ultimately denied the appeal of the vulture funds in *NML Capital Ltd. and EM Ltd. V. Banco Central de la Republica Argentina* (2011) paints Argentina in a manner which reveals the contempt which the court held for such an irresponsible track record. He cites the 'sorry history of defaults on sovereign debt' in Argentina's history, and references its 'diplomacy of default' to indicate its status as chronic debtor. In perhaps a more damning comment, right before ultimately denying NML's claim for discovery, he argues (referencing Argentine writer Jorge Luis Borges),

> One need not have what Argentina's great gift to literature termed 'a case of prodigious memory' to recall the Republic's appalling record of keeping its promises to its creditors. [...] Argentina's record in global bond markets has given new meaning to the concept of *caveat emptor*. Even when the Argentine people offer a substantial premium to those adventurous souls who risk a loan to the country, for many investors, the experience of being a creditor to the Republic has been a profile in disappointment. (652 F.3d 172 2011)

Poignantly, the characterization here is not just that Argentina, as sovereign nation, is irresponsible and a chronic debtor, but also an active cheater and risk to those who choose to loan it money. Investors are buyers, and vultures buying already distressed and highly discounted bonds are not distinguished from the adventurous souls who bravely lend money to those in need when promised potentially high returns.

Publicity around the 2014 ruling

The appearance of 'reasonable' and 'responsible' legal subjectivity in contract law favors holdout creditors, as the relation between these private equity firms and sovereign nations becomes a relation of the parity of individual parties under contract law. We see this reflected in a more popular form in the reporting on *NML Capital v. Argentina* in the mainstream press of the Global North. On July 31,

2014, the *New York Times*, along with most of the major US and UK papers, reported that Argentina had once again gone into default after a declaration by the rating agency Standard and Poor's. There was a contentious debate between the Argentine national government and those who benefitted from the rating agency's position. On July 31st the Kirchner-sympathetic Argentine daily *Página 12* bore a bold headline '*No Hubo Stay y No Hay Default*' (*There was no stay and there is no default*) accompanied with an image of Finance Minister Axel Kicilof, and many pages of analysis rejecting the claim that the frozen monthly bond payments that were destined to go to the 93% of the exchange bondholders who had indeed agreed to the renegotiated terms, was an artificial default event brought about by Judge Griesa's rulings.

Página 12 employed the vulture image in dozens of graphic covers throughout the 2014 hearings in New York, and was likely one of the unnamed source referenced by US commentators frustrated with what appeared to be a disrespectful attitude toward Judge Griesa, the private equity funds, and the process itself. A variety of sources engaged in the coordinated portrayal of the litigation and the U.S. parties involved as extortionate and vulture-like. Infographics explaining the complexities of the *fondos buitres* and the litigation in New York from the news network *Telesur* reference the Argentine ministry of the Economy, *Telam* (a national news agency), *Nodal* (a Latin American news agency) and *Página 12* as their sources. Throughout Buenos Aires and other major Argentine centers buildings and billboards were plastered with images of vultures and the American flag, symbol of the imperialist impulse of the vultures, and clearly intended to set a tone of resistance to the authority of the American courts and American investment capital. On the day of the purported default, US scholar Barbara Kotschwar of the Georgetown Center for Latin American Studies, and specialist in foreign direct investment and free trade, was cited extensively in the *New York Times*:

> 'I think that many people buy the argument that Argentina did not default, and buy into the hatred of the evil vultures,' she said, referring to the government's attempt to vilify the hedge fund holdouts. 'The story to watch, however, is what conclusion Argentines will draw in the medium term if their country's economy and their personal welfare is affected and their daily lives become more complicated.' (Stevenson and Caselli 2014, p. 6)

Here the term 'vulture,' coupled with 'evil,' is used by a proponent of the holdout creditor position in order to show the exaggeration and hyperbole of Argentina's position. To call holdout creditors vultures, it is implied, is to vilify creditors and invoke hatred amongst the people for their activities. Inherent in this framing is a sharp contrast between the emotion of hatred and insult with the logic and moral rectitude of a business or contract position. The government here is painted as at risk of irrationally subjecting its people to misery because of its reckless emotional response to a relatively standard creditor–debtor relationship.

The narrative of immaturity and adolescent petulance is also prevalent among editorials in the international press. Apart from *The Economist's* likening of Argentina to Luis Suarez (a Uruguayan footballer who bit another player while on the field in the 2014 World Cup and was subsequently ridiculed as childish in the international press) there were numerous insulting portrayals of the Argentine position, framing it as not only irresponsible but also fundamentally stupid. For example, just prior to the psuedo-default, Heidi Moore of *The Guardian* writes:

> This is the first time something quite this stupid is happening, so we'll have to keep watching. [...] As anyone who has written a check to a terrible landlord or cold-hearted credit-card company knows, disliking someone is not a good reason not to pay what you owe. Any American who has feared foreclosure can enjoy a bitter laugh: if you didn't pay your mortgage or credit cards for 13 years, you would be on the street. Argentina just gets to throw a tantrum.

Representations of the conflict between the vulture funds and the Argentine state may have varied in their tone throughout the press, but moralizing from the position of the holdout creditors quite effectively neutralizes power relations by using rational legal subjects as equal agents in a larger equation.

Daniel Pollack, a court-appointed mediator to the talks between NML Capital and Argentina, was cited in the *New York Times* just after the psuedo-default. Against Argentina's claim that they had not in fact defaulted, he responded:

> Default is not a mere 'technical' condition, but rather a real and painful event that will hurt real people: these include all ordinary Argentine citizens, the exchange bondholders (who will not receive their interest) and the holdouts (who will not receive payment of the judgments they obtained in court). (Stevenson, *New York Times*, 30 July 2014)

This representation of the situation paints the citizens of Argentina (a normally neglected party, and indeed a relatively vulnerable population with a high incidence of poverty), as in equal danger with the people who are exchange bondholders (many of whom are large banks and other institutional investors), and the holdouts (who we now identify with the hedge funds managed by Singer among others). The equation of a vulnerable population who could actually lose access to clean water, public medicine, electricity and heat, is leveled against the margins of the wealthiest investors in the world.

Conclusion

The financial pages in the *New York Times* on 1 August 2014 paint a narrative well outside of the performance of position waged by the holdout creditors and Argentina. The financialized reality of modern debt trading in times of crisis is revealed, in a statement from the International Swaps and Derivatives Association, to be far more complex than two contractually linked parties participating in a traditional lending relationship:

> Argentina's failure to make a payment on its bonds earlier this week would activate credit default swaps on the country's debt. In the coming days, investors who used the swaps to insure against the default will collect money from investors on the other side of trade. (*New York Times*, 1 August 2014)

As is the case in derivatives markets and the increasing layers of complex financial instruments, the idea that securitized debt involves a 'lender' and a 'borrower' who must pay the lender back is becoming increasingly divorced from reality. The epistemological obscurity of these debt markets only increases the stake of each actor in the performance of position through metaphors and language in order to present a distilled and persuasive version of the problem. While traders in finance are seeking arbitrage opportunities on volatile markets, usually outside of the public eye, in the legal battle between NML and Argentina we see the simple logic of contracts pitted against the moral logic of vultures. The use of the vulture metaphor was a very promising development in Argentina's positioning against the vulture funds. The metaphor undoubtedly helped to garner international support from the United Nations, contribute to a global discourse against the speculative and predatory strategy of litigation, and bolster efforts in non-US jurisdictions to create and enforce CACs. Nonetheless, the rhetoric of responsibility and maturity leveraged against Argentina by the vulture funds was ultimately more successful in legal terms, as it complemented the already codified norms of contract law.

The strategy of accumulation through litigated dispossession employed by modern vulture funds can be considered anachronistic. It necessarily involves a public relations campaign, active lobbying, and a cunning use of language in order to position itself as legitimately engaging with the legal system. While the returns are potentially high, and while NML's campaign was undoubtedly successful, it looks painfully antiquated when compared to the nuances of modern trading. We have explored the development of the vulture metaphor from its economic meaning in connection to a debt-relationship in Elizabethan England to this speculative strategy in contemporary finance. And in the history of champerty and maintenance, offenses so obscure they were considered to be obsolete in the nineteenth century, the return of vulture litigation appears to render it most relevant again, despite the aversion in contemporary jurisprudence to admit its currency. Just as Venus threatened Adonis' very wellbeing with her relentless lust, contemporary vultures threaten not only the wellbeing of the debtor nations they target – for these of course are the nations whose debts are the most unbearable and difficult to pay – but they also threaten the logic of debt renegotiation and global capital, despite discourse to the contrary. One need only look to the post-vulture Argentine debt landscape to see that economic growth and the wellbeing of the vulnerable members of Argentina's population is in critical disarray.

With the shift from Cristina Fernandez de Kirchner's government to the business-oriented government of Mauricio Macri in 2015, both the discourse of debt (and vultures) and the discourse around Argentina's attitude and place in the world have shifted dramatically. After campaigning on the promise to repay vulture funds, and following through on these promises in 2016, the *buitres* no longer figure as a character within the country's sovereign debt narrative. But with all current economic indicators pointing to another severe crisis, potentially even another default, and with new loans and conditionalities from the IMF, and a forecast of one hundred years of debt servicing, the serial drama of Argentine debt is certainly not nearing a close. Many concur that a major crisis which could potentially involve another default or similar event is inevitable in the next few years. The 'case of the century' – *NML Capital v. the Republic of Argentina* – will certainly bear importance should its sovereign debt once again be relegated to secondary markets and open to the predatory eye of future vultures.

Notes

1. Paul Singer is a US hedge fund manager who is notorious for his 'activist' investment strategies that often involve litigation against debtors (be they major firms or sovereign nations). His firm Elliot Management manages $34 Billion in assets (Forbes 2018).
2. Statute 32, Henry VIII, 1540 c. 9, also titled the *Maintenance and Enbracery Act 1540.*
3. All references to Shakespeare's *Venus and Adonis* are made with the poem's line numbers, as found in Rolfe (Ed.), 1890.
4. While not all privatization efforts were immediately successful, Kogut and Macpherson (2008) note that 'The diffusion of privatization policies began with the British and Chilean privatizations of the late 1970s and early 1980s that demonstrated the feasibility of large-scale privatization' (p. 110).
5. It should be noted that caution is needed when approaching these issues, as this particular military dictatorship was particularly brutal, repressive and destructive with approximately 30,000 people, primarily from the organized left, disappeared, tortured and killed during its tenure. Additionally, voice and attitudes towards economic thought were not unified within the ruling structure of the dictatorship.
6. Note that predatory capitalism today does not simply refer to the intentional taking of distressed debts or assets, but is also used to refer to systemic inequalities in wealth that grant disproportionate levels of power to corporate economies of scale and to finance capital. This is, some argue, the capitalism that seeks government protection of corporations and big finance in order to maintain inequalities and to avoid the pitfalls of genuine competition in the market (Chomsky 2005).
7. See Muse-Fisher (2014), Samples (2014), Vernengo (2014), Megliani (2015) and Rossi (2016) for legal defense of the use of sovereign debt-renegotiation, and the problems presented by *NML v. Argentina* for the defense of sovereign nations in future vulture fund litigation.
8. Stiglitz and Guzman (2016) refer to this particular case as 'perhaps the most complex trial in history between a sovereign nation [...] and its bondholders'.
9. This is best represented by the right-leaning Argentine dailies *Clarín* and *La Nación.*
10. This is best represented by left-leaning Latin American sources such as the news network *Telesur*, the South American Monthly *Le Monde Diplomatique* (Southern Cone Edition), and the Argentine daily *Página 12.*
11. The ATFA is a lobby group promoting the contract rights of holdout creditors in the case of sovereign debt litigation, specializing in Argentina post-2001 economic crisis Paul Singer was one of the major supporters of this group, at the same time that his private equity fund NML Capital stood the most to gain from successful litigation. Mike Lasusa (2014) notes that 'ATFA executive director Robert Raben told the *Huffington Post* in that the group's mission is to 'do whatever we can to get our government and media's attention focused on what a bad actor Argentina is' [...]. The organization also placed full-page ads in the *Washington Post*, the *Financial Times*, and the *Wall Street Journal*, as well as prominent Argentine media outlets such as *Clarín* and *La Nación* as 'an answer to a campaign of misinformation being waged by the Argentine government, specifically by its Economy Minister Axel Kicillof' (https://www.counterpunch.org/2014/07/18/fact-checking-fact-check-argentina/).

Disclosure statement

No potential conflict of interest was reported by the author.

References

Albany Law Journal. 1892. *Albany Law Journal*, 45, 21–40.

Bello, W., 2014. The Luis Suarez of International Finance: Argentina's debt stand-off reflects a teenage attitude that rules are made to be broken, *The Economist*, 412 (8894) July 5, 31.

Bianchi, Andrés, ed., 1985. *La Deuda Externa Latinoamericana*. Buenos Aires: Emece Editores.

Billiet, Johan, 2016. *International investment arbitration: a practical handbook*. Portland: Maklu.

Blackman, Jonathan, and Mukhi, Rahul, 2010. The evolution of modern sovereign debt litigation: vultures, Alter Egos and other legal Fauna. *Law and Contemporary Problems*, 73 (4), 47–61.

Boughton, James, 2000. *The IMF and the silent revolution: global finance and development in the 1980s*. Washington, DC: International Monetary Fund.

Braham, L., 2001. Vulture investing: money managers are snapping up the debt of disconnected telecom companies. *Businessweek*, 27 Aug, p. 166.

Burgueño, Carlos, 2014. *Los buitres: Historia oculta de la mayor operación financiera contra la Argentina*. Buenos Aires: Edhasa.

Cantamutto, Francisco, and Ozarow, Daniel, 2016. Serial payers, serial losers? The political economy of Argentina's public debt. *Economy and Society*, 45 (1), 123–147.

Carletti, Elena, *et al.*, 2017. The price of law: the case of the Eurozone collective action clauses. Duke Law School Public Law & Legal Theory Series No. 2016-1, Swiss Finance Institute Research Paper No. 17-35. SSRN: https://ssrn.com/abstract = 2686879.

Chomsky, Noam, 2005. *Chomsky on anarchism*. Ed. Barry Pateman. Oakland: AK Press.

Cline, William, 2003. *Restoring economic growth in Argentina*. World Bank Policy Research Working Paper 3158.

Cohen, Michael, 2015. *La Economía en Tiempos de default: Recuperación y Crecimiento de la Argentina*. Buenos Aires: Eudeba, Universidad de Buenos Aires.

Doyran, Mine, 2014. The Argentine dilemma: 'vulture funds' and the risks posed to developing economies. *Class, Race and Corporate Power*, 2 (3), Article 7. http://digitalcommons.fiu.edu/classracecorporatepower/vol2/iss3/7.

Duncan-Jones, Katherine, 1993. Much ado with red and white: the earliest reader's of Shakespeare's *Venus and Adonis* (1593). *Review of English Studies*, 44 (176), 479–501.

Eavis, Peter, 2014. Argentina default is ruled a credit event for swaps. *The New York Times*, 1 August, p. x.

Elliot Associates, LP v. Republic of Peru, 1998. U.S. District Court for the Southern District of New York. 12 F. Supp. 2d 328 (S.D.N.Y. 1998), 6 August 1998.

Forbes., 2018. Forbes 400: The definitive ranking of the wealthiest Americans. *Forbes*, Oct 3. Available from: https://www.forbes.com/forbes-400/#78671aee7e2f.

Fridman, Daniel, 2010. A new mentality for a new economy: performing the *homo economicus* in Argentina (1976–1983). *Economy and Society*, 39 (2), 271–302.

Griffith-Jones, Stephany, 1988. *Deuda externa, renegociación y ajuste en la América Latina*. Mexico: Fondo de Cultura Económica.

Halverson Cross, Karen, 2015. The extraterritorial reach of sovereign debt enforcement. *Berkeley Business Law Journal*, 12 (1), 111–143.

Hansmann, Henry, and Kraakman, Reinier, 2004. The end of history for corporate law. *Georgetown Law Journal*, 89, 439–461.

Hernández Vigueras, Juan, 2015. *Los Fondos Buitres, Capitalismo Depredador: Actores políticos, judiciales y económicos de un negocio global*. Buenos Aires: Capital Intelectual.

Kogut, Bruce and Macpherson, J.M., 2008. The decision to privatize: economists and the construction of ideas and policies. *In:* B. Simmons, F. Doblin, and G. Garrett, eds. *The global diffusion of markets and democracy*. Cambridge: Cambridge University Press, 104–140.

Kolb, Robert, 2015. The virtue of vultures: distressed debt investors in the sovereign debt market. *Journal of Social, Political and Economic Studies*, 40 (4), 368–412.

Lasusa, M., 2014. Fact-checking "Fact-Check Argentina." *Counterpunch*, 18 July. Available from: https://www.counterpunch.org/2014/07/18/fact-checking-fact-check-argentina/.

Martínez de Hoz, J. A., 1981. *Bases para una Argentina moderna. 1976–80*. Buenos Aires: No name of publisher available.

Martínez de Hoz, J. A., 1991. *Quince años después*. Buenos Aires: Emecé.

Megliani, Mauro, 2015. Vultures in courts: Why the UNCTAD Principles on responsible financing cannot stop litigation. *Leiden Journal of International Law*, 28 (4), 849–862.

Merle, R., 2016. How one hedge fund made $2 billion from Argentina's economic collapse. *The Washington Post*, 29 Mar.). Available from: https://www.washingtonpost.com/news/business/wp/2016/03/29/how-one-hedge-fund-made-2-billion-from-argentinas-economic-collapse/?utm_term=.a4c7040e588b.

Michalowki, Sabine, 2007. *Unconstitutional regimes and the validity of sovereign debt: a legal perspective*. Burlington, VT: Ashgate.

Muse-Fisher, John, 2014. Starving the vultures: *NML Capital v. Republic of Argentina* and solutions to the problem of distressed-debt funds. *California Law Review*, 102 (6), 1671–1725.

New South Wales Law Reform Commission, 1994. *Barratry, maintenance and champerty*. Sydney. Discussion Paper 36.

Oregon Supreme Court, 1892. Champerty. *Albany Law Journal*, 45 (2), 28–30.

Pereyra, Victor Abel, 2014. *Year executive deference, sovereign immunity, and NML capital v. Argentina: a constitutional analysis of sovereign immunity litigation*. Illinois Public Law and Legal Theory Resarch Paper Series No.14-28, 1–34. SSRN: http://papers.ssrn.com/abstract = 2396192.

Roddick, Jackie, 1988. *The dance of millions: Latin America and the debt crisis*. London: Latin American Bureau.

Rossi, Julieta, 2016. Sovereign debt restructuring, national development and Human rights. *Sur International Journal on Human Rights*, 13 (23), 185–196.

Ruiz, F., 2005. *El señor de los mercados: 'ambito Financiero', la City y el poder del periodismo económico de Martínez de Hoz a Cavallo*. Buenos Aires: El Ateneo.

Samples, Tim, 2014. Rogue trends in sovereign debt: Argentina, vulture funds and *pari passu* under New York Law. *Northwestern Journal of International Law & Business*, 35 (1), 49–86.

Schultze, G. and Lewis, J. 2012. *The art of vulture investing: adventures in distressed securities management*. New Jersey: Wiley.

Schumacher, Julian, Trebesh, Christoph, and Enderlein, Henrick, 2018. *Sovereign defaults in court*. ECB Working Paper No. 2135. SSRN: https://ssrn.com/abstract = 3134528.

Shakespeare, William, 1890. *Shakespeare's Poems: Venus and Adonis, Lucrece, Sonnets, Etc*. Ed. William J. Rolfe. New York: Harper and Brothers.

Sookun, Devi, 2010. *Stop vulture fund lawsuits: a Handbook*. London: Commonwealth Secretariat.

Stevenson, A., 2014. S&P says Argentina has defaulted. *New York Times*, 30 July. Available from: https://dealbook.nytimes.com/2014/07/30/s-p-says-argentina-has-defaulted/.

Stevenson, A. and Caselli, I., 2014. Argentina is in default and also maybe in denial. *New York Times*, 1 Aug, 6b.

Stiglitz, J. and Guzman, M., 2016. How to hold a country for ransom. *New York Times*, 1 Apr, p. 25a.

Ugarteche, Oscar, 2016. *Historia Crítica del FMI: el gendarme de las finanzas*. Buenos Aires: Capital Intelectual.

Valdés, Juan Gabriel, 1995. *Pinochet's economists: the Chicago School in Chile*. Cambridge: Cambridge University Press.

Vernengo, Matías, 2014. Argentina, vulture funds, and the American justice system. *Challenge*, 57 (6), 46–55.

Washington Post. 1978. Finance. *The Washington Post*, 1 Oct, 2–3 m.

Weidemaier, Mark, 2014. Sovereign immunity and sovereign debt. *University of Illinois Law Review*, 2014 (1), 67–113.

Western Law Journal. 1851. John Wright v. William Meek et al. *Western Law Journal*, 537–548.

Winfield, Percy Henry, 1912. *History of conspiracy and abuse of legal procedure*. Cambridge: Cambridge University Press.

Confronting Spain's crises: from the language of the plazas to the rise of *Podemos*

Jose Luis Carretero Miramar and Christopher Bradd[1]

'PSOE, PP, la misma mierda es'[2]

Introduction: Activist literature and the language of the plazas

In 1978 a new era of Spanish history began. By the end of the year a new constitution was introduced, formally ending the dictatorship, which had governed the country since the end of the Civil War (1939). Following the death of General Francisco Franco in 1975, a period of political and institutional compromise ensued. The outcome was the establishment of a new democracy – purportedly free of the unresolved antagonisms between fascism and the left that had characterized Spanish society since the Civil War. This period of compromise is known, simply, as '*la Transición*.'

In the years following the Transition, Spain sought acceptance within the European community (and subsequently the European Union) by developing macro-economic policies that conformed to the market liberalism requisite for membership. Since the transition period, only two parties have shared power, each following a relatively similar economic plan reliant upon real estate and tourism, and conforming to EU economic criteria: the conservative *Partido Popular* (PP) and the social-democratic *Partido Socialista Obrero Español* (PSOE). Despite being competing parties, they have governed the country as part of a bipartisan pact since the time of the new constitution.

In 2010 two major crises hit Spain as its massive real estate bubble burst. One was economic and had disastrous effects in all sectors of Spanish society. The other, a crisis of political legitimacy, called into question the validity of the very political institutions created during the Transition. With the economic crisis the European dream was dashed. Spain became among the first of many 'peripheral' European nations to bring about a larger Eurozone crisis, challenging the wisdom of its monetary union (Streek, 2015). At the same time the 'return to democracy' effected in the Transition was revealed as a misnomer, a set of compromises that had stifled the radical impulses of the left and the more general capacity of civil society groups to engage actively in the political realm. Now the very institutions of the state were being questioned, as was the neoliberal order upon which they had so heavily banked.

In this chapter we explore Spain's many responses to this dual set of crises. The voices of activists and political organizers are set alongside the voices of scholars because of the central role activists have played in developing new language with the capacity to challenge the economic and political orders that gave rise to Spain's crises in the first place. The expression of political and economic ideas, desires and imaginings has been increasingly constrained and contained in the contemporary neoliberal order, even as crises touch upon the lives of millions across the world, radically altering material realities and promising futures. This is especially true in Spain prior to 2010 as the many compromises made during the Transition reinforced much of the top-down authority of Francoist Spain, severely limiting the discursive capacity for political and economic dissent. The indictment of neoliberalism by cultural critic Henry Giroux, applies resoundingly to the Spanish case.

> Neoliberalism on both the domestic and international front has become the most dangerous ideology of the current historical moment. Not only does it assault all things public and sabotage the basic contradictions between democratic values and market fundamentalism. It also weakens any viable notion of political agency by offering no language capable of connecting private considerations to public issues. (p. 141)

And yet the absence of public spaces within which to express dissent or present economic alternatives, and the absence of a popular language through which to speak of individual experience in a way that connects to the social whole, were dramatically challenged by popular protest in Spain in 2011. What is particularly unique about Spain's experience is that, by putting people in serious economic peril, the financial crisis opened a dialogue about the lost opportunities in the transition from fascism to democracy. The rapid politicization of a massive proportion of Spanish society post-crisis amounted to a collective awakening, perhaps best captured by a popular slogan of protest in 2011 – '*dormíamos, despertamos*' ['we slept, we awoke'].

By exploring the *language of the plazas* – language that we come to know through experience, activism and critical engagement – within the context of Spain's economic and political crises, we attend also to subsequent legislative responses, including the rise of the *Podemos* ['We Can'] party and the new municipalism of several major centers. While Dierdre McCloskey's work, for example, has traced what she terms the 'rhetoric of economics' (1998), here we trace the *rhetoric of economic dissent*. This dissent is not necessarily coherently organized, nor locatable in any single critical or intellectual tradition. In many cases it does not even pertain to a specific text, existing instead in 'tropes that surround us' (Villanueva, 2015, p. 62). It is grounded in the opposition to the neoliberal practices of the Spanish state pre- and post-crisis. And most importantly, this language of dissent represents a concerted attempt to produce 'opportunities for translating private worries into public concerns, and individual discontent into collective struggle' (Giroux, 2005, p. 142).

The 15-M protests of 2011 were an important turning point in this linguistic development in Spain. The protesters, who occupied Madrid's central Puerta del Sol by the tens of thousands, were soon referred to as *indignados* ['the indignant'] in the press. The strength and momentum of the protest began what many have described as a historically unique movement (Taibo, 2011a; Antentas, 2017), and what others describe as the precursor to *Podemos* as a 'movement-party' (Lobera, 2015; Calvo and Alvarez, 2015; Martín 2015). The *indignados* focused on both the economic crisis that began in 2007, culminating in the 2010 bursting of the Spanish real estate bubble, *and* the crisis of political legitimacy that had begun to emerge. Discursively, the focus of 15-M protests was not merely on a particular political party or set of principles, but rather on the very nature of the transition to democracy in the late 1970s that had conditioned Spanish political and social landscapes for decades. The Spanish transition from dictatorship to democracy has been labeled as an 'exemplary' case by scholars and European political bodies alike. As such, it has been used as a model for other nations undergoing similar political transitions (Fernandes, 2015). Over thirty years later, however, during the 2011 15-M protests and the movements that followed, the Transition process itself was decisively called into question in and through a collective act of remembering and critique. 'In the summer of 2011,' writes Kornetis (2014), 'the trend of evoking Francoism as a direct precedent of repression and accusing the Transition of creating weak democratic foundations and a feeble political system was consolidated as a protest frame with the appearance of the *indignados*' (p. 86).

Some have described the period after the Transition as a 'great lapse in memory,' or even an 'abyss,' that dominated politics and culture (Vilarós, 1998). The challenge made against this culture, and against the austerity of post-crisis Europe demanded both a new culture and new modes of explanation. The sociopolitical landscape of post-2011 Spain bears a wider discursive and ideological register today than any time since the Civil War. Through popular collective enunciations such as chants, slogans, metaphors and even the very naming of movements, *language from below* has served a particularly important function in this respect. In part, this is because the economic impact of the crisis was so brutal that a large formerly apathetic and disenfranchised proportion of the population became rapidly politicized. Along with this wave of political consciousness came a wave of linguistic development. Tracing some of the history of the language of the plazas from the most important post-crisis protests to the language of institutional change (embodied most clearly by *Podemos*' bid for parliamentary power from 2014 onwards), reveals both the profound effects of the global financial crisis as well as the cultural and generational shift in the contemporary political arena.

The first section of this chapter traces the process of social rupture that accompanied the Spanish real estate crisis in the context of the global financial crisis, which began in 2007. The second section identifies the emergent organizations of social resistance to the economic adjustments and cuts made by the Spanish government. This includes the appearance of the 15-M movement, which manifested itself through a language charged with novelty and rupture, breaking with articulations of previous social movements that had adopted the state-sanctioned majoritarian discourse of the Transition. The third section narrates the process by which electoral alternatives were constituted by these new social movements, including the appearance of popular parties like *Podemos*, with a language and political imaginary of its own, and the new municipalism that swept major centers such as Madrid and Barcelona. The final section considers the future of the social movements that have been resisting the neoliberal project in Spain over the course of the last decade.

The great bubble and its dual crises

'We've hit the bottom. So recovery begins now, and it will exceed all expectations.' So affirmed the Spanish Treasury Minister Cristobal Montoro in September of 2013, still under the effects of the worst crisis suffered by Spain since the constitution of the parliamentary regime in 1978 (*La Vanguardia*, 2013). Indeed, this was a brutal crisis that left Spaniards in a protracted state of ruin. Unemployment reached 25.93 percent in the first four months of 2014, with some regions reaching near 40 percent (such as in the Andalucian locality of Jerez). Two million families found themselves with every member unemployed. There were hundreds of thousands of evictions and house repossessions (Salgado, 2017). And, according to a government report made to foreign investors, over 400,000 jobs were cut from the public sector (Martinez Matute and Perez, 2017).

The 2010 bursting of Spain's real estate bubble – the largest in its history – signaled the inevitability of the subsequent economic crisis. After the intensification of global processes of neoliberal financialization in previous decades, the Spanish State tailored its legislation and public policy to facilitate investment and speculation in construction, real estate and large-scale tourism.[3] Sparked by speculative real estate activity, the domestic crisis could never have reached such a magnitude if it were not also for the particular nature of the Spanish banking system. Indeed, the Spanish case differed from other countries in the periphery of the EU such as Italy.

> Banks in Spain (to be precise, the *cajas*) turbocharged a property bubble, funded through short-term capital inflows, which resulted in high net foreign debt.[4] The implosion of this property bubble coupled with dependence on wholesale market liabilities in addition to the depth of the economic crisis, meant trouble for the Spanish *cajas*, triggering a traditional banking crisis. The *cajas*, unlike Italian banks and Spanish large commercial banks, suffered heavy losses and 'banked on the state' for financial support. [...] A balance of payments crisis followed, due to sudden and significant capital outflows. The Spanish government did not have sufficient funds to recapitalize its ailing banks, resorting instead to euroarea funds. (Quaglia and Royo, pp. 502–503)

This credit-driven real estate crisis and its subsequent fallout can be understood as a result of a long-term strategy for economic stimulation and growth that political economist Robert Brenner (2006) has called 'asset price Keynesianism.' With the traditional Keynesian approach, public debt is taken on by the government in order to stimulate economic growth. With asset-price Keynesianism, however,

> demand is 'subsidized' by means of corporations and wealthy households incurring of rising *private* deficits so as to spend more than they make, encouraged to do so by the increased paper wealth that they effortlessly accrue by virtue of the appreciation of the value of their stocks, or other assets. (p. 293)

Lopez and Rodriguez (2010) suggest that combined with extremely high levels of home ownership (87 percent in 2007), asset-price Keynesianism in Spain made for a particularly volatile economic bubble, with private levels of debt at unprecedented heights. 'To put it synthetically, deficit spending in the years 1997–2007 was decisively transferred from the Spanish state to private households, which, in the final years of the cycle, became net demanders of financing' (2010, p. 11). This was brought about by a vicious cycle in which the increase in the price of housing, provoked by speculation and gentrification and favored by business-friendly public policy, operated as a guarantee for credit given by financial entities to encourage increased consumer credit-based spending and investment in new housing projects.

These policies aimed at the real estate sector involved policy measures such as the decrease of tax rates on monies used to buy housing, the change of urban planning legislation to increase land designated for development and to limit services and maintenance of public lands that were once required of building developers. New policy also allowed for things as concrete as a modification to the Mortgage Law in order to oblige those who register their home to include prior sales contracts without qualifying or annulling the void or abusive clauses contained therein. Finally, in Spain there is a peculiarity in legislation, especially favorable to the interests of speculators, which states that, even after the bank repossesses an individual's property and sells it by judicial auction, the mortgage holder still owes whatever remaining amount that has not been paid. People who are evicted and have had their homes repossessed, while still owing money for any remaining debts on their homes are called *desahucios*. Because of the short-term success of the asset-price Keynesian approach (and its complementary public policy support in the promotion of real estate speculation) the nominal asset values of Spanish households in 2007 had reached eight trillion euros, eight times the country's GDP. In large part, this was a result of the increase in home ownership and in the increase in value of the homes owned (Lopez and Rodriguez, 2010).

But the apparent prosperity of this period had what Spaniards termed *pies de barro* ['feet of clay']. As consumer activity increased, wages decreased, and a two-tiered (and increasingly precarious) labor market emerged. Over 90 percent of work contracts made during this period were seasonal. In 1995 the average household debt was €188,000. By 2007 the average household debt of Spaniards was €933,000, nearly a 500 percent increase. Of this credit, 95 percent was issued by the financial sector and served as mortgages with which to purchase homes. During this period, mortgage credit grew to almost three times its initial volume, and from the beginning of 1997 until 2005 nearly nine million homes were bought and sold in Spain – nearly 40 percent of the national supply of housing. In 1995, debt represented about 62 percent of household income in Spain. By 2008 it had soared to over 130 percent (Lopez and Rodriguez, 2010).

The frailty of the foundations of household wealth, especially among the lower classes, became glaringly apparent, and wealth inequality grew significantly as the crisis progressed. According to Spanish national data 'the Gini index for net wealth rose by almost a tenth of a percent over the period from 2008 to 2014, after a period in which it had remained stable [2002–7]' (Anghel et al.,

2018, p. 387). The rates of home ownership fell dramatically during this same period. In 2008, for example, '78 percent of households in the first two income deciles were homeowners, this percentage had dropped to 67 percent by 2014, in contrast with the decline in this percentage in the ninth decile, which was just 3 percent ' (p. 388).

Some within the European context have argued that the high level of Spanish debt pre-crisis was the result of a cultural tendency toward indebtedness. Such a characterization of peoples of the Global South or the Southern region of the Eurozone as inherently irresponsible and lazy represents a certain form of paternalism. In a March 2017 interview with the *Frankfurter Allgemeine Zeitung* the president of the Eurogroup, Jeroen Dijsselbloem of the Netherlands, when asked about solidarity within the Eurozone, responded that

> in the Euro crisis, the countries of the North have shown themselves to be in solidarity with those affected by the crisis. As a social democrat, I give exceptional importance to solidarity. But those who seek solidarity also have obligations. I cannot spend all my money on women and drink and then later ask you to come to my aid. (Suanzes, 2017)[5]

Indeed, it has become commonplace in certain media and political discourse in northern European countries such as Germany, the Netherlands or Finland to characterize citizens from the South of the European Union as lazy, seeking handouts and welfare in order to spend carelessly and engage in irresponsible lifestyle choices.

In reality, of course, we know that this indebtedness of Spaniards was the result of public policy and a dynamic actively cultivated by business interests (predominantly the large state banks, real estate developers and real estate agencies) in order to create a niche for the valorization of national capital in the face of the abandonment of the very industrial policy that the European Union had required of Spain for entry into the union in the first place. Recourse to the national financialized economy by almost all Spaniards, coupled with easy access to credit (primarily with money of European origin) and markedly neoliberal policies, corresponded with a continuous diminution of salary in relation to the national income, regardless of whichever of the two happened to be in power. The seeds of the economic crisis in Spain were thus sown by decades of neoliberal policy and Spain's particular version of a financialized real-estate-driven economy.

During the worst moments of the Spanish economic fallout between 2010 and 2011, the bipartisan nature of the Spanish political system, with the conservative *Partido Popular* (PP) and the social democratic *Partido Socialista Obrero Español* (PSOE) representing the two parties taking turns as national governing powers since the end of the Francoist era in 1978, was likewise beginning to experience the onset of a crisis of legitimacy. This came to the surface in the 2011 protests that began to question the legitimacy of the post-Transition political system. The crisis of the Spanish democratic system appears at this moment as a parallel to the economic crisis described above. How could the nature of political institutions be separated from their social and economic policy? This was broader than an ideological or economic critique. It was also calling into question the history and nature of Spanish democracy and the possibilities for political participation for the great majority of the population.

The crisis of political legitimacy did not emerge out of thin air. By the late 1990s generalized feelings of discontent with the post-dictatorship democratic order had begun to appear in forms of intellectual and cultural critique. In its early stages this discontent did not yet appear as part of mainstream public sentiment. But by 2007 political discussions grew around the victims of the civil war, opening up space for dissenting opinion over how the transition to democracy had served its citizens. Kornetis (2014) discusses the ways in which, decades after the civil war, the 'careful sealings of the past were overturned' (p. 85). In 2000, mass graves filled with the dead from the civil war were starting to be exhumed, and the controversial *Ley de Memoria Histórica* was drafted in 2001.

> In 2007 socialist Prime Minister Zapatero introduced the so-called 'historical memory law,' recognizing the rights of victims of violence during the civil war. He did this not only because of the passage of time but also due to *Partido Socialista Obrero Español* (PSOE)'s new team of progressives. Mariano Rajoy, leader of the opposition People's Party at the time, reiterated that he was 'against reopening old wounds.' (Ibid.)

Among other things this allowed political discourse to begin to contend with questions of the legitimacy of the Transition, and open up spaces for memory and past grievances that had been suppressed in the process of democratization.

The question of memory was central to the emergence of debate over the failures and successes of the transition to democracy in public discourse. Vilarós (1998) gives us particular insight into the way in which the framing of the Transition within a specific historical narrative affected the capacity of later generations to deal with much of the trauma of both the civil war and the dictatorship. She argues that Franco's death had become for most a *punto cero* ['year zero'] of Spanish history, the point from which a radical paradigm shift was perceived to have been completed, and a new Spanish state emerged, clearly and absolutely separated from the past. As such, what has popularly been called a compromise and bipartisan pact, could be better understood as what Vilarós terms the '*pacto del olvido*' ['pact of forgetting']. This 'abyss' or 'void,' which emerged as sort of a cultural and political lapse in memory, has had the effect of erasing much of the meaning of the dictatorship and the struggles of the civil war that preceded it.

> The collapse of the big utopic projects from the left is a part of the *pacto del olivdo*, which is the moment of Franco's death that initiated a new present in a radical manner: after '75, as Spaniards we dedicated ourselves with desperate passion to 'erasing,' to 'not mentioning.' As a result, in the period of transition from dictatorship to democracy Spanish society, still voting massively in favour of the socialist party, rejected the ideological aspirations that were painstakingly and patiently incubated throughout the Francoist era by leftist sectors. (Vilarós, p. 8)

Even though the Transition was presented politically as a reformist project, it entered the collective unconscious as an absolute rupture with the past (ibid.).[6]

Following an initial burst of academic publications shortly after the Transition process itself – we see edited collections and many journal issues dedicated to the Spanish process of democratization, which was viewed as exemplary by many (Kornetis, 2014) – a renewal of this scholarship has taken place subsequent to the crisis of legitimacy as it became popularized through the 2011 protests. Fernandes (2015) argues that the Spanish project of democratization served a depoliticizing function in Spanish civil society, leading ultimately to a decrease in social and political participation along with diminished institutionalized forums for diversity of political position. The pathway to democracy was 'guided from above' and 'mainly oriented towards basic institutional and political change' because 'elites simply had no plan for altering the basic social and economic structures of society; nor was there any opportunity to be taken by popular-sector civil society organizations' (pp. 1087–1088).

We can see the compromise and continuity with the dominant interests from the dictatorship in a variety of ways. First, following the Moncloa Pact of 1977, the left compromised on many of its more radical aims, many of which were incubated as resistance to Franco's regime, limiting its capacity to promote socially engaged civil society (Fernandes, p. 1088). Second, the established powers such as the church and the military were enshrined within the new institutional framework, and in this way guaranteed impunity and the continued exercise of social control for many of those who had exerted a great deal of power within the Francoist regime (Maravall and Santamaría, 1986, p. 88). Third, the constitution of 1978, despite its promotion of the principle of the freedom of association, nonetheless 'maintained the requirement of a *declaración de utlidad pública* ['declaration of public utility'], granted through very discretionary mechanisms' (Fernandes, p. 1091). This allowed for the repression or dissolution of associations that were critical of the state if Spanish authorities saw fit. Finally, many undemocratic forces persisted throughout the Transition.

> The army was never systematically purged [and] continued occasionally to exercise judicial power over civilian critics even during the peak periods of democratic euphoria, and almost brought the democratic experiment to an abrupt end with the coup attempt of February 23, 1981. (Malefakis, 1982, p. 216)

Even in 1982 'the police, the judiciary, the bureaucracy and the educational institutions are still staffed in large part by Franco appointees' (ibid.). Thus there was a need for the Transition to be popularly considered as a rupture with the past in order to downplay the many points of continuity from the dictatorship, which may have served to delegitimize Spain's new democratic era.

The diverse authors from the 15-M movement who published the 2012 collection entitled *CT: o la Cultura de la Transición: Crítica a 35 años de cultura española* (Acevedo et al.) came to affirm the claim that the so-called consensus of the Spanish Transition imposed a limited public space upon Spanish society, along with the extreme limitation of all antagonistic discourse. The ossifying and repressive legacy of the Transition was felt to be so strong in this period that a discourse emerged among activists in which the culture legitimizing the Transition itself (CT) is often described as having its very own agency. Here we cite a current municipal councillor of Madrid, and activist from the 15-M movement, Guillermo Zapata.

> The CT is a static cultural system, which attempts to assign positions to everyone. In this way, the CT accepts dissent as long as it occurs in the way that the CT determines that dissent should occur. Thus, the CT has allowed for many years the existence of parties that are from the right or the left, according to a cultural pact and in predefined identities with a series of untouchable limits. Since the beginning the logic which functions in the CT is a logic that determines boundaries and assigns a role to 'the other'. Fixed positions, tight rows. We could call this type of politics 'enemy politics.' An enemy that gives me meaning, that defines me and that allows me to affirm a set of common spaces. CT wants to determine reality, to put a name on everything and to classify it. (Acevedo et al., 2012, pp. 146–147)

Thus the great social outrage that emerged in and through the 15-M movement was that the CT generated a dynamic in which the economic corruption of politicians and businesspeople linked to 'bricks' flourished; that is, those linked to the accelerated process of housing speculation associated with a construction boom. Moreover, preceding the crisis, municipalities in Spain survived on taxes that were linked to the growth of the housing bubble, which generated the emergence of patterns of illegal business between political parties, town planning councils, land developers and financial institutions. This was a fundamentally corrupt dynamic that permeated the entire social structure and carried through to the various levels of public administration, from former ministers who became (and who continue to be) advisors to large firms, to local committees who could (and can) grant concessions of works, subsidies and municipal aid.

Historically, we have seen that the Transition produced both generalized social apathy in sectors of civil society, as well as corruption within political institutions in their relation to the economic order. With the combination of public debt, the austerity practices following the global financial crisis of 2007, and the fallout from the real estate bubble in 2010, people found themselves in a particularly desperate economic situation by the spring of 2011. A new language and a new form of politics would prove necessary to address the dual crises besieging Spain.

Madrid on the 15th of May 2011: *¡No nos representan!*

Within this unique situation, and on the heels of a period of significant social apathy, on May 14, 2011, just a week before a crucial municipal election, a demonstration was held in Madrid, convened by different youth platforms, which ended in riots in the center of the city. Several people were arrested. But something had changed. Empowered by the images of Cairo's Tahrir Square, which had flooded televisions across Spain in the previous months, a group of protesters decided to camp in Madrid's central plaza of Puerta del Sol. Initially there were not many participants. And yet they managed not to be removed by the police. This had the effect of a beacon call that filled the square with young people, tents and makeshift stalls. The police attempted to evict the demonstrators from this space, but their efforts were pre-empted by massive peaceful rallies in the square. By the time the municipal elections were held on the 22nd of May, Puerta del Sol was still occupied by the public, and dramatic images of thousands of protesters surrounded by riot vans had gone viral throughout the whole of Spain.

The occupation of Puerta del Sol acted as a catalyst for popular discontent, provoking a pronounced re-politicization of daily life. Thousands of people went to the assemblies of the plaza, where there was active debate on political and social issues. But the most profound impact also occurred outside the plaza: televisions were now animated by images of the Puerta del Sol activists, and everyday conversations started to become politicized (*Diario Público*, 2011). On the buses, in work centers, in the neighborhoods, conversations took place, even among people who did not know each other, focusing on what was happening and on the general political and social situation. Many observers commented that this degree of diffuse and informal political activity had not occurred in Spanish society since the period of the Transition. Activist Amador Fernández Savater (2012) describes the nature of this explosion of public political discourse:

> Speaking specifically about the Sol occupation that I personally experienced, it always seemed to me that the activists knew that their strength was 'outside' of Puerta de Sol. Or, rather, that their strength was in the living link with what a friend calls 'the still part of the movement': the population touched and affected by the protest in the Puerta de Sol, even though they did not participate directly in the protest. The occupation of Sol never sought to be set apart from the rest of society, and so raised so many flows of solidarity both inside and outside (on only the third day, they had to make an appeal so that fellow citizens of Madrid would stop bringing so much food as they did not know where to store it). It was never conceptualized as a utopian outside or as another possible world, but rather as an 'invitation' to the unknown other to fight together on an equal footing. (pp. 49–50)

This process of accelerated politicization bolstered the decision of the Sol activists to expand the popular assemblies held in the square to the rest of Madrid's neighborhoods and to other localities in the country. In the squares of the different districts, spaces for debate and common decision-making were generated, while popular assemblies and public activities were organized in almost all the towns and cities of Spain. Thousands of people participated in these spaces. In Madrid, in popular neighborhoods such as Pacífico or Vallecas, both with a strong tradition of worker and neighborhood mobilization, those attending the first assemblies came by the hundreds. The process of politicization reached all social strata: youth, elders, women, workers, as well as professionals, former activists and people without any known past in the previous social movements.

In September 2011, Carlos Taibo, professor of political science at the University of Madrid, and anarchist activist, began to narrate the importance of the political shift embodied by the 15-M movement.

> 15-M configures, on the one hand, an unprecedented space for experimentation through the assembly and has allowed, on the other, the meeting of very different people, with an attitude of general respect for differences. [...] Most members of the movement ask for more, much more, than the reform of the electoral law and the introduction of measures that punish corruption. [...] The chant – 'it's going to end, it's going to end, the social peace is going to end' – authentically portrays the underlying meaning of the minimum program of these hours. [...] Although the task in this regard is anything but simple, many activists are increasingly clearly aware that the future of 15-M goes through its consolidation in the form of a movement that, through assembly and self-management, faces capitalism in all orders of life and does it, in addition, from anti-patriarchal, anti-development and internationalist perspectives. (Taibo, 2011a)

This popular process was driven by certain technological instruments facilitated by the extension of Internet access of previous years, and developed its own ideological and theoretical codes, with a clear autonomy from prior dominant discourse in society.

Scholars have commented on the importance of digital technology in the rapid and widespread uptake of the ideas of the *indignados*. This, coupled with the broad inclusionary attitude of activists, was exceptional ground for a massive mobilization: 'The *indiganados* strove to build a movement of 'anyone' based on an extremely inclusive 'we' that aimed to go beyond ideological or partisan affiliations and the auto-referential dynamics, organized forms, discourses and identities of traditional social movements' (Romanos and Sadaba, 2016, p. 3). The inclusivity of the movement and the prominent role of tech-activists in the digital public sphere (Sampedro and Avidad, 2018) allowed for 'democratic innovation,' (Romanos and Sadaba, p. 10) and ensured that the political sentiment of discontent and rupture that was beginning to develop in the plazas would later take root in new political parties such as *Podemos*. Indeed, not only did the inclusivity of the movement have a widespread and cross-sectional audience, but the reception of the 15-M movement was exceptionally positive across most sectors of Spanish society. From 2011 until 2013, 75 percent of Spaniards supported its main political arguments, and 50 percent approved of its strategies of protest (Sampedro and Lobera, 2014). Further, 'this far-reaching appeal of the *indignados* also applies to attitudes toward actions that display overtones of challenging the political system' (Sampedro and Lobera, p. 75).

The questions that were raised in this newly emergent popular discourse were not only about the economic ills of the day (though those were certainly predominant on the minds of the youth who were involved) but also explicitly about the previously shared narratives about the 1970s and the transition to democracy itself. Kornetis (2014) argues that 'the 1970s themselves became an issue of open contestation, instead of the civil war or the Francoist period, as had been the case thus far' (p. 87). The very subjectivity of the Transition, which had come from the aftermath of forty years of dictatorship, was being called into question, reconsidered, recollected. This was particularly important given that much of the new debate over the period and its implications for economic and political life was being carried out by a younger generation that was born just as this transition took place, or even a decade afterward. Pablo Beas Marín argues that the rupture did more than break with the acceptance of a particular institutional arrangement, but rather served as a 'profanation' of the established conception of legitimate political life.

> Agamben uses the term 'profanation' to refer to those things that once having been sacred, were disconnected from that sacred space and were restored to the common man. The 15-M profaned the 'Culture of the Transition' because it returned to public debate many elements that the CT apparatus had relegated to a

> sacred space. Restored to the people was the debate on monarchy, on bipartisanship, on *desahucios*, on the nature of the crisis, pointing out the guilty, on liberal democracy as a closure of the political, etc. There came a heretical way of thinking in which guilt no longer belonged to everyone, but only to a select few: 'we are not merchandise in the hands of politicians and bankers.' (Beas Marín, n.d.)

This profanation spurred a shift in consciousness about economic policy, political legitimacy, the dominant narratives of Spanish history, and collective dreams of the future. But it was still seeking positive forms of articulation in a newly radicalized population.

As such the language of the plazas manifested itself most poignantly in the many collective enunciations that became popularized throughout the country, a rising call against the powers of the Eurozone who had encouraged neoliberal reforms and threatened austerity as a response to its crises, and against the very Spanish State that had capitulated to such economic demands for decades. One of the most important chants of the movement to this effect was: '*Que no, que no, que no nos representan*' ['They don't, they don't, they don't represent us'], which also calls into question the political status quo in place since the Transition of the 1970s. As Antentas (2017) explains rather eloquently, 'the slogan *No nos representan* synthesized perfectly the visceral rejection of a political system hijacked by financial power' (p. 111). This was accompanied by another popular chant – '*PSOE, PP, la misma mierda es*' ['PSOE, PP, it's all the same shit'], revealing that both the legacy of bipartisanship and the economic strategies of the state were now fully in the public eye. But perhaps even more importantly, these collective public enunciations draw attention to the nature of the dual crisis that Spain was experiencing in 2011, both of the long-standing and coordinated program of neoliberal integration into the European economic project and the failures of both the PP and PSOE to provide any meaningful alternative to the post-crisis austerity plans. The latter were perceived to be that same legacy of the Transition, and more and more enunciations emerged as a form of discrediting the past pact between economic liberalization and continuity with the ruling interests from the dictatorship.

It cannot be emphasized enough that it was in these moments in 2011 in the plazas when the characterization of the contemporary Spanish parliamentary monarchy as the 'Regime of 78' became popular. The shift in historical perspective was both broad and radical. The government was now characterized as a political regime stemming from an internal revision of the Franco regime, and not a democratic break from it. This was the most important shift in the popular historical understanding of the 15-M movement. The fundamental assertion of this understanding was that the democratic break was *not* accomplished in the late 1970s as prior political history would have claimed. The protest movement of the plazas forced previous historical narratives from the CT, from the *pacto del olvido*, into question. As a result, activists, journalists and many intellectuals began to characterize the regime as corrupt, inequitable and lacking the characteristics necessary for a serious and substantive democracy in Spain (Gil, 2017; Errejón, 2013).

The discourse of the plazas addressed not only the illegitimacy of the Regime of 78, but also the awakening of popular political consciousness and the clear statement of political aims in the wake of the crisis. For example, '*Dormíamos, despertamos*' ['We slept, we awoke']: a reference to the harsh awakening from the period of unbridled consumption facilitated by the housing bubble, and from the historical amnesia inherent to the political culture that had dominated for over thirty years. '*No somos mercancía en manos de políticos y banqueros*' ['We are not merchandise in the hands of politicians and bankers']: a reference to the lack of agency and the conditions of exploitation of those who were protesting. '*Vamos despacio porque vamos muy lejos*' ['Let's go slowly, because we are going very far']: a reference to the aims and proclaimed radicalism of the movement, which was not merely seeking a change of government but proposed much more ambitious goals. Likewise, other recurring collective enunciations of the movement refer to the challenge posed by the mobilizations against global financial powers; '*Este crisis no la pagamos*' ['We will not pay for this crisis'] and '*El miedo va a cambiar de bando*' ['Fear will change sides'].

The most politicized and politically radical sectors of the movement, on the other hand, were more direct in their aims. They were able to popularize chants from previous social movements, such as '*A, Anti, Anticapitalista*' [A, Anti, Anticapitalist']. These sentiments, while not expressing the majority-held position, nonetheless occupied a considerable place in the demonstrations and assemblies. This politicized sector also tried to link the protests with the demands and speeches of the grassroots and combative workers' movement using chants such as '*La lucha es el único camino*' ['The struggle is the only way'] and '*Que viva la lucha de la clase obrera*' ['Long live the struggle of the working class']. Most notably, '*A, Anti, Anticapitalista*' even tried, during the cycle of 15-M struggles, to provoke a general strike organized without the help of the large labor unions. What remained to be seen, from this intensive moment of collective reimagining and budding political action, was how these new conceptions of Spanish history, political legitimacy and economic justice would find a place in the institutions of Spain.

Municipalism and *Podemos*: From the plazas to the institutional assault

In the subsequent months and years, the dual crises in Spain generated an emergence of new social movements that became increasingly popular in nature, and made substantive demands on redressing some of the fundamental structural issues that gave rise to both the economic and political crises in the first place. In addition to the growth and increasing success of *el nuevo municipalismo* ['the new municipalism'] of Barcelona and Madrid, the *Podemos* party achieved a resounding electoral success in the EU elections of 2014, finally breaking away from the bipartisan model that had governed since the Transition.[7] Many new forms of political participation and action sprung up in ways that were not encapsulated within formal political frames. Cooperative projects, soup kitchens, consumer networks and all kinds of self-managed initiatives spread throughout the social body, with a dimension that had not been seen in the years since the Transition (Taibo, 2011b; Pérez Orozco, 2014; Carretero Miramar, 2013). As Arribas Lozano (2015) points out, the spring of 2011 represented a new stage of political history.

> [S]elf-organization became common sense, and we saw unfolding and strengthening a multiplicity of knowledge and collective practices: the '*mareas ciudadanas*' [citizen waves] in defense of education and public health; the networks linked to social economy, cooperatives, ethical banking, barter systems, and alternative currencies; collectives and networks against evictions, with the role of the *Plataforma de Afectados por la Hipoteca* (PAH) [Platform of Those Affected by Mortgages]; the experiences of social ecology, urban gardens, self-organized consumer networks; spaces for self-development, bookshops, alternative presses, etc. In this way the grassroots initiatives became major players, setting the political agenda in the months after the 15-M movement. (p. 158)

An especially powerful form of direct action was found in groups dedicated to developing strategies for squatting houses repossessed by the banks and housing projects that were left vacant. A group named '*okupatutambien*' ['you occupy it too'] released a free '*Manual de Okupación*' (2014) with legal, economic and political strategies of occupation, particularly focusing on reclaiming housing repossessed by banks all while leaving its former occupants in debt. Those who participated in these movements ranged from the radical left to the formerly moderate middle class including schoolteachers and care workers who now faced significant economic challenges. The diversity of the class and ideological background of the participants revealed the widespread nature of the crisis and the growing legitimacy of radical economic interventions.

As projects of informal and institutional change and resistance were mounted, so too was state repression. A growing level of state repression was the product of a legislative dynamic that engaged in a clear authoritarian drift toward to the denial of certain civil liberties, especially during the latter part of the parliamentary period of 2011–2014 (Durán, 2018). Approved projects that hardened the legal stance against protest and public demonstration included the '*Ley de Seguridad Ciudadana*' ['Law of Citizen Security'], popularly called '*Ley Mordaza*' ['Gag Law']. This law sanctioned the issue of administrative fines for many activities typically carried out by activists at protests, and included serious restrictions on spontaneous assembly and on organizers themselves (Amnesty International, 2014). The fines were based primarily on anecdotal evidence from the observations of individual police officers. More strikingly still, modifications to the Spanish Criminal Code were made in order to strengthen the repressive control of the state by instituting new definitions of what was to constitute security and crime.

The impact on social mobilization was palpable. Activists were imprisoned 'preventively.' A total of 300 trade unionists were sentenced to hundreds of years of prison sentences for activities carried out during general strikes. Allegations of mistreatment and arbitrary police attacks on protesters and detainees grew significantly, while the state security forces attempted to normalize things like the detention and interrogation of protestors who had worn balaclavas, or the judicial disciplining of lawyers of activists who counseled their clients to not give testimony while under investigation at police stations.[8] Ultimately this increased repression had a significant impact upon the context of protest in Spain, and even upon the state of democratic rights. As Cristina Flesher-Fominaya (2017) has written,

> Legal restrictions and criminal and civic costs associated with peaceful protest, therefore, form a crucial part of political opportunity structures, as we would expect. But what we also see is that mass mobilization also has increased restrictions as an unintended *consequence* of pro-democracy mobilization, leading to *fewer* rather than greater democratic rights. (p. 13)

It is thus not surprising that by mid-2013, the fatigue of many activists became evident, as burnout and sentiments of exhaustion began to spread among those who saw that the continuous mobilizations of the past few years had not given the results that had been hoped for or expected. How could this exhaustion not return to the previous state of political slumber? Decades of social anomie had generated such an intense de-politicization of the population that many people had thought that the simple fact of massive demonstrations would have been enough to convince the political regime to throw in the towel. Instead, there was a generalized sense of surprise that, even when publicly shamed, weakened and exposed to a new sort of popular '*sentido común*' ['common sense'], the political regime's levers of power remained nearly completely intact, as did the adjustment policies imposed by transnational finance.

Inspired by the example of the Bolivarian perspectives in Latin America, numerous groups and sectors linked to the protests attempted to generate a general electoral front that would accumulate the power of a majority social alliance to combat the neoliberal austerity measures that had been imposed thus far as a conditionality of bailout euroarea funds. The essential narrative thus turned from the '*No nos representan*' ['They do not represent us'] of the Plazas of May 15, to a search for mechanisms of confluence in order to unite political actors from the parliamentary left and certain parts of the broader protest movement. It was thus in this context that attempts to carry out what came to be called the '*asalto institucional*,' ['institutional assault'] emerged. Representatives of the popular movements thus entered the institutional realm, and did so in two tactical areas that, while distinct, became increasingly convergent: a new municipalism, on the one hand, and on the other a construction of political alliances capable of breaking the PP–PSOE bipartisanship, and eventually leading to the emergence of the *Podemos* party.

Many have asserted that the broad scope and inclusivity of *Podemos*' goals demonstrates it is a 'movement-party' (Calvo and Alvarez, 2015; Lobera, 2015; Martín, 2015; Atentas, 2017). Irene Martín (2015) gives examples of similar movement-parties, which arose out of crises, such as *Syriza* in Greece, and *Movimiento al Socialismo* (MAS) in Bolivia. The lines of continuity between 15-M and *Podemos* are clear, and can be seen in the shared use of a certain type of language.[9] In addition to the fact that 15-M – like *Podemos* – attempted, and generally succeeded, in avoiding the typical rhetoric of left and right, a set of shared tropes demonstrate a common discursive register between the two groups as well. This is evident in the following statement made by *Podemos*' primary spokesperson, the now deputy Pablo Iglesias Turrión.

> We can be citizens by doing politics. Politics is too important to leave in the hands of the elite, in the hands of those who have ultimately become bank stewards [...] *Podemos* wants to be just that, politics back in the hands of normal people. *Podemos* is seeking *transversal representation*, representation beyond labels. [...] We have said that the fundamental dichotomy is between people and caste, between oligarchy and democracy, between the social majority and a minority of privileged people who are using politics to defend their wealth and income. That is why [...] we do not accept the rules of the political board that plays with parliamentary concepts such as 'left' and 'right.' (Rivero, 2014, emphasis added)

Martín (2015) explains that 'there is no doubt of the continuity between '*no nos representan*' and the use of the term 'caste' to refer to political and economic elites whose interests run counter to those of the public' (p. 110). Within the differential continuity from 15-M to *Podemos*, the newly born party formed a new way for popular protest to find access to institutionalized politics (Calvo and Alvarez, 2015).

Born four months before the 2014 European Union elections, *Podemos* was an alliance between a group of professors who had recently achieved access to mainstream media in their role as 'representatives' of mass protests, and popular groups such as the post-Trotskyist '*Izquierda Anticapitalista*' ['Anticapitalist Left'] party, and the '*Juventud Sin Futuro*' ['Youth without Future'] activist group from the 15-M protests of May of 2011. From its inception, the party's links with the Bolivarian perspectives from Latin America were evident, even in and through the professional trajectories of its academic promoters.[10] Even with a high level of voter abstention and a widespread rise in left wing parties, *Podemos* was able to win five seats with over 1.2 million votes in the 2014 EU election.

As we have seen, its ideological project was clearly rooted in a democratic populism that rejected the traditional categories of left and right and sought 'new ways of doing politics.'[11] This bridging strategy began with a certain form of charismatic leadership (facilitated by the media notoriety of its spokespersons), and was combined with forms of popular participation and organizing. The latter, as in the case of municipalism in both Madrid and Barcelona, was rather complicated and limited in its capacity for horizontal decision-making. *Podemos*' attempt at broad-based horizontalist decision-making took the form of the *Círculos Podemos* ['Podemos Circles'].

The *Círculos Podemos* had their origins in the assemblies of the 15-M movement and had the aim of providing a forum for participatory democracy. Their real decision-making capacity was limited, however, by the organizational principles of the party that tended toward online and plebiscitary democracy, and relied heavily on the public persona of its leader. As a result many social activists were able to connect with people who were both previously depoliticized and disenchanted with the traditional parties. As a new political configuration and set of alliances, *Podemos* was destined to take advantage of the growing decomposition of Spanish bipartisanship. It did so within a discourse that referred, in its early stages, to the reopening of the foundational process that ended the regime of 1978.

The unexpected success of the *Podemos* party in the 2014 European Union elections played a major role in shifting the scales in favor of preexisting municipalist movements, ultimately leading them to gain greater popular support and to increase their level of institutional representation. Municipalism was represented by sectors directly linked to social movements, which saw the possibility of influencing the local level in order to short-circuit the processes that had reproduced the dynamics of financialization and dispossession. Perhaps the most shining example of this form of resistance can be seen in the *Plataforma de Afectados por la Hipoteca (PAH)* [Platform for Those Affected by Mortgages] that was formed in February 2009 in Barcelona by housing rights activists who had belonged to previous movements such as *V de Vivienda* [H for Housing] along with people who, in great numbers, were being evicted from their homes by financial institutions. Indeed, the surge in unemployment and the reduction of wages had left many people homeless.[12] The ideological perspectives held within these sectors bore strong resonances with the traditions of pre-Civil War federal republicanism, which was one of the foundations of Spanish anarchism. Municipalism was initially attempted by the *Candidaturas de Unidad Popular* ['Candidacies of Popular Unity'] of Catalonia, employing a discourse that stressed both Catalan independence and a radical ideological identity.[13]

In Madrid, municipalist tendencies were founded mainly by activists from the autonomous movement of the 1990s, and gained strength from initiatives such as the *Observatorio Metropolitano* ['Metropolitan Observatory'] and the *Fundación de los Comunes* ['Foundation of the Commons'].[14] Key to the success of this movement was the active association between the central Madrid organizations and other sectors, including most importantly the local mayoral candidacies of suburban populations. The basic ideological perspective that fed these initiatives, and that drew from disparate sources such as Murray Bookchin (1986) or the German Greens, is summarized in this fragment of the text *La apuesta municipalista: La democracia empieza por lo cercano* [*The Municipalist Bet: democracy begins close at hand*] of the Metropolitan Observatory.

> If we take the institutions that are most immediate to the citizens, the municipalities, and we turn them into areas of direct decision making, we can make a real democracy worthy of such a name. It would be enough to re-establish areas of direct participation: new citizen *agoras* with real power and real choices. According to this scheme, the essential prerequisite lies in the eviction of the current political class. The first task is therefore to clean house: we must evict the current oligarchs in order to end corruption. (Observatorio Metropolitano, 2014, p. 143)

The language of municipalism in Spain, no doubt relating back to its anarchist roots, has a decisively housing-related imagery. The metaphors of 'evicting' oligarchs and 'cleaning house' link not only the desire to oust the corrupt economic class who had been busy evicting tens of thousands of Spaniards in bankruptcy after the crisis, but also those who have occupied positions of political and social power since the dictatorship.

Thus, in the local elections of 2015, there were many municipalist candidates elected throughout the country. The resounding success of these campaigns was evidenced by the election of municipalist mayors in both Barcelona and Madrid, the country's two largest cities. In Madrid, the slate of candidates that ran under the name *Ahora Madrid* ['Madrid Now'] was a somewhat unstable amalgam of different forces headed by the judge Manuela Carmena. The forces backing this slate included the traditional parties of the left such as the *Izquierda Unida* ['United Left'], new movement parties such as *Podemos* and groups linked to the social movements of the city, such as the *Ganemos* ['Let's Win'] municipal platform. The campaign's promises of a citizen audit of the municipal debt, the remunicipalization of public services previously privatized and outsourced by the city council, the end of evictions within the municipality and compliance with the law of historical memory were only partially kept due to a confluence of countervailing forces. In particular, the plurality of interests supporting the candidates, the hegemonic presence of *Podemos* in the media in the following years, the mild reformism of leader Manuela Carmena, as well as the need to seek support from the PSOE in order to continue governing, limited the depth of changes brought about by the new municipal government. Likewise, in Barcelona, the PAH activist Ada Colau won the seat of Mayor, thanks to a pluralist set of political forces.

New language in old institutions: Unresolved crises in Spain

In October of 2014, at the Palacio de Vistalegre in Madrid, *Podemos* held its founding assembly – a kind of popular caucus where its organic structure and the content of speeches for the following electoral cycle were debated. Despite the competing ideological and strategic tendencies[15] that emerged during this assembly, an aggressive electoral strategy designed to win at all costs came to dominate the party. Using militaristic metaphors, it was proposed that *Podemos* would be converted into an 'electoral war machine' that would lead the path to victory in subsequent elections. This ultimately displaced many of the horitzontalist ideals that stemmed from the party's origins as a popular and spontaneous movement. As activist Emmanuel Rodríguez López (2016) argued in his book *La política en el ocaso de la clase media: El ciclo 15M – Podemos* [*Politics in the decline of the middle class: the 15M-Podemos cycle*], there was a '*hipótesis Podemos*' [Podemos hypothesis], which included 'the promise of achieving the electoral majority, and as its implicit shadow, the taking of the State, the only reliable strategy for a project in a society deemed to be pulverized and impotent' (p. 99).

Yet *Podemos*' strategy of Vistalegre did not yield the desired results. In the general elections of December 20, 2015, *Podemos* entered the Spanish Parliament with strength, obtaining 42 deputies in the Congress alone, and another 27 if one includes the representation of regional forces affiliated with *Podemos*. The conservative *Partido Popular* (PP), however, once again won the elections and the *Partido Socialista Obrero Español* (PSOE) remained the first opposition, with 90 deputies to its name. In the subsequent election campaign of 2016, *Podemos*, excited by the polls that indicated the possibility of surpassing the PSOE, agreed to a joint bid with the United Left becoming *Unidos Podemos* ['United We Can'].

The election results of 2016 were bittersweet. In a fragmented Congress without a clear majority, *Unidos Podemos* and its allies obtained 61 seats, less than had been won in previous elections. In total, over a million votes less than the previous elections went to the *Unidos Podemos* coalition. In December of 2016 the conservative PP finally formed a government with the support of the center-right party *Ciudadanos* ['Citizens']. Thus *Podemos* faced the end of the electoral cycle that had begun in 2014. This end was characterized, on the one hand, by a growing social demobilization, with many activists moving from popular movements in the streets to the formalized institutional context, and, on the other, with emerging hostility from the party apparatus toward the self-organizing tendencies of its allies and members who it was not able to control. The internal tensions within *Podemos* thus began to emerge in the context of a growing erosion of the image of the leaders in the media, and fatigue in the face of a project that was becoming increasingly removed from both the discourse and practice of the now-defunct 15-M movement.

The general consensus within activist circles closely linked with 15-M is that this recent electoral turn of events represents a 'lost opportunity' for *Podemos*. Activists have argued that the party was undermined by its vigorous and agonistic discourse focused on the imperative of winning at all costs. The '15-M cycle,' however, produced intense lived experiences and politicized large sectors of Spanish society in a marked fashion. The *hipótesis Podemos* (the agency-affirming 'Podemos hypothesis') had thus been its political expression. The normalization of *Podemos*' political ideas (including strong positions on sensitive issues such as the critique of the Regime of 78) and the idea of opening a 'constituent process,' has served to draw attention to both what they have termed 'the political caste of the regime' and the corruption that has sustained the conservative PP. *Podemos* brought these critiques into sharp focus once it was able to normalize both its presence and its leadership amongst the constitutional political class.

The financial crisis of 2010 ignited a retroactive re-signification of Spain's history, its understanding of democracy and its relationship to dictatorship and its authoritarian past. Returning to the claim that neoliberalism weakens political agency by offering no language to connect seemingly private concerns to public issues, we see that the language of popular resistance to the promises of liberal democracy and neoliberal austerity in fact succeeded for a moment in doing just that. The financial crisis brought about a crack in history, and activists pried open this crack in order to challenge the historical narrative of democratic progress, initiating a larger national crisis – the crisis of a historical consciousness of the present. This question of political legitimacy in Spain ultimately became a question of how to bring popular language from below (which we see in the collective enunciations of 15-M) to a language capable of engaging with institutions and the state.

The problem becomes: how to speak within an institution without becoming one? How does a movement-party resist speaking from above? In many ways, *Podemos*' failure to convert the vital social momentum of 15-M and popular movements into a political majority can be attributed to strategies that too closely resembled those of the opposition they wished to defeat. How could a movement-party resist succumbing to the institutional logics set into motion by the Transition? Indeed, modern Spanish history seems to suggest something basic about authoritarianism and its relation to democracy: namely, that it takes a long time and a great deal of struggle to move past the influence, culture and language of authoritarian institutions, especially when these institutions were integrated in many important ways into the new democratic order as a pact of political compromise. Just like the success of the real-estate-driven and credit-fueled pre-crisis economy, Spanish contemporary democracy also stands on feet of clay, and requires more time and a stronger civil society to fully awaken from an institutionalized political imagination and its language of bipartisanship and neoliberal economic programs.

Through a concerted and prolonged period of political organizing – from mass social movements, to municipalism in major centers and *Podemos*' bid at the national level – new language in Spain has come to reflect the political consciousness of a generation *que se ha despertado* ['that has awoken']; neither beholden to the neoliberal dream of the Eurozone nor to the mythologies of the Transition. The increasing political and ideological bankruptcy and crisis of the 'Regime of 78' brought out by the 15-M movement, seems irreversible. Youth in Spain are increasingly resistant toward the discourse of the old parties. While the social movements are comparatively less fervent than in 2011, and while *Podemos* could not complete its 'institutional assault,' popular critical spirit has not retreated into obscurity as during the years preceding the crises. Something is still moving in the underground of Spanish society.

Notes

1. This essay was translated from Spanish by Sonya Marie Scott.
2. 'PSOE, PP, it's all the same shit,' a popular chant of the 15-M protests in May 2011.

3. The real estate sector was fueled by easy state-sponsored credit and led to massive projects such as high-speed rail throughout low density regions, massive neighborhoods of new apartment blocks without any preexisting services or infrastructure and huge airports all over the country. Most of the buildings and airports lay abandoned after the crisis, veritable '*elefantes blancos*' (or 'white elephants') on the Spanish landscape. Most notably perhaps is the Don Quijote International Airport of Ciudad Real in the province of La Mancha, situated in the middle of the desert about one and a half hours by rail from Madrid. The 4,000-meter runway is one of the longest in all of Europe. The airport was slated to be a hub servicing Madrid via high speed rail. Yet the railway station was never completed. And while the airport did have limited operations for several years, using subsidies to entice discount airlines to add it to their routes, eventually service was cut off and the local government was forced to put it up for sale for a fraction of its cost. It remains abandoned today.
4. *Cajas*, unlike large commercial banks, are regionally based savings and loan banks. Stein, Capepe and Gallego (2012) explain that while *cajas* and commercial banks coexist, 'one of the differences between *cajas* and banks is that decision making in *cajas* is influenced by public authorities. Founded with the backing of regional and local governments, *cajas* are not-for-profit and so their surplus, after reserves and provisions, is used to finance welfare and cultural provisions' (p.3). Just as the community-based dimensions of *cajas* makes them fundamentally more integrated to and impactful upon their constituencies, it also proved, prior to the crisis, to make many of them more susceptible to corruption and direct political influence. In 2011 'of a total of 26 banks and *cajas* that were subjected to stress tests [in order to discern the viability of their capital structure], five (all of them *cajas*) failed' (ibid.).
5. Some scholars have expressed concern that this stereotype of an economically irresponsible Spanish cultural sensibility was also internalized within the Spanish middle class. Alonso et al. (2015) have found through interviews with focus groups that even Spanish discourse and reflection about the crisis had come to mirror the disciplinary tones of the North, including personal guilt around household overspending and a moral association with appropriate (i.e. financially responsible) levels of consumption. It should be noted, however, that participants generally held a more critical and sophisticated analysis of the factors contributing to household debt in subsequent years of study (Alonso et al., 2017).
6. It should be noted, however, that while this critique of the Transition has gained legitimacy and voice, perspectives on this issue are varied. See, for example, the work of Spanish historian Santos Juliá (2010), who celebrates the Transition as a great achievement of compromise and democratization. Many in Spanish society framed the Transition as an institutionalized form of inclusivity that smoothed the way for democracy in a very divided political arena. Critique became necessary in the throes of the 2010 crisis in part because of how unquestioningly celebratory mainstream attitudes had previously been toward the process.
7. While we will focus on the development from the 15-M movement to the rise of municipalism and new parliamentary parties such as *Podemos*, it should be noted that the growth in number of local assemblies and collectives of all kinds likewise allowed for an accelerated social dissemination of the ideas of self-management and self-organization. A sweeping radical engagement had taken Spain, with the spirit of the *indignados* affecting civil society groups in all sectors.
8. Amnesty International has expressed significant concern about the curtailment of the freedom of expression due the Gag Law and other measures in Spain, even up until present. See: www.es.amnesty.org/en-que-estamos/espana/libertad-de-expresion/.
9. It should be noted, however, that many of 15-M's goals were developed spontaneously as the movement was emerging in the plazas of 2011. Much of what they sought to accomplish was not clearly or coherently delineated as a political platform, nor capable of being institutionally organized within Spanish parliamentary politics (Lobera 2015).
10. For example, Iñigo Errejón, one of Iglesias' collaborators, wrote his doctoral thesis on Boliva's MAS party and their strategies during its first formed government (Martín 2015).
11. Regarding the new categories of political language popularized by the leaders of *Podemos*, among which the concept of a 'new politics' stands out, see '*Podemos instaura sus términos en el lenguaje de los políticos españoles*' ['Podemos establishes its terms in the language of Spanish Politicians'] in *Vozpopuli* (2014). Available at: www.vozpopuli.com/espana/Pablo_Iglesias-Juan_Carlos_Monedero-Cristobal_Montoro-Pedro_Sanchez-Partido_Socialista_Obrero_Espanol_PSOE-Podemos_0_716928332.html
12. For an excellent discussion and chronology of the PAH see Flesher Fominaya (2015) pp. 470–472.
13. The *Candidaturas de Unidad Popular* (CUP), after making the leap into the Catalan autonomous chamber, was to become decisive in future parliamentary dynamics. The CUP was to have an important role in the independence

process that led to the declaration of the Catalan Republic after the referendum of self-determination on October 1, 2017. The autonomous deputies of the CUP, who were essential to the absolute majority gained by the independence movement in the Catalan Chamber, would later try to give a strong social content to the newly born Republic, after forcing the resignation of the Catalan President Artur Mas, linked by the press with cases of political corruption, and replaced by Carles Puigdemont, who would finally make the declaration of independence in Parliament and then seek exile in Brussels in late 2017.

14. Foundations of the commons (https://fundaciondeloscomunes.net/) and Metropolitan Observatory (www.observatoriometropolitano.org/) are both inititatives from the autonomous movement of Madrid that have participated in the municipalist candidacy Ahora Madrid.
15. The two competing tendencies held fundamental differences. On the one hand, the university professors who founded the movement – Pablo Iglesias and Iñigo Errejón – maintained a markedly populist discourse by fiercely rejecting both the 'political caste' and the 'militant old left' that dominated prior to the genesis of *Podemos*. And yet while horizontalism had be the founding mantra of the party, a commitment to a fundamentally vertical organizational structure emerged as the *Círculos Podemos* began to lose many of their self-appointed powers leading up the elections. On the other hand an opposition to this hierarchal structure of party governance emerged from the post-Trotskyist *Izquierda Anticapitalista* (IA) ['Anticapitalist Left'] party. The IA attempted to reinstate the organizing principles from the 15-M movement and from the preexisting radical left, but was ultimately not successful in doing so.

Works Cited

Acevedo, C. et al., 2012. *CT o la Cultura de la Transición: Crítica a 35 años de cultura española*. Barcelona: Debolsillo.

Alonso, L.E. et al., 2015. From consumerism to guilt: economic crisis and discourses about consumption in Spain. *Journal of Consumer Culture*, 15 (1), 66–85.

Alonso, L.E. et al., 2017. 'I think the middle class is disappearing': crisis perceptions and consumption patterns in Spain. *International Journal of Consumer Studies*, 41, 389–396.

Amnesty International, 2014. *Spain: The Right to Protest Under Threat*. London: Amnesty International Publications. Available at: www.amnesty.org.uk/files/spain_-the_right_to_protest_under_threat_0.pdf.

Anghel, B., Basso, H., Bover, O. et al., 2018. Income, Consumption and Wealth Inequality in Spain. *SERIEs: Journal of the Spanish Economic Association*, 9 (4), 351–387.

Antentas, J.M., 2017. Spain: from the *indignados* rebellion to regime crisis (2011–2016). *Labour History*, 58 (1), 106–131.

Arribas Lozano, A., 2015. 'Recordar el 15M para reimaginar el presente. Los movimientos sociales en España más allá del ciclo electoral de 2015.' *Interface: A journal for and about social movements*, 7 (1), 150–164.

Beas Marín, P. (n.d.). El 15-M y la Cultura de la Transición: Elogio de una profanación. *Proyecto Brandaris*. Available at: https://proyectobrandaris.com/2017/02/24/el-15-m-y-la-cultura-de-la-transicion-elogio-de-una-profanacion/.

Bookchin, M., 1986. *The Limits of the City*. Montreal: Black Rose Books.

Brenner, R., 2006. *The Economics of Global Turbulence: The Advanced Capitalist Economies from Boom to Long Downturn, 1945–2005*. New York: Verso.

Calvo, K. and Alvarez, I., 2015. Limitaciones y exclusiones en la institutionalización de la indignación: del 15-M a Podemos. *Revista Española de Sociología*, 24, 115–122.

Carretero Miramar, J.L., 2013. *La autogestión viva: proyectos y experiencias de la otra economía al calor de la crisis*. Madrid: Queimada.

Diario Público, 2011. Cronología de la acampada indignada en la Puerta del Sol, Diario Publico, May 31. Available at: www.publico.es/actualidad/cronologia-acampada-indignada-puerta-del.html.

Durán, R., 2018. Enfoques mediáticos sobre libertad y seguridad. La Ley española de Seguridad Ciudadana como estudio de caso. *Política y Sociedad* 55 (1), 211–234.

Errejón, J., 2013. El crisis del régimen del 78. *Viento Sur*. 9 January. Available at: http://vientosur.info/spip.php?article7571.

Fernandes, T., 2015. Rethinking pathways to democracy: civil society in Portugal and Spain, 1960s-2000s. *Democratization*, 22 (6), 1074–1104.

Fernández Savater, A., 2012. El 15-M y la crisis de la política consensual en España. *Periférica Internacional: revista para el análisis de la cultura y el territorio*, 13, 63–71.

Flesher Fominaya, C., 2015. Redefining the crisis/redefining democracy: mobilising for the right to housing in Spain's PAH movement. *South European Society and Politics*, 20 (4), 465–485.

Flesher Fominaya, C., 2017. European anti-austerity and pro-democracy protess in the wake of the global financial crisis. *Social Movement Studies*, 16 (1), 1–20.

Gil, A., 2017. Del15-M al 1-O: el desborde del régimen del 78. *El Diario*. October 2. Available at: www.eldiario.es/politica/15M-1o-desborde-regimen-78_0_692931368.html.

Giroux, H.A., 2005. Globalizing Dissent and Radicalizing Democracy: Politics, Pedagogy and the Responsibility of Critical Intellectuals *In*: Gray-Rosendale and Rosendale, Eds., *Radical Relevance: Toward a Scholarship of the Whole Left*. Albany, N.Y.: State University of New York Press, 141–159.

Juliá, S., 2010. 'Cosas que de la transición se cuentan' *Ayer: Revista de Historia Contemporánea*, 79, 297–319.

Kornetis, K., 2014. 'Is there a future in the past?' Analyzing 15M's intricate relationship to the Transición. *Journal of Spanish Cultural Studies*, 15 (1–2), 83–98.

La Vanguardia, 2013 Montoro dice que España supera los pronósticos en su recuperación económica. *La Vanguardia*, 6 September. Available at: www.lavanguardia.com/economia/20130906/54380086500/montoro-dice-espana-supera-pronosticos-recuperacion-economica.html.

Lobera, J., 2015. De movimientos a partidos. La cristalización electoral de la protesta. *Revista Española de Sociología*, 24, 97–105.

Lopez, I. and Rodriguez, E., 2010. *Fin de ciclo: Financiarización, territorio y sociedad de propietarios en la onda larga del capitalismo hispano (1959–2010)*. Madrid: Traficantes de Sueños.

Lopez, I. and Rodriguez, E., 2011. The Spanish Model, *New Left Review*, 69, 5–28.

Malefakis, E., 1982. Spain and Its Francoist Legacy. *In*: John Herz Ed., *From Dictatorship to Democracy: Coping with the Legacies of Authoritarianism and Totalitarianism*. London: Greenwood Press, 215–230.

Manual de Okupación. 2nd ed. Madrid: n.p., 2014.

Maravall, J.M. and Santamaría, J., 1986. Political Change in Spain and the Prospects for Democracy. *In*: O'Donnell, P., Schmitter, C., and Whitehead, L., Eds., *Transitions from Authoritarian Rule. Southern Europe*. Baltimore, MA: Johns Hopkins University Press, 71–108.

Martín, I., 2015. Podemos y otros modelos de partido-movimiento. *Revista Española de Sociología*, 24, 107–114.

Martinez Matute, M. and Perez, J., 2017. General Public Employment in the Last Decade. *Banco de España, Economic Bulletin 4*, November 7. Available at: www.bde.es/f/webbde/SES/Secciones/Publicaciones/InformesBoletinesRevistas/NotasEconomicas/T4/files/bene1704-nec12e.pdf.

McCloskey, D., 1998. *The Rhetoric of Economics*. Madison, WI: University of Wisconsin Press.

Observatorio Metropolitano, 2014. *La Apuesta Municipalista: la democracía empieza por lo cercano*. Madrid: Traficantes de sueños.

Pérez Orozco, A., 2014. *Subversión feminista de la economía. Aportes para un debate sobre el conflicto capital-vida*. Madrid: Traficantes de Sueños.

Quaglia, Lucia and Royo. S., 2015. Banks and the political economy of the sovereign debt crisis in Italy and Spain. *Review of International Political Economy*, 22 (3), 485–507.

Rodríguez López, E., 2016. *La política en el ocaso de la clase media: El ciclo 15M – Podemos*. Madrid: Traficantes de Sueños.

Romanos, E. and Sádaba, I., 2016. From the street to institutions through the app: digitally enabled political outcomes of the Spanish indignados movement. *Revista Internacional de Sociologia*, 74 (4), 1–14.

Salgado, R., 2017. Es la hora de que la recuperación de la economía se refleje en la sociedad. *La Razón*, 17 July. Available at: www.larazon.es/economia/es-la-hora-de-que-la-recuperacion-de-la-economia-se-refleje-en-la-sociedad-LD156111390.

Sampedro, V. and Lobera, J., 2014. The Spanish 15-M Movement: a consensual dissent? *Journal of Spanish Cultural Studies*, 15 (1–2), pp. 61–80.

Sampedro, V. and Martínez Avidad, M., 2018. The digital public sphere: an alternative and counterhegemonic space? The case of Spain. *International Journal of Communication* 12, 23–44.

Solis, J., 2014. Podemos instaura sus términos en el lenguaje de los politicos españoles. *Vozpopuli*, 20 July. Available at: www.vozpopuli.com/espana/Pablo_Iglesias-Juan_Carlos_Monedero-Cristobal_Montoro-Pedro_Sanchez-Partido_Socialista_Obrero_Espanol_PSOE-Podemos_0_716928332.html.

Stein, G., Capape, J. and Gallego, M., 2012. Corporate Governance in Spanish Banks: 2011. *IESE Business School Working Paper No. 946*. Available at SSRN: https://ssrn.com/abstract=2079572 or http://dx.doi.org/10.2139/ssrn.2079572 .

Streek, W., 2015. Why the euro divides Europe. *New Left Review* 95, 5–26.

Suanzes, P., 2017. Dijsselbloem se niega a disculparse por decir que los países del sur se gastan la ayuda 'en copas y mujeres' *El Mundo*, March 21. Available at: www.elmundo.es/economia/2017/03/21/58d15c9cca47413d5a8b45f9.html.

Taibo, C., 2011a. *Nada será como antes: Sobre el movimiento 15-M*. Madrid: Catarata.

Taibo C., 2011b, Cinco razones para confiar en el 15-M. Crónica popular, September 14. Avalaible at: www.cronicapopular.es/2011/09/cinco-razones-para-confiar-en-el-15-m/.

Vilarós, T., 1998. *El mono del desencanto: Una crítica cultural de la transición española (1973–1993)*. Madrid: Siglo Veintiuno.

Villanueva, V., 2015. Puerto Rico. *Journal of Cultural Economy* 8 (1), 62–74.

Recuperating and (re)learning the language of *autogestión* in Argentina's *empresas recuperadas* worker cooperatives

Marcelo Vieta

ABSTRACT

This article homes in on the recuperative and learning dimensions of Argentina's *empresas recuperadas por sus trabajadores* worker cooperatives (ERTs, worker-recuperated enterprises). Drawing on the author's sociological, ethnographic, and political economic work with Argentina's ERTs since 2005, the article theorizes *autogestión* – the collective self-management of associated labour – from its take up by ERT movement protagonists. The article explores and theorizes how ERT workers come to practice *autogestión*, what they actually take back in the process of occupying and controlling the formerly capitalist workplaces that had employed them, and how their projects of cooperative production are ensconced in a 'language of *autogestión*' – recuperating and (re)learning other economic notions and practices against and beyond capitalocentric discourses. Grounded in a class-struggle Marxist perspective, the paper ultimately proposes that ERT workers collectively recuperate three overarching dimensions of productive life from capital: (1) *the self-valorization of living labour*, (2) *cooperation in the labour process*, and (3) *the socialization of surpluses and wealth*. These recuperations of *autogestión*, the article concludes, (their 'language of *autogestión*') offer evocative suggestions for envisioning less-exploitive forms of work, more socially just and democratic workplaces, and for challenging and beginning to move beyond neoliberal logics.

> Argentina's social movements reverberate with infrequently used words, charged with old political content: *solidaridad, autonomía, autogestión* .... The experiences that originate this conceptual resurrection so contrary to neo-liberalism surge more from a creative and combative response to necessity rather than from a theoretical understanding of world history and workers' own past because there was nobody – much less after the killings of the last Argentine dictatorship – to transmit and care for this historical memory. But the very fact that thousands of workers in different parts of Argentina and in other countries simultaneously relied on the same methods and ideas reveals the existence of a profound and hidden subterranean historical conscience. (Almeyra 2004, p. 182)

Marxist researcher, historian, and journalist Guillermo Almeyra wrote these words in the thick of the long Argentine December of 2001. This was a period of deep political crisis and socio-economic distress in the country that, while coalescing into the mass protests of 19-20 December 2001, reverberated throughout the years spanning the turn of the millennium. This period was not only riddled with the temporary implosion of the country's neoliberal model. It was also impassioned by myriad grassroots movements gripped with transformational ideas of how to refashion the social, economic, and political fibres of life from below. These initiatives, impelled both by crisis and a contagion of anti-systemic struggles, began to resurrect the 'historical memory' of a praxical language 'charged with old political content', as Almeyra suggests. Reviving working-class protagonism, these grassroots movements rebelled against the system *and* proposed alternatives. Underscoring them was a reawakened 'historical conscience' embedded in old working-class practices catalyzed anew by material and existential crisis. The crisis, in turn, was wrought by a neoliberal system that had reached saturation and laid bare the false promises of 'trickle-down economics'. This historical period offered a rare moment when the true source of exploitation and marginalization, usually 'obscured and secured' by the class compromise (Burawoy 1985, p. 32), was put into relief for working people.

In this article I home in on one of the grassroots movements at the front lines of these struggles in turn-of-millennium Argentina – the *empresas recuperadas por sus trabajadores* (ERTs, worker-recuperated enterprises). I particularly focus on how its worker-protagonists have been recuperating and (re)learning the concept and practices of *autogestión* since first coming onto the scene in the mid-to-late 1990s. In the process of recuperating workplaces and converting them to worker cooperatives, ERT protagonists have been seized by a two-fold praxis of *rebellion* – in a subversive refusal of status-quo social relations of production – and *prefiguration* – in a foreshadowing of another way of organizing work and economic life beyond the dominative logics of existing property-based capitalist relations. This once dormant historical conscience and working-class self-activity of rebellion and prefiguration – temporarily silenced by state-sanctioned torture, disappearances, and economic repression that gave birth to Argentina's neoliberal model (Patroni 2004, Petras and Veltmeyer 2004) – was resuscitated by working people via the openings afforded by a crumbling neoliberal order and, in its ashes, the alternative economic language and practices of possibility that the grassroots developed. Ever since, ERT protagonists' conversions of formerly capitalist workplaces to cooperatives have been at the forefront of reconceptualizing production for working people and communities, and rearticulating in practice the potential for *autogestión*.

This article's two central concepts, then, are *autogestión* – workers' or a community's collective self-determination of their labour in association – and *recuperation* – to bring back what was once lost, to mend, to make anew again. Taking up an alternative economic language of organizing, producing, and distributing wealth (Gibson-Graham 2006, p. 57), ERT workers recuperate *autogestión* via a process of collective learning that over time enunciates their creative acts of forging new worker cooperatives out of formerly capitalist enterprises. This creativity is first mobilized by workers living through crisis as defensive moves to save jobs. Eventually, workers' direct actions of occupying firms and converting them to cooperatives, as we will see, catalyze the transformation of their subjectivities from managed employees to self-managed workers and open up new vistas for their working lives that articulate a new language of collective production and reproduction. ERTs thus begin to unleash enterprises, labour processes, and the (re)distribution of surpluses from 'a capitalocentric discourse [that] condenses economic difference' (p. 56). Capitalocentrism equates anything to do with the economy 'as circulating around capitalism' (p. 56), in effect making absent or disqualifying other ways of doing economy (de Sausa Santos 2004). ERT protagonists, as I will show in this article, begin to directly contest capitalocentric discourses by recuperating and *re*learning another economic language – the language of *autogestión*.

Drawing on my sociological, ethnographic, and political economic work with Argentina's ERTs since 2005 (Vieta and Ruggeri 2009, Vieta 2010, 2012, 2013, 2014a, 2014b, forthcoming, Ruggeri and Vieta 2015) and grounding my analysis in class-struggle Marxism, I seek to theorize *autogestión* from its take up by the ERT movement's worker protagonists, how they come to learn and practice it, and what they actually recuperate in the process of occupying and controlling the formerly capitalist workplaces that had employed them. To organize the article's empirical evidence and draw out the language of *autogestión*, I appeal to 'the diverse economy' framework (Gibson-Graham 2006). The 'language of the diverse economy' considers the economy expansively by explicitly recognizing that transactions, labour, and enterprises are diversely configured in a plurality of practices which include capitalist, alternative capitalist, and non-capitalist relations (p. 60). Inspired by this approach, I ultimately propose that ERT protagonists' practices and lived experiences of *autogestión* are recuperating three overarching dimensions of productive life from capital in ways that directly speak and make visible an economy that had been silenced by capitalocentric discourses: (1) reconfigured and re-humanized labour relations through the *self-valorization of living labour*, (2) democratically rearticulated enterprises privileging *cooperation in the labour process*, and (3) 'de-marketized' and community-focused transactions via the *socialization of surpluses and wealth*. I ultimately contend that ERT workers' recuperative practices and lived understandings of *autogestión* – their language of *autogestión* – offer evocative suggestions for projects thinking through less-exploitive forms of work and social justice in the workplace, and for challenging and beginning to move beyond neoliberal logics.

Class-Struggle, living labour, and cooperation

The paper extends out from the very concepts, actions, and experiences of the ERT protagonists I have interviewed and worked with over the years. To better understand the recuperative and prefigurative dimensions of ERT protagonists' projects of *autogestión*, I draw on the class-struggle Marxist tradition.

The self-valorization of living labour and the political economy of the working class

While the class-struggle Marxist tradition is best known through autonomist Marxism (*autonomia operaia*), it also encapsulates other critical theoretical streams such as Open Marxism and libertarian socialism (Dyer-Witheford 1999). Most broadly, the tradition highlights the centrality of class struggle in the capital–labour relation, moving beyond a strict focus on the structural features and laws of capital and homing in on the self-determination still embedded in *labour*, or working people's 'productive activity' (Wolff 2002, p. 31, 124). Class-struggle Marxism specifically 'traces the conflict between exploiters and exploited' (Dyer-Witheford 1999, p. 62), pinpointing the ways that workers can and do struggle to move beyond the dominative logics of capitalism, even while being integrally situated within it as alienated labour. But labour is not just this, class-struggle Marxists underscore. Workers' lived experiences overflow the production of capitalist value, already always remaining more than wage-labour; that is, workers are more than simply the bearers of the commodity labour-power. As McNally (2004) points out, contesting Postone's primary focus on the alienating drive of capitalist production, 'purely alienated, instrumentalised labour as an accomplished brute fact of capitalism, rather than a tendential drive ... [is a] ... one dimensional account of labour' (p. 198). For McNally, this focus forgets 'the *dual nature* of commodity producing labour and the critical charge this concept carries' (p. 198, emphasis added).

Class-struggle Marxists draw out this critical charge by returning to Marx's consistent analysis of the two-fold character of labour within capitalism, 'concrete' *and* 'abstract' labour (Marx 1967, pp. 41–46), beginning with how the capitalist labour process at the same time produces 'use-values and values' (McNally 2004, p. 198). Highlighting its two-fold character recognizes that labour exists in capitalism contradictorily, as both constitutive of but also antagonistic to capital (Bonefeld 1994). On the one hand, capitalist production – fundamentally the production of surplus value (Marx 1967, p. 509) – is reliant on abstract labour (i.e. averaged out, socially commensurable labour) which both values commodities and alienates the worker from the work, the means of production, other workers, and their very humanity as creative beings (Marx 2007). The capitalist valorization process relies on the manifestation of labour as an abstracted and alienated form, a process deeply inscribed within capitalist labour processes creating commodities for market exchange (Bonefeld 1994, Postone 1996, Holloway 2002). In this sense, capital is an alien power commanding over the worker and diminishing their human potential (Colletti 1972). On the other hand, labour is also concrete (i.e. living and creative), producing use-values and useful products and services appropriated by people to meet their commodified *and* non-commodified needs and wants. Concrete labour is already always living in working people, it is the manifestation of labour rooted in workers' boundless capacities for conceptualizing and making things in cooperation. Crucially, as 'sentient, embodied, thinking, self-conscious labour' (McNally 2004, p. 198), concrete labour remains antagonistic to capital's tendency of command and control. This two-fold character of labour, in short, is at the heart of class struggle. As McNally (2004) asserts: 'one manifestation of this oppositional determination of labour – of its antagonistic dual structure – is *class struggle*' (p. 198, emphasis added).

I must be clear here; the class-struggle analysis I appeal to does not reify capital or treat labour as separate or apart from capital as its dichotomous opposite. This is a major criticism that has been levelled against this tradition, especially targeting autonomists such as Tronti and Negri (Bonefeld 1994, Toms 2008, Rigi 2015). Agreeing with Dyer-Witheford (1999, p. 68), the most convincing class-struggle analysis acknowledges that labour sits, rather, in an antagonistic 'in and against' relation with capital. While this acknowledges that in a capitalist economic system labour is perversely alienated by and, indeed, remains beholden to capital for the things it needs for its own subsistence and reproduction, this is not commensurable to capital's dependence on labour for its valorization and accumulation processes and, thus, for its very continuation as a system. As Bonefeld's (1994) nuanced analysis of the capital–labour relation rightly points out, 'labour is not external to "capital". Labour exists in and against capital, while capital ... exists only in and through labour' (p. 47, emphasis added). That is, while labour is the 'substance of value' (and, thus, the source of surplus value for capital), capital, however, is not equally the 'substance' of labour. As Marx (1967) reminds us, 'the labourer alone is productive' (p. 509) as living labour, the 'form-giving fire' of creativity in production (1973, p. 361). Capital, on the other hand, opportunistically draws on labour's capacities to value commodities for market exchange via the exploitative methods of the capitalist labour process.[1] This is why we can say that labour is constitutive of capital in a way that capital is not so of labour (Cleaver 1992, Bonefeld 1994).

Taking up seriously the socio-political and -economic implications of living labour in their analyses of working-class self-activity, class-struggle Marxists thus move beyond the diagnosis of capitalism's ills by also striving to highlight the 'self-valorizing' capacities of living labour – the ability for workers to not only valorize capital, but also to struggle against and innovate social and economic life beyond it, by and for themselves (Cleaver 1992). And working people often come to an awareness of their real situation within the capital–labour relation and strive for another socio-economic reality when the alienating and exploitative tendencies of this social relation are brought to relief: when, for instance, the wage-labour contract is violated or the conditions of work become unbearable. These situations often occur during moments of micro-economic downturns or broader macro-economic crises resulting in downsizings, mass redundancies, or outsourcing, as happened with workers that went on to create ERTs in Argentina at the turn-of-the millennium. Indeed, when working people have historically combined, unionized, sabotaged, resisted, refused, or occupied workplaces, they have also brought to the fore labour's two-fold character: what constitutes them as labour within capital as the source of value, *and also* how they push back against the valorization process.

As history has shown, then, workers can and do attempt to create mitigations against capitalist alienation while also inventing alternative moments and spaces for self-valorized work and self-actualized life. Marx termed this perspective 'the political economy of the working class' (Marx 1978a, p. 517), which for him was most clearly illustrated in the British working class's fight for the 10-hour workday and the emergence of 'co-operative factories' (pp. 517–518). Especially pertinent for understanding the recuperations and prefigurations of ERTs, worker cooperatives not only revealed for Marx the superfluousness of capitalist ownership and management, but most crucially the gratuitousness of capital as mediator of productive life and for satisfying people's material needs (Marx 1981, 1985, 1988). The experiences of Argentina's ERTs, I argue, delineate a contemporary instance of the political economy of the working class and an attempt by workers themselves, however provisionally and imperfectly, to self-valorize their work as living labour and against abstracted and alienated manifestations of their creativity.

The radical potential of worker cooperatives

Although Marx was generally supportive of worker cooperatives (Jossa 2005), illustrating for him the political economy of the working class, his theory of co-ops was underdeveloped and ambivalent. Ever since, their potential for social change as alternatives to capitalist production has been contested in radical-left debates (i.e. Ratner 2015, Gindin 2016, Sandoval 2016). Marxist critics of cooperatives, such as Luxemburg (2006), Bordiga (cited in Thoburn 2003, p. 110), and others, have pointed to their chequered history in the capitalist era and how they supposedly always replicate the deficiencies of capitalist production within the totality of a system driven by surplus-value extraction. Left critiques of cooperatives and workers' self-management also emphasize how these experiments have usually been short-lived and thus not up to the task of organizing revolutionary social change. They also argue that cooperatives have too often been co-opted by the capitalist system, forced as they are to continue to produce under the constraints of socially necessary labour times and competitive markets (McNally 1993). As Marx also theorized, workers cooperatively managing enterprises in order to produce commodities for markets 'naturally reproduce in all cases, in their present organization, all the defects of the existing system', becoming 'their own capitalist' (Marx 1981, p. 571). The implicit assumption in these critiques is that, without a broader seizure of power by the working class or a complete return of 'the process of production itself to the control of the workers' (Braverman 1974, p. 446), cooperatives remain inadequate for the project of moving beyond capitalism.

Undoubtedly, much of the historical cooperative movement has been seduced by business discourses that emphasize cooperatives' capacities for efficient production, innovation, and entrepreneurship (Sandoval 2016). While co-ops have even been proposed by heterodox economists as being central to a 'human-faced' economic system (Restakis 2010), left-critics argue that this humanization is nullified if the bulk of the capitalist system still remains intact (Ratner 2015). I, too, recognize how the democratic potential of co-ops is challenged by having to operate within competitive markets (Atzeni and Vieta 2014, Vieta 2012). Nevertheless, following a number of contemporary cooperative theorists of the left (i.e. Jossa 2005, 2014, P. Marcuse 2015, Sandoval 2016, Audebrand 2017), I take Marx's more farsighted view of co-ops.

Suggesting 'the emergence of a new form [of work organization]' that, while still a part of the capitalist system, begins to abolish 'the opposition between capital and labour' (Marx 1981, p. 571), worker co-ops offer 'an alternative to the economic paradigm' (Audebrand 2017, 370). Formally, worker cooperatives are 'voluntary association(s) of [workers] who own the co-operative and operate it democratically ... with one vote each, like citizens in a political democracy' (Vieta *et al.* 2016, p. 437; also see Ellerman 1990). They are thus not designed to be organized by non-producing owner-investors to control labour in order to maximize profits but, instead, are meant to be co-organized by labour itself in order to maximize workers' control of capital and production and, in the best of cases, their own wellbeing (Pérotin 2014, Rothschild 2016). Unlike investor-owned firms, in the worker co-op rights to control and co-own the firm, as well as to decision taking over returns/earnings, disbursements, and re-investments, are linked to members' work contributions rather than monetary investments. Moreover, all members, again unlike in investor-owned firms, have an equal vote not linked to their shares but to their identity as worker-members (Oakeshott 1990).

As Audebrand (2017) concisely puts it, what distinguishes a worker co-op from other firms is that they are *worker controlled*, *worker owned*, and *worker benefiting* (p. 372). Worker controlled means that worker co-ops are set up to be democratic workplaces, bestowing participation and decision-making rights on workers who can decide to run the firm themselves or hire (and fire) external managers. Worker owned means that property is socialized among members and workers themselves decide what to do with revenues. And worker benefiting means that labour processes and the conditions of work are shaped by workers themselves, enabling worker-members to directly address workplace stressors and challenges, preserve jobs by striving not to fire workers in economically difficult times (by, for instance, temporarily lowering salaries), and, in socially focused co-ops such as Argentina's ERTs, contribute to the wellbeing of surrounding communities. For these and other reasons, worker co-ops are productive organizations where the capital–labour relation begins to be contested (Jossa 2014). In theory and practically, worker co-ops underscore how non- or less-capitalist workplaces can be organized by encouraging horizontalized labour processes and directly democratic practices (Zevi *et al.* 2011, Jensen 2012, Vieta *et al.* 2016).

Additionally, worker co-ops are not inherently co-optable into the capitalist system by design. They most usually become so in national contexts not fully supportive of cooperatives and workplace democracy (Craig 1993), or when left to fend for themselves within extremely competitive market sectors (McNally 1993). Indeed, some class-struggle Marxists have pointed out how worker cooperatives, especially those with strong worker- and community-focused projects such as ERTs, embrace a 'labour commons' rooted in associated labour and socialized production (de Peuter and Dyer-Witheford 2010).

Argentina has one of the oldest cooperative sectors in the world (Shaffer 1999) and worker co-ops have existed in the country since at least the 1920s (Vuotto 2014). ERTs, however, can be seen as a new form of worker co-operative. Unlike more traditional cooperative development strategies, whereby a collective from the same sector organize a co-op business to either provision better products, market related goods, or guarantee the delivery of services based on the mutual needs of members, Argentina's ERTs took off in the 2000s as part of a new wave of co-ops that directly responded to the dire situation of workers (Fajn 2003, Vieta and Ruggeri 2009, Vieta 2012). During this period, two types of new worker co-ops emerged in the country: state-sanctioned cooperatives linked to the delivery of welfare plans (Vuotto 2014), and ERTs, which were driven at first by workers' desire to save jobs and keep companies afloat, with the cooperative model an already available form from which to re-organize production under their own control (Fajn 2003, Ruggeri *et al.* 2005, Rebón 2007). What distinguishes ERTs from traditional, ideologically driven, and strictly member-benefiting cooperatives, or state-sanctioned, assistentialist co-ops, is that ERT workers did not originally envision starting a co-op, nor did they have much, if any, state support. Rather, ERTs are a part of what I have called elsewhere 'the new cooperativism' – anti-systemic experiments in alternative organizing that respond directly to crises, that are driven initially by the material needs of working people, and that take on values and practices of horizontalism and solidarity as viable alternatives to the crises from which they emerge (Vieta 2016, 2018). Over time, as I will shortly show, ERT protagonists learn the ins-and-outs of cooperation and *autogestión* praxically and through collective struggle, eventually realizing the value of organizing workplaces democratically and advocating for workers' control and cooperation.

While not without challenges, the continued presence and growth of Argentina's ERT movement and its new forms of solidarity-based cooperativism suggest that the *tout court* dismissal of worker cooperatives and self-management by left critics is too hasty, forcing those on the left seeking alternatives to re-evaluate co-ops' theoretical and concrete potential.

From neoliberal crisis to rebellion: the emergence of Argentina's *empresas recuperadas*

Commentators informed by class-struggle approaches have suggested that crisis moments are both threatening instances of disorganization for the status quo's socio-economic order as well as opportunities for alternatives (i.e. H. Marcuse 1969, Bell and Cleaver 2002, Lazzarato 2003). Crises place into relief the contradictions of the capitalist system of production and can even stimulate a contagion of resistance and alternative proposals (H. Marcuse 1969). Illustrative of these crises-driven social upheavals and alternatives in Latin America were the rebellions and social re-compositions that emerged in response to the temporary collapse of the neoliberal model in Argentina at the turn of the millennium.

Throughout the 1990s, Argentina embraced a series of neoliberal policies that included privatizing much of its public-sector services and assets, fixing the peso to the US dollar, deregulating barriers to direct foreign investment, and dismantling long-established labour guarantees (Forcinito and

Basualdo 2007, Pozzi and Nigra 2015). Ostensibly designed to curb the hyperinflation of the late 1980s and kick-start a floundering economy, the results of these policies were ultimately counterproductive; by the mid 1990s, capital began to flow out of Argentina and local SMEs (small- and medium-sized enterprises) became uncompetitive (Palomino 2003, Patroni 2004). With the implosion of this economic model by late 2001, and via a 'reactivation' of 'communitarian social experience' and self-organization from below (Svampa and Pereyra 2004, p. 233), countless locally based social movements that had been slowly emerging since the mid 1990s had by 2001 blanketed Argentina's urban centres and public spaces. They created alternative organizations rooted in directly democratic decision-making structures that temporarily filled the void left by systemic socio-economic breakdown and a crumbling and impotent nation-state (Colectivo Situaciones 2002, Sitrin 2012, Zibechi 2012).

As rebellions against the socio-economic and -political status quo, the turn-of-millennium social movements contributed to further choking the main institutional arteries of neoliberal capital. For instance, with no bosses to rail against or workplaces to strike, the *piqueteros* – organized groups of the growing unemployed masses – would go on to cut off the main distributive veins of capitalism. By occupying Argentina's national roads and barricading themselves in, the *piqueteros* would temporarily shut down the distribution of commodities, recuperating the pavement for places of horizontal organizing. At the same time, neighbourhood assemblies would occupy the public sites of reproduction of life and labour, such as local parks and plazas, recuperating directly democratic processes for local governance by creating people's assemblies where the failing state's grip on power was contested and state authoritarianism refuted. Local barter clubs and alternative currencies would directly challenge and circumvent the circuits of finance and exchange, capitalism's main channels of accumulation. And ERTs, in turn, would seize workplaces, capitalism's points of production, recuperating them as sites of associated (rather than exploited) labour, as well as reconstituting them as open spaces for socialized production and the production of culture, as we will soon see.

What needs to be underscored is that the popular rebellions of turn-of-millennium Argentina were not mere protests limited by a politics of demand. They were, rather, both actual counter-offensives by working people against the worst effects of neoliberal enclosure *and* experiments in creating new, community-driven socio-economic institutions from below. Both of these aspects were embedded in the collective cry of fury heard around the world during Argentina's mass uprisings of 19-20 December 2001: '*¡Que se vayan todos!*' ('Everyone [in the political and economic establishment] leave now!') (Almeyra 2004, Dinerstein 2015). Implicit in this slogan – and in the concept of *autogestión* – was thus the two-fold practices of rebellion *and* prefigurative (re)invention, which would bring together social movements like the *piqueteros*, neighbourhood assemblies, barter clubs, community self-provisioning experiments, and ERTs. On the one hand, the cry of '*¡Que se vayan todos!*' underscored a collective desire of refusal by rebellious subjects who had had enough of corruption, socio-economic immiseration, and socio-political collapse. On the other hand, '*¡Que se vayan todos!*' implied the willing actions of countless grassroots groups throughout the country as they collectively conceptualized and co-produced other socio-economic and -political institutions and practices counter to neoliberal austerity and stagnant institutions of constituted power. It is true that many of the voices that joined the cry of '*¡Que se vayan todos!*' belonged to the middle class, motivated to protest due to their frozen bank accounts and loss of purchasing power. But it was also undeniably a working-class and marginalized people's rebellion that brought to the fore the need for alternative experiments in economic transactions, labour, and production that, while already existing, had been silenced and absenced by the status-quo system (de Sausa Santos 2004).

I have drawn theoretical inspiration from E.P. Thompson (1963) to understand how the grassroots rebellions and reinventions of working people at the turn of the millennium were driven, to a large extent, by *a moral economy of work* (Vieta 2014b, forthcoming). Spearheading the emergence of ERTs, for instance, a wave of workplace occupations swelled as the exploitation workers experienced on shop floors became increasingly intolerable, as labour contracts were explicitly violated by employers, and as the political economic system which had delivered workplace security and social benefits in the past evaporated with the neoliberal juggernaut (also see Atzeni 2010). With increasing impunity during moments of deep capitalist crises, employers often resort to rationalization drives, lockouts, wage rollbacks, and other infringements of employment contracts. But often during these moments, the exploitative social relations of the capitalist labour process are also made visible to workers as work is intensified, salaries cut, and firings increase. In turn-of-millennium Argentina, at a time when the fluid class compromise between labour, employers, and the state ruptured,[2] the solution for more and more workers was to, at first, engage in spontaneous acts of workplace occupations and, eventually, the conscious reconceptualization of once-capitalist workplaces as cooperatives. To do so, these workers would rely on the solidarity that they had already been forging over the years on shop floors and that had been solidifying during the period of acute economic crisis, eventually refashioning their work, workplaces, and labour processes within the rubric of *autogestión* (Rebón 2007, Ruggeri 2014, Vieta 2014b).

As SME bankruptcies, mass layoffs, and unemployment rates soared to record levels throughout the late 1990s and early 2000s (Magnani 2009), and as business owners, often in collusion with court trustees, began to engage in nefarious asset-stripping schemes to stay afloat or seek to benefit personally from insolvencies, an increasing number of workers from a broad cross-section of Argentina's urban-based economy began taking matters into their own hands (Fajn 2003, Rebón 2007, Vieta 2010, 2012, Ruggeri 2014). By the early 2000s, more and more threatened workers' collectives would occupy the companies, clinics, factories, and workshops that had employed them, setting them to work again as cooperatives. Evocatively articulating the three major stages needed to convert workplaces to co-ops in Argentina, some ERT protagonists have borrowed the slogan *ocupar, resistir, producir* (occupy, resist, produce) from Brazil's landless workers' and peasants' movement. ERT protagonists would learn these three stages to *autogestión* collectively, informally, and in the thick of struggles to save their working lives, or '*sobre la marcha*' ('on the path of doing'), as various ERT workers have told me (Vieta 2014b). In the process, they have been recuperating the historical Argentine working-class tactics of factory occupations and street protests of the 1950s, 1960s, 1970s, and 1980s (Wyczykier 2009). Their embrace of *autogestión* also suggests ERT protagonists' social memories of other Argentine working-class traditions, including: a long history of activist unionism, cooperativism, and union-based democratic shop-floor organs, such as *comisones internas* (internal workers' commissions), *asambleas* (workers' assemblies), and *cuerpos de delegados* (shop stewards' committees) (Munck *et al.* 1987). At the turn of the millennium, these social memories and working-class traditions would merge with contemporary social movement practices of occupations of public spaces, experiments in collective self-provision, and local participatory democracy (Almeyra 2004, Zibechi 2012).

While ERTs usually first emerge as workers' localized and defensive strategies for saving jobs and livelihoods, going through the struggle to take over a troubled firm eventually radicalizes some workers, as we will soon review. In the ensuing years since they first appeared over two decades ago, ERTs have become a new dimension of the Argentine labour movement, a world-renowned icon of resistance against neoliberal capitalist excess, and a twenty-first century beacon of workers' self-management (Vieta 2010, 2012, Ozarow and Croucher 2014, Ruggeri and Vieta 2015). ERTs are now a legitimate solution to business closure and unemployment; have formed into numerous umbrella networks and organizations representing the interests of self-managed and cooperative workers throughout the country (some affiliated with the country's broader union movement or parties of the left, some remaining more autonomous); and have mobilized to influence the reform of bankruptcy laws and expropriation legislation to assist in the conversion of troubled firms to cooperatives (Ruggeri and Vieta 2015, Ranis 2016). Today, almost 400 ERTs exist throughout the country involving close to 16,000 workers across the urban-based economy in sectors such as printing and publishing, metallurgy, construction, ship building, wood work, newspapers and media, restaurants, food stuffs, and health care (Ruggeri and Vieta 2015, Ruggeri 2016). And they continue to emerge in response to a new wave of anti-labour legislation, business closures, unemployment and precarity, and myriad other socio-economic challenges unleashed since early 2016 by the centre-right coalition government of President Mauricio Macri (Ruggeri 2016, de Assis 2018).

From rebellion to *autogestión*: recuperating productive life

In this section I assess some of the evidence for ERT protagonists' articulation of the language and practices of *autogestión* as they begin to recuperate from capital three overarching dimensions of productive life: *self-valorization of living labour*, which reconfigures and rehumanizes labour relations; *cooperation in the labour process*, which democratically rearticulates enterprises; and *socialization of surpluses and wealth*, which can be said to begin to 'de-marketize' economic transactions by privileging the community over competitive markets. All of the ERTs I have visited over the years have begun to recuperate these dimensions to varying degrees. Before exploring them, I first more fully define *autogestión* and *recuperation*, this article's key concepts.

Autogestión

The Spanish word *autogestión* has etymological roots in the Greek *autós* (self, same) and the Latin *gerere* (to bear, to carry, to manage) (Farmer 1979, p. 59). *Autogestión* has deep resonances with the history of workers' self-activity and is intertwined with the development of capitalism in the political economy of the working class (Ruggeri 2018, Vieta 2014a). As lived by formerly waged workers desiring to cooperatively self-determine their productive lives, *autogestión* embraces the notion of becoming something other than wage-labour (Vieta 2014a). In line with the two-fold notion of rebellion/prefiguration engrained in Argentina's turn-of-millennium social movements, Brazilian social theorists Sardá de Faria and Novaes (2011) remind us that experiments in *autogestión* are enfolded into the history of global capitalism, emerging 'either in the context of revolutionary outbreak or in the intensification of class conflict ... [uniting] the two sides of the associative principle: resistance and the production of the means of life' (p. 40).

In Argentina, as in other parts of Latin America, the concept of *autogestión* encapsulates working people's collective experiments with socio-cultural and socio-economic self-determination (Peixoto de Albaquerque 2004, Sitrin 2012, Zibechi 2012). It alludes to a processual and embodied movement of collective self-creation and self-conception, having socio-political relevance in its implicit potentiality of becoming something other than capital. ERT workers themselves use the word *autogestión* in their promotional materials, in communicating their initiatives to outsiders, and in the everyday conversations between themselves, both to describe their new ways of organizing work and as reminders of the collective struggles that led them to re-appropriate their workplaces as cooperatives (Vieta 2012, 2014b). A former president of the ERT newspaper *Comercio y Justicia* in the city of Córdoba, Javier De Pascuale, defined *autogestión* for me from his own lived experience as:

> the possibility that we – all people – have to realize ourselves professionally, economically, and, in our capacities to labour. It emerges from within ourselves and together with the people with whom we want to share this realization, but without sacrificing personal freedom, without sacrificing personal dignity, and from our own developmental potential. It is, in other words, about the possibility of the full development of the person. (De Pascuale, cited in Vieta 2014b)

Recuperation

The word 'recuperate' comes from Latin, formed by the prefix *re* (back) and the verb *capere* (to take) (Oxford 2018). The preeminent Spanish language dictionary, Real Academia Española, defines the verb *recuperar* as follows: '*to take back* or *acquire again* what was once had'; '*to put back into service or use* that which was at one time unusable'; 'to work for a determined period in order *to make up for what had not been done* for some reason'; '*to return* to itself, or to a former state' (Real Academia 2018, emphases added).

In what can also be seen as 'a language of recuperation', these definitions highlight what is at stake for ERT protagonists' living labour when they occupy their places of work and re-open them as worker cooperatives. For instance, in recuperating a failing or failed capitalist firm, ERT workers 'put back into service or use that which was at one time unusable'. In recuperating their workplaces and the machines and tools therein and in setting the means of production to work once again, ERT protagonists 'take back or acquire again' what was once historically, and especially in traditional and craft-based work, firmly under the control of the direct producers. And in taking back control over the labour process and the conception and creation of the final products of their work, ERT protagonists 'return to [themselves]' the self-determination and ultimate control over the fundamental human capacities that began to get lost or forgotten in the real subsumption of labour by capital – that is, the capacities for workers to conceptualize, plan, coordinate, and cooperatively produce, as well as to distribute the social wealth needed to not only survive, but also to thrive.

In sum, in the very actions of taking over and self-managing once-capitalist firms, ERT protagonists begin to prefiguratively show how to un-alienate their labour and take back the labour process. As Sitrin and Azzellini (2012) underscore in their assessment of the Occupy movement, in affinity with the ethico-political force of ERT workers' understanding and take-up of the concept of recuperation:

> [t]he term *recuperate*, in an emancipatory context, refers to the *re-appropriation* of something concrete, conceptual, or historical, by the people. This is anything from a factory to historical memory. The prefix '*re*' indicates that it *is understood as having belonged to the people before*. (p. 56, emphasis added)

It must also be mentioned, however, that we can also identify a tension with the word *recuperation* between ERT workers' conceptions of it in their language and practices and the state's co-optation and deployment of the term in its policies and discourses. The centre-left Peronist governments headed by Presidents Nestor Kirchner and Cristina Fernández de Kirchner (2003–2015) also spoke of 'recuperating' the economy and national productivity from neoliberal crises, embracing notions of *recuperar el empleo* (recover employment), *recuperar los salarios* (recover salaries), and other economic *recuperaciones* in socio-economic policies and political speeches (Wylde 2012, Kulfas 2016). Indeed, the Ministry of Labour's Programa Trabajo Autogestionado, for instance, a salary top-up and technical assistance programme for ERTs and other self-managed firms established in 2004, as well as the reform of Argentina's banckruptcy law in 2011, explicitly took up the notion of *recuperar empresas*. These and other developmentalist programmes and policies geared to ERTs, the 'informal' sector, and social and solidarity economy initiatives contributed to the attempt to institutionalize self-management initiatives by *kirchnerismo* as not only paths to saving businesses in crises, for combatting under- and unemployment, and for developing local economies, but also as 'social containment' strategies that aimed to co-opt and essentially de-politicize these initiatives (Dinerstein 2007). How ERT workers have interpreted and taken up the notion of recuperation, however, differs from the state-institutional deployment of the concept. ERT protagonists, as we will explore next, have been using the concept in a more profound and farsighted way: to articulate paths to regaining life security, saving jobs, and recomposing and reinventing work and the workplace along more humanized, democratized, and community-focused paths. These are all minimized or bracketed out by state-institutional uses of the term.[3]

Three overarching recuperations of autogestión

Self-valorization of living labour

What ERT protagonists' projects of *autogestión* most fundamentally recuperate, I argue, is control over their living labour. Here they begin to revive the diverse economies of creatively working and producing the things we need and desire that is otherwise silenced by capital, a conceptualization of labour situated beyond wage-labour. More precisely, in taking over their places of employment and self-managing them as cooperatives, ERT workers take back control over and begin to decommodifiy their *labour-power* – their capacities to transform raw materials into useful things, to work collaboratively, and to create value. It is these capacities that purchasers of labour-power (i.e. the capitalist) most crucially seize when paying wages for work done, a seizure that is legally sanctioned in the employment contract. Tellingly, the capitalist fundamentally pays wages not out of concern for the wellbeing of workers but, rather, as a cost of production in order to trigger and appropriate the capitalist valorization process. On the other hand, in controlling their own living labour and pulling themselves out of the circuits of the buying and selling of wage-labour, ERT protagonists essentially de-commodify their labour-power and begin to un-alienate themselves.

In short, Argentina's ERTs underscore how workers' capacities for value creation and productivity can be taken back by living labour and reappropriated for the purposes of self-valorization. Indeed, as self-valorizing workers, ERT protagonists show how *autogestión* contrasts sharply with the direct control of workers by the hyper-specialization of Taylorist or Fordist production regimes, or the indirect control of workers through rationalization drives, 'responsible autonomy' (Friedman 1977), or empowerment schemes of so-called post-Fordist production regimes. Now, under the auspices of *autogestión*, ERT workers re-embrace more expansive notions of work and learning, as they share myriad skills and tasks that often extend beyond their occupational specialty, including accounting, sales, administrative, and marketing know-how, and the softer skills of cooperation, solidarity, and even, as we will shortly see, community engagement. Relatedly, ERT protagonists recuperate a community centred and craft-based approach to the labour process, where workers regain control over a multiplicity of abilities and learning dimensions similar to what Sennett (2008) defines as 'making a life in common' (p. 6). Moreover, ERT protagonists are proving that innovation, risk-taking, and creativity are not the unique domain of the investor or the 'heroic entrepreneur' but are, rather, firmly ensconced in the skills and practices of working people.

These innovative and creative capacities are most outwardly visible in the fact that over 94 percent of ERTs become worker cooperatives, even though most ERT workers have not had previous experience with cooperativism (Ruggeri *et al.* 2005). There are two major reasons for the overwhelming take up of cooperativism. The first is pragmatic; the ERT movement's earliest leaders came to the realization that the worker cooperative was a readily available and sound business model for workers of troubled firms to restart production. Today, workers who are contemplating taking over and self-managing a firm soon learn about the cooperative solution from older ERT experiences, from ERT umbrella organizations or movement lawyers, or from sympathetic university researchers. The second is educative and symbolic; ERT workers themselves eventually discover that a co-op offers a viable organizational form for the collective to learn participation and self-management and for beginning to move beyond the most negative aspects of working under bosses that they had previously experienced (Vieta 2014b).

It is in the process of transitioning from employees to self-managed workers that ERT protagonists begin to learn the intricacies of cooperativism: '*Aprendimos cooperativismo sobre la marcha*' ('We learned how to be cooperators on the path of doing'), as a worker from and ERT health clinic in the city of Córdoba told me in 2009 (cited in Vieta 2014b). This type of learning is, as I have pointed out in an earlier article, *informal* and *inter*- and *intra-cooperative*, unfolding via traditional working-class methods of apprenticing and mutual aid (Vieta 2014b). Similar to what Dewey (1938) meant by experiential learning, this collective learning-by-doing begins during an ERT's first months of conflict and crises when the collective of workers of a troubled or bankrupt firm decide to occupy it and take it over. During this period, other ERTs and social movement organizations come to support the occupying workers, transferring knowledge of the political and judicial systems, as well as values of solidarity and know-how concerning how to start a cooperative.

The informal and social means of acquiring the skills for *autogestión* solidify within the recuperated workplace in what the ERT workers themselves call *compañerismo* – a strong sense of solidarity through camaraderie developed from having traversed difficulties together and from engaging in shared projects. What *compañerismo* means practically is that ERT workers are now more likely to think about the collective and to assist each other when compared to their more individualistic interests when they worked for a boss. As a founder of a Buenos Aires print shop ERT explained:

> Before, under owner-management, there was always someone marking out the rhythm of your work .... Things are now different .... Before we were 'workmates' but today we aren't workmates anymore. We're now more like *socios* (partners, members, or associates), where the problem of one member affects us all .... Before, if something happened to someone it was the owner's responsibility, but now, what binds us together is the fact that we're all responsible for this cooperative. (cited in Vieta 2012, 2014b)

Compañerismo is also reflected in how ERT workers learn across generations in ways that not only transfer on-the-job skills and know-how from expert to novice, but also pass on strategies for resisting the repressions that often come with recurrent threats of evictions, knowledge of how to combat any left-over individualist tendencies that might remain with some workers, and how to embrace shop-floor participation and democracy. This knowledge is passed on to junior workers from senior workers, who themselves draw on both their own experiences and the well-spring of historical Argentine working-class practices. Knowledge of how to carry out workplace takeovers, convert them to worker co-ops, and self-manage them are also recalled and retold by ERT workers as shared stories within each ERT and between ERTs (Ruggeri 2014, Vieta 2014b).

Informal and *sobre la marcha* knowledge acquisition and the intensity of *compañerismo* are, of course, not the same at all ERTs and for all ERT workers. As Eduardo Murúa, former president of the ERT umbrella organization Movimiento Nacional de Empresas Recuperadas (MNER, National Movement of Recuperted Enterprises) explains it:

> The change in subjectivity in some workers is much more powerful than in others. The subjectivity and culture of some workers have not changed. Some workers go to work every day and just do their tasks in the recuperated enterprise; they do them very well, perhaps with more effort than before when they worked under a boss. But they finish their job for the day and then they go home like they did in their old jobs. Other workers are different. They have re-conceptualized the factory differently. They begin to talk and think in a new way. They have come to understand how their former bosses were exploiting them. They have come to understand how the economic system functions in Argentina, how the capitalist system destroys each one of our workplaces .... (Murúa, cited in Vieta forthcoming)

Also reported by Ruggeri *et al.* (2005), ERT workers with the deepest learning and greatest take-up of *compañerismo* are founding members that directly experienced the challenges of taking over and converting their places of work into co-ops. As Murúa further underscores, ERT workers who experience the most radical change are those that 'entrenched themselves the most in the issues of the recuperation of the enterprise and that struggle to turn them into cooperatives' (Murúa, cited in Vieta forthcoming). I also found, as did Ruggeri *et al.* that *compañerismo* is stronger in smaller ERTs where each worker is more intimately familiar with the lives of their fellow workers than in larger ERTs (Vieta 2014b).

In sum, from out of macro- and micro-economic crises and collective struggles, ERTs construct more solidarity-based and less competitive social relations of production when compared to the previous capitalist firms from which they emerge. In the process, ERT workers embark on the variegated path of un-alienating themselves from capital–labour relations by beginning to self-valorize their own labour and cooperative capacities, learning *autogestión* collectively, informally, and by doing via *compañerismo*. In turn, *compañerismo* acts as a social adhesive for consolidating the worker co-op and strengthening the relations between *socios*, other ERTs, and surrounding communities (as we will shortly see) in ways unthinkable when these workers worked for bosses.

Cooperation in the labour process

One of the alternatives that the political economy of the working class is attentive to centres on what Marx characterized as 'social production' under 'freely associated labour' (Marx 1978a, 1978b, 1981). For ERTs, this is most readily palpable in the sharp uptake of cooperation in the labour process once production restarts. Here, they begin to fundamentally transform labour relations in the workplace.

In practice, this is reflected in the horizontal re-contouring of the shop, including directly democratic decision-making and administrative structures and egalitarian remuneration practices. These are all central to deep notions of *autogestión*.

As formal cooperatives, virtually all ERTs are administered by regularly elected and recallable workers' or administrative councils (*juntas directivas* or *juntas administrativas*). These usually consist of a president, secretary, treasurer and at times members-at-large (*vocales*). Almost all ERTs also engage in regular (usually monthly but often weekly) workers' assemblies, going far beyond the legal requirement for Argentine cooperatives of holding at minimum one assembly of the membership per year. Yet another clear example of how deeply *autogestión* is taken up at ERTs is the preponderance of complete or almost complete pay equity, without privileging the specific skillset or the age of the worker, although at times seniority, following traditional organized labour practices, is taken into account in some salary differentials.[4] Indeed, around two-thirds of ERTs engage in egalitarian pay practices (Fajn 2003, Ruggeri *et al.* 2005). The practice of equal pay, it should also be noted, is not necessarily common in worker cooperatives. The broad adoption of this practice across the ERT movement has become, rather, a unique social innovation that differentiates Argentina's ERTs from other forms of labour-managed firms elsewhere. Indeed, redesigning formerly capitalist firms with directly democratic governance structures and pay parity are two of the most radical non-capitalist practices innovated by ERTs. Prefiguring a different kind of productive economy by revaluing the contributions of all worker-members, whether administrators or plant workers, Argentina's ERTs thus also begin to recuperate something innovative for cooperativism – labour equity.

ERT protagonists' cooperation in the labour process also means the reconfiguration of the very notion of work, suggesting ways of turning the capitalist labour process on its head. ERT workers, for example, also strive to humanize rather than speed up work, designing many breaks into their workday (e.g. regular *mate* tea breaks), and eating and playing together regularly (e.g. daily communal lunches and weekly soccer games or barbeques). What might seem to be modest amendments to work time have brought many benefits to workers, helping to ease work-related stress and improve overall wellbeing. Of course, these re-configurations of workspaces and work rhythms are uncommon in capitalist firms with different other ideas regarding 'productive' and 'non-productive' time.[5] Other ways that capitalist notions of work are being challenged and revalued by ERTs are: refusing contracts and projects when the work proves to be too onerous or beyond the capacity of the cooperative, sharing production processes with other ERTs and cooperatives, and allowing workers regular time off to attend to personal matters.

The cooperative redesign of the labour process also serves as practical responses to ongoing production and financing challenges. These challenges are caused by various factors, including: ERT workers having to restart production from a broken capitalist enterprise and without previous administrative experience, the need to continue to engage in competitive markets for pragmatic reasons, and also from the absence of coherent public policies that could help to more quickly stabilize and consolidate these self-managed companies. In response to these challenges, ERT workers have ensured the operational functioning of the co-op in several creative ways, such as: 'just-in-time' production; having customers pay for raw materials as soon as an order is placed; or the common practice of producing *a façón*, a type of putting out system where ERTs become part of the production process of other enterprises. Some ERTs in the same sector or within the same region also actively collaborate by sharing machines and maintenance costs; practicing collective purchases of raw materials, inventories, and other production inputs; or via the social and solidarity economy strategies of bartering goods and services between ERTs or with other cooperatives or surrounding neighbourhoods. While engaging in social and solidarity economy practices, between ERTs and between ERTs and other co-ops, serves to put into question the logic of competitive markets, they also effectively put into practice the International Co-operative Alliance's sixth cooperative principal: cooperation among cooperatives.

In these cooperative practices, ERTs can be seen to be recuperating forms of craft-based pre-capitalist or early-capitalist economies where expert craftspeople shared production processes with customers or work agents. Further, ERTs' continued existence and emergence with relatively low failure rates (only around 10 percent of all ERTs that have existed since they first emerged in the 1990s have closed (Ruggeri and Vieta 2015, Ruggeri 2016) illustrates the capacities of workers to innovate and find creative fixes to continued challenges. Additionally, we can view the social and solidarity economy practices of ERTs as the self-valorization of living labour turned outwards from the cooperative to the community. We turn to these practices next.

Socialization of surpluses and wealth

Compañerismo and cooperation at ERTs also extend outwards to the community and to other cooperatives via the socialization (rather than privatization) of production and wealth creation and the broader adoption of social and solidarity economy practices. A major consequence of the cooperativization of labour processes, then, is the conversion of businesses into organizations of socialized production that redistribute surpluses rather than accumulating them for private gain. In effect, this begins to 'de-marketize' economic transactions. For example, while ERTs tend to ensure that revenues are first distributed among workers in order to meet their material needs and then to production and maintenance needs of the cooperative, any leftover surpluses – including unused spaces within the firm and remaining funds – are often shared with surrounding communities. Thus, besides providing jobs to local people and securing economic activity directly related to the main business of the firm, ERTs also contribute to the socio-economic needs of surrounding neighbourhoods and to de-marketized exchanges, creating alternative forms of economic transactions between ERTs (for instance, by bartering or sharing production inputs) and beyond the ERT movement. The two main ways that this socialized surplus and wealth creation happens is by *opening up the shop to the community* and *sharing surpluses with the community.*

First, in a manifestation of what the ERT movement calls *la fábrica abierta* (the open factory), many ERTs *open up the cooperative to the community* by dedicating portions of workspaces to other uses besides the principal activity of the cooperative. More than half of ERTs, for instance, are used outside of production hours as community or cultural centres, as free health clinics, for popular high school equivalency programmes known as *bachilleratos populares* that also emerged from the turn-of-the-millennium social movements, for multimedia initiatives, and even for neighborhood dining rooms. All are organized by workers, neighbours, or volunteers (Ruggeri *et al.* 2010, Vieta 2010, 2012, 2014b). Exemplar ERTs that have opened up their spaces to well-known and often-used community initiatives include the ceramics manufacturer Zanón/FaSinPat in the province of Neuquén; the *bachillerato popular* and the Chilavert Recupera recreation space at the Buenos Aires print shop Artes Gráficas Chilavert; La Fábrica Ciudad Cultural (the Cultural City Factory) and the popular Universidad de los Trabajadores at the Buenos Aires ERT metal shop IMPA; the 19 de Diciembre metal shop ERTs' *bachillerato popular* in the Buenos Aires suburb of San Martín; and the print shop Gráfica Patricios' health clinic and radio programme in the Buenos Aires neighbourhood of Barracas.

Second, some ERTs, such as Zanón/FaSinPat or Unión Solidaria de Trabajadores (UST) in the municipality of Avellaneda, also *extend the shop into the community* by engaging in the redistribution of surpluses in order to contribute to the needs of local communities. Zanón/FaSinPat, for instance, regularly redistributes surpluses and donates ceramics to local community initiatives, including assisting in the construction of a local hospital. UST has similarly built a local sports complex for the youth of the surrounding *barrio*, while also initiating a recycling programme, radio programming and other multimedia projects, a spin-off brick building cooperative, and a *bachillerato popular*. In addition – and with few other precedents in the worldwide worker co-op movement – UST has also built 100 attractive townhomes for its most vulnerable workers and neighbours in need of dignified housing.

There are several reasons why many ERTs open up the shop to the community or commit to the needs of local communities beyond the shop. One reason is to give back to the communities that assisted them in their most harrowing days of occupation when neighbours would arrive with bedding, clothing, food, and, in the most difficult cases, as human barriers against violent eviction attempts by the state or returning owners and their hired thugs. Another related reason is that many ERT protagonist start to see their recuperated firms as intimate parts of their neighborhoods and local communities as they come to realize that inserting themselves tightly into the neighborhoods that surround them redoubles the social value of the ERT. One direct result of this added social value is that ERTs inure themselves against future threats of eviction or closure by the state or returning owners. As has happened in numerous cases over the years, court decisions or vetoes by local governments that threaten to shutter an ERT again or return the firm to the previous owner usually unleashes the resistance not only of its workers but also the mobilizations of the surrounding community in defense of the ERT. Consequently, the social capital of ERTs grows exponentially as they open up to or extend out into the community.

A third way that ERTs are engaging in social and solidarity economy activities should be mentioned; the Argentine ERT movement has been forging new, international knowledge sharing and exchange networks with ERTs and cooperatives from other parts of Latin America and the world. While they are still incipient, several promising initiatives have unfolded over the years, such as: the regular bi-annual meetings of the International Network of the Workers' Economy (started in 2007 by Argentina's ERT movement and academics that work in solidarity with ERTs from the University of Buenos Aires's Facultad Abierta); the first and second regional gathering of ERTs from across Latin America, held in Venezuela in 2005 and 2006 with the backing of its Bolivarian government; and attempts to export ERT products with the assistance of the US non-profit The Working World (Ranis 2016). While alternative international markets of recuperated products have yet to establish themselves, promising transnational knowledge and know-how exchanges continue to occur via these and other regular gatherings and initiatives.

Soon after beginning my work with Argentina's ERTs, I learned that the participation of an ERT in ensuring broader community wellbeing becomes integral to its new *raison d'être*. With many ERTs, then, the self-valorization of its worker-protagonists' own living labour also extends into neighbouring communities. This increases exponentially the social value of the productive entity in ways that are never contemplated by the capitalist model of production. The practices of bringing the community into the shop or extending the shop into the community thus symbolically tear down the walls that contain the 'secret' work activity of the capitalist factory, transforming once-private firms into community-based work organizations and socio-cultural spaces. In sum, jobs and physical assets are not the only things recuperated by an ERT – they also begin to recuperate and socialize surpluses and wealth for the community.

(Re)Learning the language of *autogestión* 'in struggle'

To be sure, working people's initiatives to self-manage their productive lives in a sea of capitalist practices and logics, especially when still needing to produce in part for competitive markets, are deeply challenged and remain incomplete (Atzeni and Vieta 2014). This does not, however, take away from the prefigurative character of these experiments in alternative diverse economies, contributing important experiences to the political economy of the working class. But if the historical conscience of these other economic experiments in Argentina was lost to the continued enclosures, effacements, and repressions of the neoliberal project, as Almeyra articulated in the opening epigraph of this article, the language and practices of *autogestión* needed to be recuperated and *re*learned. As we have seen, the major way that ERT protagonists learn *autogestión* is in the thick of struggle, informally, and collaboratively. This form of learning by people engaged in common struggles has been conceptualized as the transformative nature of learning in social movements, in workplaces, and especially during moments of crisis where people must work together to overcome shared difficulties. ERTs are yet another example of how such spaces for working-class learning can emerge and even flourish.

Foley's (1999) research work with social movements helps us understand that much transformative learning happens in 'emancipative struggle' (p. 11), especially when people come together to overcome perceived injustices. Moments of deep crises where commonly assumed rights and ways of living are challenged bring to the surface shared grievances and a moral economy. Such moments can compel people to collectively organize, pool resources, and contest or change aspects of the world deemed unjust by learning about issues and taking up new skills, values, and practices of participation and cooperation (Hall and Clover 2005). People thus learn deeply when struggling together to overcome challenges and participating in solving common problems in constructive ways (Overwein 2000).

Similar learning-in-struggle dynamics unfold with Argentina's ERT protagonists. Most crucially during the first years of the movement, ERTs emerged out of macro-economic and social crises radiating into workplaces. What were at first workers' spontaneous occupations and defensive actions to save jobs would eventually transform for many of them into struggles to secure their *dignidad* (dignity) and future livelihoods, underscoring their transformations from managed employees to self-managed workers. '[L]ooking back on our struggle … I can see where the change in me started … ', as a founding member of a Buenos Aires print shop put it in 2005, 'it begins during your struggles … . You realize it afterwards, when time has transpired … . You start to do things that you would never imagine yourself doing' (cited in Vieta 2014b).

While ERTs are part of a social movement, they are also fundamentally places of work. And workplaces, too, as a growing body of literature suggests, are spaces of deep, social, and informal learning (Boud and Garrick 1999, Engeström 2001, Illeris 2003, Livingstone and Sawchuk 2003, Bratton *et al.* 2004, Eraut and Hirsh 2010). Labour-managed firms such as worker cooperatives are endowed with particularly strong learning environments, since members must be cognizant of each other's needs and also the needs of the broader the communities they serve (Quarter and Midha 2001, Larrabure *et al.* 2011). By their very nature, then, cooperatives are learning organizations connected to the 'associative intelligence' of people working for a common goal (MacPherson 2002, Novkovic 2008, Vieta 2014b). Indeed, participatory worker organizations have long been understood as educational and potentially emancipatory for the working class by reformers and radical thinkers such as Owen (1991), Proudhon (1989), Bakunin (1990), Gramsci (2000), GDH Cole (1920), and others (Vieta 2014a, Ruggeri 2018). And while Marx remained cautious regarding the revolutionary potential of worker cooperatives, they too, for him, served what can be seen as an educational and prefigurative function for the working class (Marx 1978c, 1981, 1985, 1988). Gramsci (2000), in particular, homed in on the educative and future-oriented force of working-class organizations and associations, viewing them as forerunners to a broader workers' democracy since they contained the possibility to 'stimulate [working-class] thought and action' (p. 79). As Pateman (1970), Schugurensky (2000), Rothschild (2016), P. Marcuse (2015), Jossa (2005, 2014), and other critical theorists have contended, workplace democracy promotes participation beyond the workplace as people learn not only citizenship but also potentially revolutionary practice by 'doing' democracy.

Conversions of firms to co-ops, such as ERTs, are particularly strong moments of learning for workers. An 'expansive' kind of learning occurs in these situations, as contradictions and ruptures problematize workers' previous experiences and cognitive schemas, potentially opening them up to new understandings and practices (Engeström 2001). This type of learning can happen in critical moments, such as during threats of mass firings, the closure of one's place of employment, or during periods of crises in the broader political economy. In contexts with amenable enabling environments including traditions of working-class militancy and shop-floor democracy (as in Argentina) or a supportive cooperative movement (as in Italy), such moments can translate the moral economy of work into workers' radical acts, such as taking over the firms that employed them and creating new co-ops (Vieta 2012, forthcoming, Vieta *et al.* 2017). Delahaye (2005) highlights the emancipatory potential of expansive and informal learning in worker-driven conversions of firms, where skills and values must be acquired in order to overcome a 'traumatic and uncertain environment where the disorienting dilemma of bankruptcy … [challenges] … all former belief systems and values underpinning the older firm and its workers' (pp.45–48). Likewise, in an earlier study of worker-recuperated firms of the 1970s and 1980s, Paton (1989) pointed out how '[e]ach takeover is an intense learning process for the workforce as an organization as well as for individuals – there is a change of social roles, new attitudes are required' (p. 48).

Recuperating *autogestión*, prefiguring other economic realities

Through collective struggle, much transformative, expansive, or paradigm shifting learning unfolds when employees of troubled capitalist firms take on projects of *autogestión* by first occupying their former places of employment and then converting them to co-ops. In other words, Argentina's ERT workers collectively learn over the months and years how to best articulate the language of *autogestión* 'in struggle'. In short, much of the learning that takes place within ERTs is intensive, social, and informal, taking shape within concentrated moments of struggle that transform into processes of collaborative learning by doing *autogestión*. ERTs are, in fact, as sites of expansive and transformative learning, the most radical forms of organizational change and ultimately transformative organizations for workers, for workplaces, and for communities (Vieta 2014b).

While ERT workers must be pragmatic in how they engage with the state, markets, and other institutions of capital, and even though ERTs' radical political potential is still incomplete, they nevertheless continue to prefigure ways of re-organizing work beyond capital. These prefigurations are made visible and articulated in the three overarching dimensions of productive life that ERTs begin to recuperate from capital – the *self-valorization of living labour*, which reconfigures and rehumanizes labour relations; *cooperation in the labour process*, which democratically rearticulates enterprises; and the *socialization of surpluses and wealth*, which 'de-marketizes' economic transactions, privileging community over profits. Saturated with values of *compañerismo* forged in solidarity and in the thick of struggle, ERT protagonists collectively mobilize their self-management projects into new social relations of production and new, community-oriented enterprises that begin to contest neoliberal capitalist discourses and values.

In the process, ERT protagonists have begun to articulate and recuperate another economy via the language of *autogestión*. This is part of the 'language of the diverse economy', contingent on other forms of interactions and social relations that begin to push against 'an [economic] landscape we have always read as capitalist' by articulating and making evident in their actions and new discourses a reality of economic plurality and difference (Gibson-Graham 2006, p. 54). ERT protagonists express this other economic language of *autogestión* through the stories they recount to each other and to others; through the concepts they learn, deploy, and use; and, most importantly, in their very actions and practices that concretely express to themselves and others what their projects of *autogestión* are inherently about and in direct contrast with the previous capitalist firm they emerged from.

But, as with other labour-managed firms surrounded by capitalist logics, it cannot be forgotten that Argentina's ERTs exist in a dual reality, placing their projects of *autogestión* in tension with the continued existence of competitive markets, uneven state supports, and counterproductive regulations (Fajn and Rebón 2005, Vieta forthcoming). ERTs must, on the one hand, produce at least in part for the market and engage with local and national governments to address outstanding legal issues, secure workers' control of the company, or attempt to access state-sponsored programmes. This has been viewed by some commentators as risking the most radical potential of ERTs while seeing them legitimating the capitalist state by permitting official programmes to 'insitutionalize' them (Heller 2004, Atzeni and Ghigliani 2007, Dinerstein 2007). On the other hand, ERTs to date must engage in such activities pragmatically for survival while they also push back against such institutionalization and capitalist pressures in the numerous ways we have seen in this article. Moreover, in their very existence as converted, formerly capitalist firms, ERTs are counterfactual realities to the status quo, prefiguring other modes of organizing local economies and work organizations (Ruggeri 2014, Vieta forthcoming).

While Marx was also sensitive to the dual reality of worker co-ops, he nevertheless consistently articulated how they pointed to the possibility for another form of production without the need for supervisors or private owners. The utopian socialists before him, anarchist and socialist contemporaries, and other Marxists and anarchists since, have also emphasized the prefigurative and educative potential of co-ops and workplace democracy for organizing in association the economic life of the working class. Inspired by this tradition, I too have attempted to articulate the most radical – if still unfinished – promises of ERTs in this article. Articulating a language of *autogestión*, ERT protagonists start to recuperate the skills and capacities of their very living labour unleashed by collective creativity, a capacity for innovation that remains obscured from workers in capitalist labour processes. Restructured under cooperative values, equitable remuneration, and community service that problematize competitive tendencies, differentiated wages, and the pursuit of private profit, such alternative forms of production and wealth creation are possible because (being worker cooperatives) labour at ERTs employ capital and not vice versa, and workers (rather than administrators or bosses) decide what to work on, and when and how to do that work. These are not minor points; they fundamentally differentiate ERTs (as associated and cooperative workplaces) from capitalist work organizations and are exemplars of the diverse economies existing within, but that begin to step beyond, capitalocentric realities.

Notes

1. 'Capital', wrote Marx, 'is dead labour, that, vampire-like, only lives by sucking living labour, and lives the more, the more labour it sucks' (Marx 1967, p. 233).
2. In Argentina this class compromise has included union–state–employer social compacts dating back to Perón's first presidency in the mid-to-late 1940s and extending into the early-to-mid 1970s, and then again intermittently between the early 1980s to today. Various periods of socio-political turbulence throughout the country's political economic history have threatened or ruptured this class compromise, such as during the dictatorship of Ongania in the late 1960s, during the genocidal Proceso de Reorganización Nacional of the 1976–1983 dictatorships (the test-phase of Argentina's experiments in neoliberalism), in moments of Alfonsin's troubled presidency in the 1980s, during President Menem's sharp neoliberal austerity programme of the 1990s, and now, again, with the austerity policies of President Macri's Cambiemos coalition.
3. As Dinerstein (2007), Atzeni and Ghigliani (2007), and others have noted, tying the delivery of social assistance programmes to the 'normalization' and 'formalization' of social and solidarity economy initiatives risks depoliticizing and containing them. This has occurred, for instance, when decreeing waste recycler (*cartonero*) groups seeking access to the Plan Argentina Trabaja scheme to formally register on state lists and form into cooperatives (Vuotto 2014), or forcing ERTs to meet minute and often unreasonable work safety norms in order to receive subsidies (Ruggeri and Vieta 2015). This institutionalization has attempted to redirect these experiences from their most promising political work and has in some cases co-opted them by canalizing their protagonists' and workers' activities into more mundane and bureaucratized tasks.
4. Additionally, it should be noted that some ERTs also top up salaries for administrative duty or community engagement work, but the pay differentials here are negligible when compared to those of capitalist firms.
5. Elsewhere I have theorized that ERTs thus start to practice what Marcuse termed 'work as free play', or the merger of work and play (H. Marcuse, cited in Vieta 2014a, 2017).

Disclosure statement

No potential conflict of interest was reported by the author.

References

Almeyra, G., 2004. *La protesta social en la Argentina, 1990–2004: Fábricas recuperadas, piquetes, cacerolazos, asambleas populares*. Buenos Aires: Continente Pax.

Atzeni, M., 2010. *Workplace conflict: mobilization and solidarity in Argentina*. Houndmills, Basingstoke, UK: Palgrave Macmillan.

Atzeni, M. and Ghigliani, P., 2007. Labour process and decision-making in factories under workers' self-management: empirical evidence from Argentina. *Work, Employment and Society*, 21 (4), 653–671.

Atzeni, M. and Vieta, M., 2014. Between class and the market: self-management in theory and in the practice of worker-recuperated enterprises in Argentina. *In*: M. Parker, G. Cheney, V. Fournier, and C. Land, eds. *The Routledge companion to alternative organization*. London: Routledge, 47–63.

Audebrand, L., 2017. Expanding the scope of paradox scholarship on social enterprise: the case for (re)introducing worker cooperatives. *M@n@gement*, 20 (4), 368–393.

Bakunin, M., 1990 [1873]. *Statism and anarchy*. Cambridge: Cambridge University Press.

Bell, P. and Cleaver, H., 2002. Marx's theory of crisis as a theory of class struggle. *The Commoner* [online], 5 (Autumn). Available from: http://www.commoner.org.uk/cleaver05.pdf.

Bonefeld, W., 1994. Human practice and perversion: beyond autonomy and structure. *Common Sense*, 15, 43–52.

Boud, D. and Garrick, J., eds., 1999. *Understanding learning at work*. London: Routledge.

Bratton, J., *et al.*, 2004. *Workplace learning: a critical introduction*. Aurora, ON: Garamond Press.

Braverman, H., 1974. *Labor and monopoly capital: the degradation of work in the twentieth century*. New York: Monthly Review Press.

Burawoy, M., 1985. *The politics of production: factory regimes under capitalism and socialism*. London: Verso.

Cleaver, H., 1992. The inversion of class perspective in Marxian theory: from valorization to self-valorization. *In*: W. Bonefeld, R. Gunn, and K. Psychopedis, eds. *Open Marxism, volume II: theory and practice*. London: Pluto, 106–145.

Cole, G.D.H., 1920. *Guild socialism restated*. London: Leonard Parsons.

Colectivo Situaciones, 2002. Asambleas, cacerolas, y piquetes (sobre las nuevas formas de protagonismo social). *Boradores de investigación* [online], 3. Available from: http://www.nodo50.org/colectivosituaciones/borradores_03.html.

Colletti, L., 1972. *From Rousseau to Lenin: studies in ideology and society*. London: New Left Books.

Craig, J.G., 1993. *The nature of co-operation*. Montreal: Black Rose Books.

de Assis, C., 2018. Argentine newspapers recuperated by workers' cooperatives. *Socialist Project: The Bullet* [online], April 10. Available from: https://socialistproject.ca/2018/04/argentine-newspapers-recuperated-by-workers-cooperatives/.

de Peuter, G. and Dyer-Witheford, N., 2010. Commons and cooperatives. *Affinities*, 4 (1), 30–56.

de Sausa Santos, B., 2004. The WSF: toward a counter-hegemonic globalization. *In*: J. Sen, A. Anand, A. Escobar, and P. Waterman, eds. *World social forum: challenging empires*. New Delhi: The Viveka Foundation, 234–245.

Delahaye, B., 2005. *Human resource development: adult learning and knowledge management*. Milton, Australia: John Wiley and Sons.

Dewey, J., 1938. *Experience and education*. New York: Collier Books.

Dinerstein, A.C., 2007. Workers' factory takeovers and new state policies in Argentina: towards an 'institutionalisation' of non-governmental public action?. *Policy and Politics*, 35 (3), 529–550.

Dinerstein, A.C., 2015, *The politics of autonomy in Latin America: the art of organizing hope*. Houndmills, Basingstoke, UK: Palgrave Macmillan.

Dyer-Witheford, N., 1999. *Cyber-Marx: cycles and circuits of struggle in high-technology capitalism*. Chicago: University of Illinois Press.

Ellerman, D., 1990. *The democratic worker-owned firm: a new model for the east and the west*. Boston: Unwin Hyman.

Engeström, Y., 2001. Expansive learning at work: toward an activity theoretical reconceptualization. *Journal of Education and Work*, 14 (1), 133–156.

Eraut, M. and Hirsh, W., 2010. *The significance of workplace learning for individuals, groups and organisations*. Oxford, UK: Oxford University Press.

Fajn, G., 2003. *Fábricas y empresas recuperadas: Protesta social, auotgestión, y rupturas en la subjectividad*. Buenos Aires: Centro Cultural de la Cooperación/ Instituto Movilizador de Fondos Cooperativos.

Fajn, G. and Rebón, J., 2005. El taller ¿sin cronometro? Apuntes acerca de las empresas recuperadas. *Herramienta* [online], 28. Available at: http://www.herramienta.com.ar/revista-herramienta-n-28/el-taller-sin-cronometro-apuntes-acerca-de-las-empresas-recuperadas.

Farmer, P., 1979. Enjoying language: an adventure with words. *The English Journal*, 68 (5), 58–61.

Foley, G., 1999. *Learning in social action: a contribution to understanding informal education*. London: Zed Books.

Forcinito, K. and Basualdo, V., eds., 2007. *Transformaciones recientes en la economía argentina: Tendencias y perspectivas*. Buenos Aires and Los Polvorines: Prometeo Libros and Universidad Nacional de General Sarmiento.

Friedman, A., 1977. *Industry and labour: class struggle at work and monopoly capitalism*. London: Macmillan.

Gibson-Graham, J.K., 2006. *A postcapitalist politics*. Minneapolis: University of Minnesota Press.
Gindin, S., 2016. Chasing utopia: worker ownership and cooperatives will not succeed by competing on capitalism's terms. *Jacobin* [online], March 10. Available from: https://www.jacobinmag.com/2016/03/workers-control-coops-wright-wolff-alperovitz/.
Gramsci, A., 2000 [1919]. Workers' democracy. *In*: D. Forgacs, ed., *The Antonio Gramsci reader: selected writings, 1916–1935*. New York: New York University Press, 79–82.
Hall, B. and Clover, D., 2005. Social movement learning. *In*: L.M. English, ed., *International encyclopaedia of adult education*. Houndmills, Basingstoke, UK: Palgrave Macmillan, 584–589.
Heller, P., 2004. *Fábricas recuperadas: Argentina 2000–2004*. Buenos Aires: Ediciones Rumbos.
Holloway, J., 2002. *Change the world without taking power: the meaning of revolution today*. London: Pluto.
Illeris, K., 2003. Workplace learning and learning theory. *Journal of Workplace Learning*, 15 (4), 167–178.
Jensen, A., 2012. *Insolvency, employee rights, and employee buy-outs: a strategy for restructuring. Unpublished doctoral dissertation*. University of Sydney, Sydney, Australia.
Jossa, B., 2005. Marx, Marxism and the cooperative movement. *Cambridge Journal of Economics*, 29 (1), 3–18.
Jossa, B., 2014. *Producer cooperatives as a new mode of production*. London: Routledge.
Kulfas, M., 2016. *Los tres kirchnerismos: una historia de la economía argentina, 2003–2015*. Buenos Aires: Siglo Veintiuno Editores.
Larrabure, M., Vieta, M., and Schugurensky, D., 2011. The 'new cooperativism' in Latin America: worker-recuperated enterprises and socialist production units. *Studies in the Education of Adults*, 43 (2), 181–196.
Lazzarato, M. 2003. Struggle, event, media. *RepubicArt* [online]. Available from: http://republicart.net/disc/representations/lazzarato01_en.htms.
Livingstone, D. and Sawchuk, P., 2003. *Hidden knowledge: organized labour in the information age*. Toronto: University of Toronto Press.
Luxemburg, R., 2006 [1900]. *Reform or revolution and other writings*. Mineola, NY: Dover Publications.
MacPherson, I., 2002. Encouraging associative intelligence: co-operatives, shared learning and responsible citizenship. *Journal of Co-Operative Studies*, 35 (2), 86–98.
Magnani, E., 2009. *The silent change: recovered businesses in Argentina*. Buenos Aires: Teseo.
Marcuse, H., 1969. *An essay on liberation*. Boston: Beacon.
Marcuse, P., 2015. Cooperatives on the path to socialism? *Monthly Review*, 66 (9), 31–38.
Marx, K., 1967 [1867]. *Capital: a critique of political economy, volume I: a critical analysis of capitalist production*. New York: International Publishers.
Marx, K., 1973 [1857-1861]. *Grundrisse: foundations of the critique of political economy (rough draft)*. London: Penguin.
Marx, K., 1978a [1864]. Inaugural address of the Working Men's International Association. *In*: R.C. Tucker, ed. *The Marx-Engels reader*. New York: W.W. Norton, 512–519.
Marx, K., 1978b [1875]. The critique of the gotha program. *In*: R.C. Tucker, ed. *The Marx-Engels reader*. New York: W.W. Norton, 525–541.
Marx, K., 1978c [1871]. The civil war in France. *In*: R.C. Tucker, ed. *The Marx-Engels reader*. New York: W.W. Norton, 618–652.
Marx, K., 1981 [1894]. *Capital: a critique of political economy, volume III*. London: Penguin.
Marx, K., 1985 [1866–67]. Instructions for the delegates of the provisional general council. The different questions, 5. Co-operative labour. *In*: *Marx and Engels collected works, volume 20 (Marx and Engels: 1864–68)*. London: Lawrence and Wishart, 190.
Marx, K., 1988 [1863]. A) cooperation. *In*: *Marx and Engels collected works, volume 30 (Karl Marx: 1861–63 [Marx's economic manuscripts of 1861–1863])*. London: Lawrence and Wishart, 255–264.
Marx, K., 2007 [1844]. *Economic and philosophic manuscripts of 1844*. Mineola, NY: Dover Publications.
McNally, D., 1993. *Against the market: political economy, market socialism and the Marxist critique*. London: Verso.
McNally, D., 2004. The dual form of labour in capitalist society and the struggle over meaning: comments on Postone. *Historical Materialism*, 12 (3), 189–208.
Munck, R., Falcón, R. and Galitelli, B., 1987. *Argentina: from anarchism to peronism: workers, unions, and politics, 1855–1985*. London: Zed Books.
Novkovic, S., 2008. Defining the co-operative difference. *The Journal of Socio-Economics*, 37 (6), 2168–2177.
Oakeshott, R., 1990. *The case for workers' co-ops*. Houndmills, Basingstoke, UK: Palgrave Macmillan.
Overwien, B., 2000. Informal learning and the role of social movements. *International Review of Education/Internationale Zeitschrift für Erziehungswissenschaft/Revue Internationale de L'éducation*, 46 (6), 621–640.
Owen, R., 1991 [1820]. Report to the County of Lanark. *In*: G. Claeys, ed. *A new view of society and other writing*. New York: Penguin, 250–308.
Oxford, 2018. Recuperate. *Oxford Living Dictionary* [online]. Available from: https://en.oxforddictionaries.com/definition/recuperate.
Ozarow, D. and Croucher, R., 2014. Workers' self-management, recovered companies and the sociology of work. *Sociology*, 48 (5), 989–1006.

Palomino, H., 2003. The workers' movement in occupied enterprises: a survey. *Canadian Journal of Latin American and Caribbean Studies*, 28 (55), 71–96.
Pateman, C., 1970. *Participation and democratic theory*. Cambridge, UK: Cambridge University Press.
Paton, R., 1989. *Reluctant entrepreneurs: the extent, achievements, and significance of worker takeovers in Europe*. Milton Keynes, UK: Open University Press.
Patroni, V., 2004. Disciplining labour, producing poverty: neo-liberal structural reforms and political conflict in Argentina. *Research in Political Economy*, 21, 91–119.
Peixoto de Albuquerque, P., 2004. Autogestión. *In*: A.D. Cattani, ed., *La otra economía*. Buenos Aires: Editorial Altamira, 39–46.
Pérotin, V., 2014. Worker cooperatives: good, sustainable jobs in the community. *Journal of Entrepreneurial and Organizational Diversity*, 2 (2), 34–47.
Petras, J. and Veltmeyer, H., eds., 2004. *Las privatizaciones y la desnacionalización de América Latina*. Buenos Aires: Promoteo Libros.
Postone, M., 1996. *Time, labor, and social domination: a reinterpretation of Marx's critical theory*. Cambridge, UK: Cambridge University Press.
Pozzi, P. and Nigra, F., 2015. Argentina a decade after the collapse: the causes of the crisis and structural changes. *Latin American Perspectives*, 42 (1), 3–10.
Proudhon, P.-J., 1989 [1851]. *General idea of the revolution in the nineteenth century*. London: Pluto.
Quarter, J. and Midha, H., 2001. Informal learning processes in a worker co-operative. The Research Network on New Approaches to Lifelong Learning (NALL), Working Paper, No. 31-2001. Available from: https://files.eric.ed.gov/fulltext/ED462537.pdf.
Ranis, P., 2016. *Cooperatives confront capitalism: challenging the neoliberal economy*. London: Zed Books.
Ratner, C., 2015. Neoliberal co-optation of leading co-op organizations, and a socialist counterpolitics of co-operation. *Monthly Review*, 66 (9), 18–30.
Real Academia, 2018. Recuperar. *In: Real Academia Española* [online]. Available from: http://dle.rae.es/?id=VXJKMGZ.
Rebón, J., 2007. *La empresa de la autonomía: trabajadores recuperando la producción*. Buenos Aires: Colectivo Ediciones-Picaso.
Restakis, J., 2010. *Humanizing the economy: co-operatives in the age of capital*. Gabriola Island, BC: New Society Publishers.
Rigi, J., 2015. The demise of the Marxian law of value? A critique of Michael Hardt and Antonio Negri. *In*: E. Fisher and C. Fuchs, eds. *Reconsidering value and labour in the digital age*. Houndmills, Basingstoke, UK: Palgrave-Macmillan, 188–204.
Rothschild, J., 2016. The logic of a co-operative economy and democracy 2.0: recovering the possibilities for autonomy, creativity, solidarity, and common purpose. *The Sociological Quarterly*, 57, 7–35.
Ruggeri, A., 2014. *¿Qué son las empresas recuperadas? autogestión de la clase obrera*. Buenos Aires: Peña Lillo/Ediciones Continente.
Ruggeri, A., 2016. *Las empresas recuperadaos por los trabajadores en los comienzos del gobierno de Mauricio Macri: Estado de situación a mayo de 2016*. Buenos Aires: Programa Facultad Abierta, Facultad de Filosofía y Letras, Universidad de Buenos Aires.
Ruggeri, A., 2018. *Autogestión y revolución: las luchas obreras autogestionarias: De las primeras cooperativas a Petrogrado y Barcelona*. Buenos Aires: Peña Lillo/Ediciones Continente.
Ruggeri, A. and Vieta, M., 2015. Argentina's worker-recuperated enterprises, 2010–2013: a synthesis of recent empirical findings. *The Journal of Entrepreneurial and Organizational Diversity*, 4 (1), 75–103.
Ruggeri, A., Martínez, C., and Trinchero, H., 2005. *Las empresas recuperadas en la Argentina*. Buenos Aires: Programa Facultad Abierta, Facultad de Filosofía y Letras, Universidad de Buenos Aires.
Ruggeri, A., *et al.*, 2010. *Informe del tercer relevamiento de empresas recuperadas por sus trabajadores: las empresas recuperadas en la Argentina, 2010*. Buenos Aires: Programa Facultad Abierta, Facultad de Filosofía y Letras, Universidad de Buenos Aires.
Sandoval, M., 2016. What would Rosa do? Co-operatives and radical politics. *Soundings*, 63 (Summer), 98–111.
Sardá de Faria, M. and Novaes, H.T., 2011. Brazilian recovered factories: the constraints of workers' control. *In*: I. Ness and D. Azzellini, eds., *Ours to master and to own: workers' control from the commune to the present*. Chicago: Haymarket Books, 400–417.
Schugurensky, D., 2000. *The forms of informal learning: towards a conceptualization of the field*. NALL Working Paper No. 19, New Approaches to Lifelong Learning (NALL), Centre for the Studies of Education and Work, Ontario Institute for Studies in Education of the University of Toronto.
Sennett, R., 2008. *The craftsman*. New Haven, CT: Yale University Press.
Shaffer, J., 1999. *Historical dictionary of the cooperative movement*. Lanham, MD: Scarecrow.
Sitrin, M., 2012. *Everyday revolutions: horizontalism and autonomy in Argentina*. London: Zed Books.
Sitrin, M. and Azzellini, D., 2012. *Occupying language: the secret rendezvous with history and the present*. New York: Zuccotti Park Press.

Svampa, M. and Pereyra, S., 2004. *Entre la ruta y el barrio: la experiencia de las organizaciones piqueteras*. Buenos Aires: Editorial Biblos.
Thoburn, N., 2003. *Deleuze, Marx and politics*. London: Routledge.
Thompson, E.P., 1963. *The making of the English working class*. New York: Vintage.
Toms, S., 2008. 'Immeasurability': a critique of Hardt and Negri. *Ephemera*, 8 (4), 433–446.
Vieta, M., 2010. The social innovations of *autogestión* in Argentina's worker-recuperated enterprises: cooperatively organizing productive life in hard times. *Labor Studies Journal*, 35 (3), 295–321.
Vieta, M., 2012. From managed employees to self-managed workers: the transformations of labour at Argentina's worker-recuperated enterprises. *In*: M. Atzeni, ed. *Alternative work organizations*. Houndmills, Basingstoke, UK: Palgrave Macmillan, 129–156.
Vieta, M., 2013. Recuperating a workplace, creating a community space: the story of Cooperativa Chilavert Artes Gráficas. *Scapegoat: Architecture, Landscape, Political Economy*, 4, 161–178.
Vieta, M., 2014a. The stream of self-determination and *autogestión*: prefiguring alternative economic realities. *Ephemera*, 14 (4), 781–809.
Vieta, M., 2014b. Learning in struggle: Argentina's new worker cooperatives as transformative learning organizations. *Relations Industrielles/Industrial Relations*, 69 (1), 186–218.
Vieta, M., 2016. *Autogestión*: prefiguring a 'new cooperativism' and 'the labour commons'. *In*: C. DuRand, ed. *Moving beyond capitalism*. London: Routledge, 55–63.
Vieta, M., 2017. Inklings of the great refusal: echoes of Marcuse's post-technological tationality today. *In*: A. Lamas, T. Wolfson and P.N. Funke, eds. *The great refusal: Herbert Marcuse and contemporary social movements*. Philadelphia: Temple University Press, 258–282.
Vieta, M., 2018. New co-operativism in Latin America: implications for Cuba. *In*: S. Novkovic and H. Veltmeyer, eds. *Cooperativism and local development in Cuba: An agenda for democratic social change*. Leiden: Brill, 51–81.
Vieta, M. forthcoming. *Workers' self-management in Argentina: contesting neo-liberalism by occupying companies, creating cooperatives, and recuperating autogestión*. Leiden and Chicago: Brill and Haymarket Books.
Vieta, M. and Ruggeri, A., 2009. Worker-recovered enterprises as workers' co-operatives: the conjunctures, challenges, and innovations of self-management in Argentina and Latin America. *In*: D. Reed and J.J. McMurtry, eds. *Co-operatives in a global economy: the challenges of co-operation across borders*. Newcastle Upon-Tyne: Cambridge Scholars Publishing, 178–225.
Vieta, M., *et al.*, 2016. Participation in worker co-operatives. *In*: D. Horton Smith, R.A. Stebbins, and J. Grotz, eds. *Palgrave handbook of volunteering, civic participation, and nonprofit associations*. Houndmills, Basingstoke, UK: Palgrave Macmillan, 436–453.
Vieta, M., Depedri, S., and Carrano, A., 2017. *The Italian road to recuperating enterprises and the Legge Marcora framework: Italy's worker buyouts in times of crisis*. Research Report No. 015-17. Trento, Italy: European Research Institute on Cooperative and Social Enterprises (EURICSE).
Vuotto, M., 2014. La economía social y las cooperativas en la Argentina. *Voces en el Fenix*, 38 (October), 46–53.
Wolff, J., 2002. *Why read Marx today?* Oxford, UK: Oxford University Press.
Wyczykier, G., 2009. *De la dependencia a la autogestión laboral: Sobre la reconstrucción de expériencias colectivas de trabajo en la Argentina contemporánea*. Buenos Aires: Universidad Nacional de General Sarmiento and Promoteo Libros.
Wylde, C., 2012. ¿Continuidad o cambio? Política económica argentina posterior a la crisis y el gobierno de Néstor Kirchner, 2003-2007. *Íconos*, 43 (mayo), 109–133.
Zevi, A., *et al.*, 2011. *Beyond the crisis: cooperatives, work, and finance: generating wealth for the long term*. Brussels: CECOP Publications.
Zibechi, R., 2012. *Territories in resistance: a cartography of Latin American social movements*. Oakland, CA: AK Press.

Making sense of precarity: talking about economic insecurity with millennials in Canada

Nancy Worth

ABSTRACT

While there are many effective metrics for quantifying economic precarity, talking to young people about their experiences in the labour and housing markets reveals a gap in explanatory language around living in/through crisis. In particular, in my research with Canadian millennials (born from the early 1980s through the mid-90s), although they could state the facts about how hard it is to get a good job or afford decent housing, what this pervasive sense of insecurity feels like is much harder to put into words. For many, a generalized sense of precariousness invades everyday life, even when work and housing are relatively secure. Thinking through this sense of anxiety, that the future might not be any better than the present and that young people might not be as well off as their parents, leads to a generational understanding of economic crisis – and for a group of young adults who came of age during the downturn of 2008–2009, examining how they talk (or cannot talk) about precarity is revealing.

While there are many effective metrics for quantifying economic precarity, talking to young people about their experiences in the labour and housing markets reveals a gap in explanatory language around living in/through crisis. In particular, in my research with Canadian millennials (born from the early 1980s through the mid-90s), although they could *state the facts* about how hard it is to get a good job or afford decent housing, the experience of this pervasive *sense of insecurity* is much harder to put into words. For many, a generalized sense of precariousness invades everyday life, even when work and housing are relatively secure. Thinking through this sense of anxiety, that the future might not be any better than the present and that young people might not be as well off as their parents, leads to a generational understanding of economic crisis – and for a group of young adults who came of age during the downturn of 2008–2009, considering why they can't talk about precarity is revealing. These observations emerge from research projects with young adults, examining precarious work and co-residence with parents (Worth 2016, Worth 2017). Because of the length and format of this commentary, there is not space to include interviewee's testimony–moreover, the substance of my comments is on what cannot be talked about. I focus here on three interconnected reflections about why it might be difficult for millennials to talk about economic insecurity: (1) precarity as an unremarkable norm, (2) the millennial 'me,' and (3) the concept of hedging, a way to deal with future uncertainty in the present. I sum up by considering how precarity can be understood as a *relation* to understand work and life. My aim is to highlight the challenge of working with an experience/concept like precarity, but also why it is vital to examine this slippery idea.

Precarity as an unremarkable norm

My work with young people began with 16–25 year olds, focusing on the process of school–work transitions. My research with this group, who had yet to enter the labour market, centred on their expectations for the future. One of my findings was that hopeful expectations of a comfortable, stable work life in the future helped young people manage current challenges (Worth 2009). In subsequent work with millennial women and their experience of work (Worth 2016) and millennials who live with their parents (Worth 2017), I was interested to find out what happened when the hoped for future of secure, meaningful well-paid work did not materialize for all. In particular, for millennials in Canada who were born between 1980 and 1995, many in the leading edge of the cohort graduated into the economic crisis of 2008–2009 meaning that permanent full-time jobs with good benefits were increasingly difficult to find.

Yet, asking millennials about their experience of work was somewhat challenging, as precarity – in the sense of a labour condition – was an unremarkable norm. Short-term, contract labour was the only kind of work that many respondents had experienced. In my research, I use the approach of 'critical moments' to organize the interview encounter (Thomson *et al.* 2002). Critical moments are highly consequential, setting young people on to one pathway or another. The importance of these moments is often recognized in hindsight, as participants remark on change and make comparisons with how things used to be and how things are now. In my research with young adults and their experience of work, I needed a different approach. In my interviews with dozens of young adults, work was just work; while they very easily told me about different jobs they had had, there were rarely any epiphanies about the consequences of these experiences, as the precarious aspects of these jobs were often expected and therefore commonplace. Moreover, as young people see the same issues (unemployment, underemployment, contract work) in the lives of their friends, precarity is normalized and typical. I wanted to understand how young adults experienced precarity in its myriad forms, so my interviews eschewed difficult 'why' questions, in favour of 'what' and 'how.' According to Silverman (2013, p. 85), qualitative research can 'locate the interactional sequences ("how") in which participants' meanings ("what") are deployed. Having established the character of some phenomenon, it can then (but only then) move on to answer "why" questions by examining how that phenomenon is organisationally embedded.' In effect, meaning can be drawn from the mundane and everyday through the interview (or conversational) dynamic. Working life stories – including the foundational *Working* by Terkel (1972), allow for insight into the 'why' of working conditions, including precarious ones, even though this is often hard to name explicitly (Foster 2013, Ba' 2014). It is important to note that my interest is not about the use of the term 'precarity' specifically; naming work as 'insecure' or 'uncertain' or any other stand-in for 'precarious' was also difficult.

Finally, Millar's (2017) work offers an important critique of the political potential of precarity that has relevance to my project with this commentary. She uses Thorkelson's (2016) research with contingent faculty in France to argue that precarité is often used in solidarity with workers, not by workers themselves. While I do not expect my respondents to be situated in this European history about the politics of precarity, the unwillingness of contingent faculty in France to use the term about themselves aligns with my findings; according to Millar (2017, p. 5), 'One reason precarity failed to resonate with the very workers it was meant to describe was that it signified an overexploited, degraded existence that few people were comfortable identifying as their own.' Moreover, many found nothing new or exceptional in this discourse as – work had always felt precarious.

The flexible, millennial 'me'

This section details how some millennials do talk about work, often in individualistic terms and through the lens of flexibility. First, when I have discussed my research with young adults at conferences and colloquia, I have been asked why millennials have not taken to the streets to protest insecure work. Yet, as the project of neoliberalism consistently tells (young) people, their success or failure is on them. Many young people have invested in a very personal conception of choice within the life course, connected to education, work, and family life. According to Gershon (2017), this extends to managing one's personal brand and marketing yourself to employers. Very few talk about the often formidable structural inequalities they face because they go unrecognized in a society that valorizes personal achievement.

Second, the language of 'insecure' versus 'flexible work' is important. For Neilson and Rossiter (2005),

> it is the doubleness of precarity that is the substrate of post-Fordist capital – a desire for greater flexibility and perceived freedom to choose one's style of work (the expressive capacity of labour-power) coupled with an increased uncertainty, not to mention frequent struggle, that is normative to the experience of life (ontological insecurity).

Discourses of flexibility can put a positive spin on precarity. Returning to the dynamics of interviews, the urge to tell a happy story, where people 'subjectively enhance the value of impending outcomes that are contrary to their own consciously held interests' – what psychologists call 'sweet lemons' can be strong (Kay *et al.* 2002). For example, rather than feeling bad that you have not been able to get a secure full-time job with benefits, the narrative shifts to idealizing short-term contracts that allow freedom and change – being successful within the world of work as it is. Few of the young adults I have worked with used flexibility solely in a positive light; those who did often had privilege of one kind or another that meant their work was inherently less risky (e.g. a partner who was willing to financially stabilize their endeavours). Yet, some young adults put a value on self-precarization as an aspect of authentic creative labour. Lorey (2006, pp. 187–88) writes about:

> the ways in which ideas of autonomy and freedom are constitutively connected with hegemonic modes of subjectivation in Western, capitalist societies. The focus of this text is accordingly on the extent to which 'self-chosen' precarization contributes to producing the conditions for being able to become an active part of neo-liberal political and economic relations.

Another part of this story that valourizes flexibility is connected to entrepreneurship and self-employment, as well as what has been termed the millennial side hustle (Thieme 2017). While entrepreneurship is a growing part of the economy in Canada, for young adults (and others) it can also be a way to disguise un/underemployment. While some of my respondents made their salary from freelancing, others simply had aspirations to support themselves through self-employment, and others wanted to avoid a perceived gap in a resume by being a 'LinkedIn CEO.' In Canada, self-employment grew in the recent economic downturn (LaRochelle-Côté 2010), and its use as a coping strategy or buffer– or even as a performance of labour market success– is a practice I would like to examine further.

Finally, across all my work with young people, participants asked me if they were typical, on some level wanting to place their experience in a wider narrative or experience. Similar to Hall's (2017) experiences, my own research encounter often involved participants asking questions to me and about me, often with pleased but resigned surprise that other people involved in the research also had a hard time getting a job or difficulty balancing a changing work schedule with caring responsibilities. So while respondents tend to put a positive spin on their working lives and personalize their 'failures,' they are relieved to hear that others are in the same boat. I see this as an opening, a small way forward, and I have returned results of research to participants so that they can see how they fit in with their cohort (Worth & Tomaszczyk 2017, Worth 2008). This section has considered individualized flexibility as one of the explanatory frameworks that young adults are comfortable using to explain their working lives, where precarity remains present but below the surface. In the following section, precarity is again revealed by its absence, young people spoke about the present and resisted talking about an uncertain future.

Hedging, uncertainty, and the collapse of long-term thinking

The previous sections discuss why young adults cannot talk about precarity, and often use the more positive language of flexibility instead. This section adds a temporal element: thinking through why many young adults find it difficult to talk about the future. According to Bauman (2007: 3):

> the collapse of long-term thinking, planning and acting, and the disappearance or weakening of social structures in which thinking, planning and acting could be inscribed for a long time to come, leads to a splicing of [...] individual lives into a series of short term projects and episodes which are in principle infinite, and do not combine into the kinds of sequences to which concepts like 'development', 'maturation', 'career' or 'progress; (all suggesting a preordained order of succession) could be meaningfully applied. A life so fragmented stimulates 'lateral rather than 'vertical' orientations.

When you no longer think in long-term plans (or even hopes), precarity becomes hidden by just-in-time decision-making and an increasingly popular language about flexibility and responsiveness to change. For the young people I spoke with in Toronto, planning for the future was not something many spent time on; it was a waste of time because they could not anticipate what would happen next. Instead, concerns centred on making sense of the present, including current work and housing challenges, looking after the 'now.' For those who contemplated the future, many spoke about a distant ideal, rather than a planned achievement – where people would, for example, someday, hopefully, have a full-time job with benefits, but young people often could not talk about how to get there from here. Berlant (2011, p. 54) writes about this as the 'historical present,' with the aim of 'explaining crisis-shaped subjectivity amid the ongoingness of adjudication, adaptation, and improvisation.' Elsewhere she describes the historical present as 'an impasse, a thick moment of ongoingness' where the fantasy of the good life is maintained and held onto (Berlant 2011, p. 200). In my work, this has emerged through some young adults' explicit acceptance of what one termed 'temporary exploitation' at work, while holding onto a somewhat elusive hope that it would change in the future.

Where the future does partially emerge (and young people talk about coping with precarity) is through the practice of hedging; Newhouse (2017, p. 512) has 'shown hedging to be the laborious and generative efforts at mediating the future [...] Hedging is also the work of attuning oneself to such radical uncertainty and being ready to jump at the arrival of the unforeseen.' In my work, millennials moving back home to live with parents functions as a hedge against future uncertainty. Not only did young adults move home (or remain at home) to manage current challenges, many explicitly used co-residence with parents to put themselves into a more stable position for the future. For example, some young people move home to save on rent, building up a down payment to get on the property ladder. Others live at home so they can afford to go to school, building up skills/experience to be more competitive in the labour market. Ettlinger (2007, p. 325) argues that

> The everydayness of precarity holds clues as to how people routinely, if implicitly, develop strategies that permit feelings of certainty amid uncertainty. People grope for the surety to navigate social, political, economic, and cultural life through everyday discursive and material practice.

It has been important for my work to understand that not everyone has the ability to hedge uncertainty in the same ways and that precarity is connected to how actors are differently situated (Zeiderman *et al.* 2015). Just as flexible work can be thought of as a form of privileged precarious work, hedges such as moving home to live with parents are not available to all.

Situating precarity/precariousness/precaritization/precariat

Precarity has been framed in diverse ways across the social sciences and humanities – and this flexibility in terminology reflects how much work this concept does. At its most straightforward, objective measures of precarity are interested in how employment has shifted away from full-time, permanent jobs with benefits to work that is increasingly part-time (see Bourdieu 1998) or contract while subjective definitions of precarity concern 'life worlds that are inflected with uncertainty and instability' (Waite 2009, p. 416). Yet, in Puar's et al. (2012) virtual roundtable with Lauren Berlant, Judith Butler, and others, the concept of precarity gets more layered. For Butler, meanings of precariousness include:

> (1) precariousness, a function of our social vulnerability and exposure that is always given some political form, and precarity as differentially distributed, and so one important dimension of the unequal distribution of conditions required for continued life; but also (2) precaritization as an ongoing process, so that we do not reduce the power of precarious to single acts or single events. Precaritization allows us to think about the slow death that happens to targeted or neglected populations over time and space. (Puar *et al.* 2012, 169)

Moreover, Lorey's work on 'self-precarization' focuses on the workplace, where 'everybody has to become "creative" and to design her/himself to sell her/his whole personality on the market of affective labor' (Puar *et al.* 2012, p. 164). In addition to these framings of precarity as a form of labour and a feeling of insecurity, Standing's (2011) *The Precariat: The New Dangerous Class* gives a class identity to the precarity discussion, where identity is no longer based on work. What emerges is that we can use precarity (in all its conceptual forms) as a *relation* to understand work and life. According to Millar (2017), 'precarity is both a socio-economic condition and an ontological experience (Neilson and Rossiter 2008). Or better yet, it aims to capture the relationship between precarious labor and precarious life.' This relational framing is quite useful conceptually; yet, this analytical depth is a signal of how difficult precarity can be to pin down in practice, as an experience/condition/feeling for people to narrate. Trying to understand the everydayness of precarity within a research encounter can be challenging.

To sum up, this commentary has considered how young adults make sense of precarity. My interest is not about whether people actually use the term 'precarity,' but instead I have been thinking through some reasons why the experience of precarity, both objective and subjective, – might be difficult to talk about. For many, precarious work is an unremarkable norm, an experience that feels common and everyday, and consequently not worth mentioning. For others, not identifying as a precarious worker is about eschewing a negative label. On top of this, there is a tendency to individualize experience; perhaps reinforced by the one-to-one research interview, where work is a personal success (or failure), and it is challenging to see oneself in the context of wider structural changes (such as the decreasing number of positions in the 'standard employment relationship' of full-time, permanent positions). Some young adults describe work that is objectively precarious through the positive framing of flexibility, and it is interesting to consider how self employment fits into young people's imaginings of 'successful' work. Finally, just as flexi bility is a way of talking about precarity, examining how young people hedge (act in the present to attempt to mitigate future uncertainty) is another way of indirectly getting at the experience of insecurity.

For my research, I have found that a generational analysis can be useful to reveal the unremarkable, as this kind of analysis examines how a cohort of people (in all their diversity) experience economic, political, and social events at a particular age. Generational thinking is explicitly a way of scaling up from individual experience and creates a context that can be revealing of difference (see also Vanderbeck 2017). In my work with millennial women, many spoke about what their mother did at the same age, as a way of reflecting on her own life. When considering how young adults (cannot) talk about the diverse concept of precarity, from a labour market condition to an affective condition or sense of ontological insecurity, how respondents speak, the words they choose, and what is not said can be just as revealing as how millennials present themselves.

Acknowledgements

Many thanks to Sonya Scott, who organized the colloquium where an earlier version of this essay was presented.

Disclosure statement

No potential conflict of interest was reported by the author.

Funding

This work was supported by the Social Sciences and Humanities Research Council of Canada under Grant 430-2015-00637.

ORCID

Nancy Worth http://orcid.org/0000-0002-2379-526X

References

Ba', S, 2014. 'A great job and a family': work narratives and the work and family interaction. *Community, Work & Family*, 17 (1), 43–59.

Bauman, Z., 2007. *Liquid Times: Living in an Age of Uncertainty*. Cambridge: Polity Press.

Berlant, L., 2011. *Cruel optimism*. Durham, NC: Duke University Press.

Bourdieu, P., 1998. *Acts of resistance: against the tyranny of the market*. New York: The New Press.

Ettlinger, N., 2007. Precarity unbound. *Alternatives: Global, Local, Political*, 32 (3), 319–340.

Foster, K., 2013. Generation and discourse in working life stories. *British Journal of Sociology*, 64 (2), 195–215.

Gershon, I., 2017. *Down and out in the new economy: how people find (or don't find) work today*. Chicago, IL: University of Chicago Press.

Hall, S.M., 2017. Personal, relational and intimate geographies of austerity: ethical and empirical considerations. *Area*, 49 (3), 303–310.

Kay, A.C., Jimenez, M.C., and Jost, J.T., 2002. Sour grapes, sweet lemons, and the anticipatory rationalization of the status Quo. *Personality and Social Psychology Bulletin*, 28 (9), 1300–1312.

LaRochelle-Côté, S., 2010. *Self-employment in the downturn*. Ottawa: StatsCan.

Lorey, I., 2006. 'Governmentality and self-precarization: on the normalization of cultural producers'. In Gerald Raunig and Gene Ray (Eds.), *Art and Contemporary Critical Practice Reinventing Institutional Critique*. London: May Fly Books. pp. 187–202.

Millar, K. M, 2017. Toward a critical politics of precarity. *Sociology Compass*, 11 (6), e12483–e12n/a.

Neilson, B. and Rossiter, N., 2005. From precarity to precariousness and back again: labour, life and unstable networks. *The Fibreculture Journal*, 5. Available from: http://five.fibreculturejournal.org/fcj-022-from-precarity-to-precariousness-and-back-again-labour-life-and-unstable-networks/.

Neilson, B. and Rossiter, N., 2008. Precarity as a political concept, or, Fordism as exception. *Theory, Culture & Society*, 25 (7–8), 51–72.

Newhouse, L.S., 2017. Uncertain futures and everyday hedging in a humanitarian city. *Transactions of the Institute of British Geographers*, 42 (4), 503–515.

Puar, J., et al., 2012. Precarity talk: a virtual roundtable with Lauren Berlant, Judith Butler, Bojana Cvejić, Isabell Lorey, Jasbir Puar, and Ana Vujanović. *TDR: The Drama Review*, 56 (4), 163–177.

Silverman, D., 2013. *A very short, fairly interesting and reasonably cheap book about qualitative research*. London: Sage.

Standing, G., 2011. *The precariat: the new dangerous class*. London: Bloomsbury Academic.

Terkel, S., 1972. *Working: people talk about what they do all day and how they feel about what they do*. New York: Pantheon.

Thieme, T.A., 2017. The hustle economy. *Progress in Human Geography*. Available from: https://doi.org/10.1177/0309132517690039.

Thomson, R., et al., 2002. Critical moments: choice, change and opportunity in young people's narratives of transition. *Sociology*, 36 (2), 335–354.
Thorkelson, E, 2016. Precarity outside: the political unconscious of French academic labor. *American Ethnologist*, 43 (3), 475–487.
Vanderbeck, R.M., 2017. Intergenerational Geographies in Theory and Practice. In T Skelton and S. Aitken (Eds.), *Establishing Geographies of Children and Young People*, Vol. 1. Singapore: Springer.
Waite, L, 2009. A place and space for a critical geography of precarity? *Geography Compass*, 3 (1), 412–433.
Worth, N., 2008. *Innovative adulthoods: what VI young people say about becoming an adult*. Leeds, UK.
Worth, N., 2009. Understanding youth transition as 'Becoming': identity, time and futurity. *Geoforum*, 40 (6), 1050–1060.
Worth, N., 2016. Feeling precarious: millennial women and work. *Environment and Planning D*, 34 (4), 601–616.
Worth, N., and Tomaszczyk, A., 2017. *GenY at home: understanding why young adults live with parents in Toronto, Canada*. Canada: Waterloo. Available at: www.genyathome.ca
Worth, N., 2017. 'The privilege of a parental safety net: millennials and the intergenerational transfer of wealth and resources'. In M. Moos, D. Pfeiffer and T. Vinodrai (Eds.), *The Millennial City: Trends, Implications, and Prospects for Urban Planning and Policy*. London: Routledge.
Zeiderman, A., et al., 2015. Uncertainty and urban life. *Public Culture*, 27 (2 (76)), 281–304.

Language, gender and crisis: An interview with Katherine Gibson

Katherine Gibson and Sonya Marie Scott

In this interview, Katherine Gibson discusses the complexity of the relationship between language, economic crisis, and gender. The interview questions draw on Gibson's notion of 'language politics' as well as concepts relating to gender and crisis in both J.K. Gibson-Graham's *The End of Capitalism (As We Knew It): A feminist critique of political economy* (1996), and J.K. Gibson-Graham, Jenny Cameron, and Stephen Healy's *Take Back the Economy: An ethical guide for transforming our communities* (2013).

For the purposes of this issue, the interview is divided into two sections. In the first section, we deal with the epistemological difficulty in determining what 'the economy' might be, and how its theoretical constitution relates to a gendered discourse. Gibson goes beyond the discussion of the economy as a contained yet malleable sphere found in *The End of Capitalism* and also addresses the construction of the financial economy as the 'authentic' economy within capitalocentric discourse. Just as a feminist exploration of phallocentric narrative practices reveals the use of the masculine as the standard by which to measure all else, a linguistic analysis of capitalocentrism allows us to see the way in which the financial economy is posited as the 'real' economy, with alternatives and other formulations being conceptualized as subordinate. The analysis of economic crises, therefore, is particularly interesting, as it runs the risk of being recuperated by a capitalocentric analysis which shows that crisis is simply an aberration of the dominant, stable and organic economy. Thus the language of crisis – if it folds into one coherent crisis narrative – has the potential to de-mobilize those concerned with economic justice, or to feed into authoritarian reactions or the logic of austerity.

In the second section, Gibson asks the poignant question: 'Is crisis part of a narrative that continually reconstructs the durability of this notion of a capitalist economic system, and to what extent can it be used to prize open spaces of opportunity and spaces for action?' As such the latter part of the interview engages with the pragmatic and popular text *Take Back the Economy*, both in terms of the language used to write the text, and the nature of reclaiming the authority to understand and participate in economic activity. We explore terms like 'economy,' 'community' and 'class' as processes, always under construction, always seeking to consider 'our interdependence with each other, with our future, and with future others.'

Section one: epistemology, language and economy

SS: Let's begin with some of the ideas from *The End of Capitalism (As We Knew It): A Feminist Critique of Political Economy*, especially picking up on the idea that capitalism serves to limit our conception of the possible, always constraining us, and then move later into the ideas about community and possibility as they emerge in your more recent work *Take Back the Economy.*

One of the guiding themes for this colloquium is the way in which language relates to economic crises. Of course, in order to take up such a theme, language has to be conceptualized in a broad manner as it can manifest itself in a multiplicity of ways. Language might be the vocalization of resistance. Language might be the codified rights granted to corporations and transnational capital as part of a more general program of austerity. Language might be austerity itself and the policy regime that attempts to write the wrongs of a volatile economy and exacerbated levels of debt. But language could also be seen through creative acts, such as recovered enterprises, political movements attempting to reframe economic debate, land recovery movements wresting property from foreign interests, or community projects including things as local as garden sustainability, to name just a few possibilities.

And so I would like to start our conversation tonight *before* the point of crisis. And, of course, going back before the point of crisis when we're talking about capitalism or capitalist economies involves going to a fictional point, because crises always accompany capitalism. Nonetheless, I'm going to proceed *as if*. I'd like therefore to begin by asking you about the relationship between language and the very constitution of this thing we call 'the economy' in the first place. In many ways, it's in this relationship that I've understood the feminist project in your earlier work in *The End of Capitalism*. So, in a general sense what would you say is the relationship between language and the way we constitute 'the economy'?

KG: What's been central to our work, is what we call a 'language politics.' For those who maybe haven't thought about language before, you might think that language just represents reality somehow. That it's just the best way of representing what's out there in the world. Now, that kind of vision is based on a kind of realist epistemology, that the thing speaks and we just register the thing in language. And our work started in that way. We started thinking: well, capitalism is the best way of registering what an economy is, and the way in which economics had documented these things was the real. And with the shift towards a more poststructuralist epistemology we started to question this relationship between reality and representation. We started to realize that representations in language, for instance, or in framings like calculative framings – like national income and product accounts – actually shape the ways we understand reality and therefore they affect how we act. So, there is a way in which language itself performs the reality that we operate within.

Now, that's not to say that we can just speak another world and suddenly the world is there. When we were first making this argument way back in the 1990s, everyone was very upset with this idea. A geographer at that time challenged us to walk through the wall in the conference room we were sitting in, since we could just kind of 'think the world away' with language. Clearly, we weren't saying that. But we were saying that the way we conceptualize an economy and the way we give meaning to it as something like a sphere that is separate from other parts of the world, other parts of social life, something that's somehow separate from ecological processes, was itself a kind of theoretical construction, and that the language we used was helping to make certain things more real and certain other things less real. Or, as someone like Boaventura de Sousa Santos working on the Global South is saying, it makes certain things 'credible' and other things 'non-credible'. So if you start to attend to language, you can see the kind of ways in which we conceptualize an economy and then act within it – seeing certain kinds of market dynamics as more important and more influential in driving economic change than other dynamics like class or power dynamics, that come out of other kinds of political formations. Why is it that we focus on certain relationships and dynamics and not others?

So this relationship between language and economy was, for us then, up for grabs. And the reason for this was that the language we'd been tutored and trained in, which was a language of Marxian political economy, seemed to be not allowing us to think outside, not allowing us to consider other kinds of ways of building a world. We were theorizing globalization and the internationalization of capital, and we felt that if we could just nail it, if we could just somehow understand every process, somehow that would lead us toward thinking beyond it. And then we realized that, actually, that wasn't happening, that all we were doing as academics or as scholars was describing more and more of this thing that we were wanting to try and get away from.

Of course, language is powerful and it had many powerful interventions in the past. And the kind of language that political economy and Marxian political economy developed had its own power in the time in which it was developed. But we felt that in the time we were working in, its power was being lost – and it's not that its power was lost totally, but its ability to help us think about other kinds of economic organization, other kinds of worlds, was being diminished. So that's why we set ourselves a project of developing a different kind of language of economy amongst other things and also a different politics of the subject and politics of collective action.

SS: In the introduction to *The End of Capitalism* you critique a series of common narratives, narratives which present capitalism as an absolute and hegemonic force, narratives which render capitalism central to any way of imagining economics otherwise. Capitalism, in this sense, is ever-present, ever-looming. As an example, you present the narrative that, "Capitalism's visage is plastic and malleable, its trajectory protean and inventive. It undergoes periodic crises and emerges regenerated in novel manifestations (thus Fordism is succeeded by post-Fordism, organized by disorganized capitalism, competitive by monopoly or global capitalism)" (9). So when I re-read this recently, I wondered, could we add to this rather contained image of capitalism, given the impact of the global financial crisis, that the productive economy has been replaced by the financialized or speculative economy, as many current explanatory modes articulate? In other words, can we now imagine the financial economy as part of the same malleable capitalism that you described in *The End of Capitalism*?

KG: Yes, I think that's a plausible hypothesis. What we're really talking about here are representations of the economy. And certainly, this makes sense if we think about the way the economy is talked about and how that has shifted and changed, say, in the last forty years. I mean, in my lifetime, I remember when there was nothing on the evening news that was called "financial news." But now, we have the news bulletin, and then we have a whole business sector where we get told what's happening to this stock exchange and to this market and the other. So the news is about the ways in which financial transactions and movements take place. It's not often about what's going on in terms of production or in terms of commodity production. It's all to do with the movement of money, and how risk is being managed, and how currencies are moving, etc., etc.

So in terms of the ways in which economies are represented to us, I think you could definitely say that the finance sector is now what the economy is, to some extent. And, that's difficult for people to react to, because for those of us who don't have shares or don't play the stock market, the fact that the economy is centered, or appears to be centered in that area means that a lot of people feel as if they are just not part of it. We're not part of that economy. So in a sense, yes, I think that the figure of the financial sector is now the figure of the capitalist economy. A lot of people have problems with that and suggest 'let's get back to the real thing.'

But this again is part of the way in which we have a very blunt language for understanding economic processes and practices. Many of the things going on in the financial sector could be seen just as gambling or scamming, having no relationship to people's material survival, and certainly a place where wealth is being destroyed. But, how do we start talking about it in a way that makes sense? It's not going to be through derivatives or the financialization of everyday life, important as an analysis of that is. I think there is a way in which the notion of capitalism gets morphed in every era to include everything, as opposed to us developing a much more specific language, to try to actually track some of these processes that are emerging and what they mean for survival, for wealth distribution, and for environmental relationships.

SS: In *The End of Capitalism* you describe the gendered component of the language of industrial production. And I've been thinking about the ways that gendered narratives or conceptions might work in the way that financial capitalism is represented.

KG: There are a number of ways to think about what a gender perspective enables with respect to 'the economy'. To back track a little bit, one thing is to see how central a feminist approach to thinking about the economy has been to our analysis. Consider the idea of capitalocentrism, the idea that all economic activity is measured against the norm of capitalism or capitalist economic practice. That analysis, that kind of framing, is definitely coming straight from a feminist perspective, where, poststructuralist feminists talked about what they called phallocentrism, the way in which woman was only ever to be found in relationship to man. Woman is always a negativity in relation to the positivity associated with the figure of the male or the man, and she can only ever be a subordinate to, or in a complementary relationship – but there is always this master signifier of the male figure or the man figure.

In the economy, there's this idea that capitalism is the real economy and everything else is somehow subordinate to it. So that is the feminist perspective that we brought into political economy, and which made us more attuned to the gendered nature of all sorts of narratives around economies, such as, only productive workers were the real workers in an economy, and people in the home were just kind of doing support work—capitalist 'reproduction'. It wasn't really where the dynamics of an economy were located. We could start to do that analysis on the financial sector, on stock market floors and derivatives trading and so on, because it is an extremely male sector.

People like geographer Linda McDowell have looked at this kind of thing. The dynamics of working in the financial sector are very much centred around aggressiveness, competitiveness, and being on a work schedule that is inconsistent with the kind of work-life balance that women would like, or are forced to have, because of the relations of care and so on. So it's a masculinist narrative – you know – who's going to win? Risk-taking and all this kind of language go along with being a successful financial investor. And where this analysis gets you, I'm not one hundred percent sure. But I think it's worth noting, though I'm more interested in a kind of more consensual feminist approach that asks us to think about why we continue to set up these binarisms and how they stand in the way of starting to think about finance and investment in a different way.

Let's take the financial out of a purely financial sphere and put it into other ways in which we invest in futures, invest in people and so on, through all sorts of mechanisms, some of which take the form of money and some of which take the form of employment equity, and so on. I think that there is a whole field to be developed there.

SS: Can you expand upon how you envision this field of possible futures?

KG: In *Take Back the Economy* (2013), we proposed a focus on investment in the broadest sense and a move away from a preoccupation with monetized finance. We pointed to people taking back the economy by mobilizing funds and human effort, investing in futures for the next generation and for the planet. Tools like crowd funding or social bonds, or policies like a Basic Income Grant, are helping to marshal this kind of investment. At the same time, people are bound into bearing the risks of mainstream financial markets through, for example, mortgages, education loans, and pension funds. These instruments are supposed to be helping secure survival and a future, but are increasingly creating a form of debt bondage. There is a need to establish mechanisms for saving and borrowing, smoothing over periods of scarcity and abundance, that serve human and planetary interests and are immune from the short term, high risk casino mentality that dominates the financial world. Only when we step back and ask ourselves 'what is finance for?' can we start to reframe it and our relationship to it.

SS: Within the discourse of crisis-analysis, or public economic discourse more generally, highly technical language often serves to exclude people at the same time that it establishes a certain authority for economists or commentators and for the parameters of truth that he or she may wish to describe. The context of the last financial crisis and its aftermath has really highlighted this for me. Authority taken, and explanations given, on the basis of a certain literacy, and ability to deploy a special and specialized, language. So, language, in such cases, may serve an exclusionary function. Do you think that, along these lines, economic crises might serve to help us see ruptures in what you have described as the definitional closure of capitalism? Do you think that crisis could serve as an opportunity to think the economy otherwise?

KG: Well, that's an interesting question. There are a number of different, and not necessarily consistent, responses to that. To some extent the idea of crisis comes out of an organic conception of the economy, where the economy goes along and reproduces itself. And suddenly it's tripped up by some sort of crisis that arises, in the Marxian political economy view through some sort of internal contradiction that produces crisis. And then, the crisis gives impetus to innovate, and this is a mixture of Keynesian vision and the Marxian vision. There are ways in which our ever-inventive entrepreneur will find a way around the crisis, and then establish a modified system, put the organism on a new plane and re-establish a different set of reproductive dynamics. So, if we stay within that kind of paradigm, crisis just becomes the impetus for a different kind of malleability. And so in this sense I don't think it becomes something that ruptures that vision of the economy. It stays within the same vision. And, we're still talking about representations here, so how do we want to define crisis and talk about crisis, and where do we want to locate it? Do we want to locate it as a *discursive entity*, or as something *actually happening*? This is the real problematic.

In some ways, I feel like we're suffering crisis fatigue at the moment, in our society. We have the climate change crisis, we have the obesity crisis, we have the housing crisis, we have the budget crisis, we have the financial crisis, and everything simply becomes a crisis, you know? One of the problems with that language is that it demobilizes any kind of response that people feel, it becomes too big, and people can't relate. So, to some extent, the notion of the language of crisis is, I think, perhaps standing in the way of the kind of productive ruptures or revelations of the incoherence that we might need in order to become more politically active, or active in a whole range of ways. To what extent is crisis part of a narrative that actually continually reconstructs the durability of the notion of a capitalist economic system? And, conversely, to what extent can crisis be used to prize open spaces of opportunity and spaces for action? I think this is the question.

Economic crisis, as it has been defined by the financial gurus, is just one thing. But we could start talking about how crisis focuses attention on one thing and not another. This is problematic because if we said it's a financial crisis, we think of all those poor investors who are losing their stock value. But why don't we talk about a crisis of wealth distribution in our society? When do we ever hear about the crisis of wealth equality and distribution? People talk about the obesity crisis, but when do we ever talk about a kind of liveability crisis in our world? So whatever it gets tied to before, the crisis suddenly gets elevated as *the* thing. That's where the crisis is located, when often I think we need to step back and say, 'What is going on here? Who's suffering? How are they suffering and what is that related to?'

I've been thinking about this question and I don't see a simple answer. I got rid of the language of crisis when I moved away from that kind of classic political economy framing, because if you start to think of the diverse economy as the radical heterogeneity of economic practices, we can't fold everything into one crisis narrative. We have to look at lots of different things happening at any time, including things that are really bad, which are absolute crises for individuals, or regions or places. The problem with the crisis narrative is that it becomes *too narrative*. It becomes then, too easy to just keep rolling it out and never getting at the responsibility to do this other work of fine-tuned mapping of what's happening in different ways.

On your other point, I think that a crisis narrative feeds into a kind of authoritarianism that is prevalent in our society at the moment, that there are certain people who are experts, and can tell you how the world is. And because of the crisis, we 'need' these strong and punitive and powerful leaders who will lead us away from crisis, who will manage our world for us. We're hearing that around the budget crisis in Australia. And the austerity argument is the same kind of thing: 'this is a crisis, therefore we need this kind of strong management.' Obviously, that kind of authoritarianism probably has a lot to do with how Mr. Trump is riding high in the US and so on. So I think we need to be very careful about these kinds of things, and question their political possibility.

SS: I was going to ask you some questions about what the economic object, as a representation, might look like today given the many crises we've seen. You have named some of them. I had other ideas, like major defaults like we saw in countries like Turkey and Argentina in the early 2000s; the food crisis of 2005-6, which is largely ignored today when we think of crisis; the global financial crisis beginning in 2007, and which is still being played out; and the current crisis in the Euro Zone. I was wondering, given these crises, what does the economic object look like today? Has it been ruptured or recuperated?

Thinking of my own research, I have found that often theories of crises and economic crisis themselves precede theories of equilibrium, which is a sort of theoretical (and likely political) desire to smooth notions of a conflictual economy into harmonious systems. What do you imagine the epistemological consequences the prominence of crisis in the popular imagination might be?

KG: About the economic object, I do think that there is a crisis in economic discourse, in university economic departments, for instance, at the moment. And the teaching of economics and the whole heterodox economics movement, which is something that graduate students have led by saying 'this kind of economics training that we're getting is just not speaking to what we're experiencing.' The way in which economic theory and economic discourse is so confined to particular schools of thought is really stopping us from developing our skills and from being able to understand things differently, this sort of autistic economic analysis, you know.

I think that in some senses you're right, that the object being set up in economics departments is still very much informed by a kind of neoclassical economics under crisis. And, that's the kind of economic thinking that's going into more and more esoteric game theory, in part to understand what's going on in the financial sector. It's getting further and further away from pressing concerns that graduate students and other people are experiencing. So I do believe that there is a crisis in economic theory. If I want to use the crisis argument, I don't think it's destabilizing many economic departments because of the way power is distributed. Clearly, most economic departments that taught pure economics are quite diminished these days in the face of business schools, which are where most economic day-to-day understanding is being promulgated. And again, it's very much in a kind of entrepreneurial form. But, you know, there are other minor streams, like forms of ecological economics which are questionable in terms of where they're getting us. In terms of academic thinking, there's a lot going on. It's not necessarily producing well-supported economic theorizing, which it could be doing if it were to have an analysis of power dynamics. Timothy Mitchell's work on tracing the relationship between certain kinds of think tanks and certain kinds of power groups and so on starts to prize open the ways in which we can see that what is taught in universities is very much a product of a certain kind of political assemblage, really. Ultimately, the end supports a particular vision that's true, but that vision is increasingly under crisis in many ways.

SS: One might attempt to work against the totalizing conception of 'the economy' or against capitalocentrism by recalling the Polyanian framework,[1] where the economic is always already embedded in the social, even though capitalism appears to be total by its recuperation of pre-capitalist or extra-capitalist forms into its fold. In this sense, despite all of the dangers of the capitalocentric discourse, and perhaps the problems with the way in which crisis points us back to 'fixing' and 'normalizing' a naturalized and singular 'economy,' could crisis not also provide a crack in what appears to be a totality, just large enough so that a conjuncture, or confluence, of previous experiences and current crises, open other radical possibilities within the social economy? Such as Worker Recuperated Enterprises in Argentina, for example, along with a whole host of other innovative forms of the social economy and social organizing?

KG: With respect to the Polyanian argument I would agree, of course, that human economies are situated and embedded within social relations. The project that I'm part of is trying to develop a language that can itself have its own power of defining how we see the world. So it's definitely in conversation with Polyanian work and has benefitted from it. So, yes, perhaps we can see the question of crisis opening things up, or peeling away layers, even potentially peeling away promises such as the American dream. The promise that everyone can get ahead, that you just have to work hard, and you'll be able to make it too, just like Donald Trump, or someone else like him.

These crises definitely peel away that narrative, the narrative that worked pretty well throughout the golden age, even through the oil crisis of the seventies and beyond, where people kept saying 'Yeah, well, you know, it's okay. It's not communism, and it's probably good because we'll still get a piece of the pie if we keep working hard.' That's kind of gone now. So, then, crisis does open up opportunities in terms of subjectivities because there need to be these alternative places to turn to, to feel like one has a role in society. And that's where I think that these alternatives that are pre-existing, already there, can come to the fore. But I wouldn't like to leave building alternative worlds and new worlds totally up to crisis, to the impetus it generates.

SS: With respect to the idea of developing a new language of economics, it might be useful to turn to *A Postcapitalist Politics*. There, you argue, the experiment with a new language of economics was necessary because the hegemonic totality of 'the economy' subsumes our imaginations, our capacity to consider life outside of 'the real' of its bounds. It also hinders our capacity to consider the very possibility of actively managing or shaping 'the economy' in the first place. Thus the capitalist economy, in this way, is often represented as "*extradiscursive*, as the ultimate real and natural form of economy" (2006, p. 55). Taking from Laclau and Mouffe (1985) you have suggested that a counter-hegemonic project involves both opening up to the notion of diverse and dispersed economies, and promoting a 'collective disidentification' with capitalism. This is so important because "we have come to accept that 'the economy' establishes the bottom line for action and 'it' makes us perform in certain ways. This ideological fantasy has become safe, even enjoyable, directing and limiting politics to certain channels, blinding us without realizing it to the possibility of other options." (*A Post-capitalist Politics* 2006, pp. 55–56)

I find this counterhegemonic move extremely appealing, especially as the power of this narrative of 'the economy' (whom our policymakers and governments appear destined to serve) continues to dominate popular discourse. At the same time, however, with the current contestation of 'truth' and the very possibility of truth claims that is dominating US politics, and politics in many other countries where the media is not generally serving to critically engage with political and economic activity but rather to play sides in a larger ideological battle, I think it is pressing also to turn our gaze back at this so-called 'economy' in order to wrench it open, in order to break with its naturalizing claims, its dominance and capacity to effect real and material crisis on a whole host of citizens.

The question is political – we know that this epistemological construction of an economy as such is, at best, deeply flawed, and at worst, as you have suggested over the course of decades now, responsible for the curtailment of public engagement and the capacity to see our lives otherwise. But we also know that the disavowal of many systemic truths about the nature and effects of capitalism (in favour of alternative truths, a new relativism bolstered by the extradiscursive universality of the market) may serve to worsen and deepen its collateral damage.

So, it seems that the question of the 'real' presents us with a contemporary double-bind. On the one hand, we are wary and suspect of this economic object that has served as a social pacifier, or as an epistemological field of containment. And on the other hand, we must tarry with its construction and those who deploy it as a legitimation of their very real actions and structural forms of redistributions (such as the latest round of intensive tax cuts to the wealthy in the US, for example). It seems that moments of crisis then, if the latter were a compelling political call, could serve in some way to undermine the legitimacy of this economic narrative. In this case, I wonder if it would bring what was extradiscurve back into a struggle over discursive meaning and accounts of lived realities, truths, and the potential for action?

KG: I think we have to be careful to distinguish between the kinds of empirical data that can be scientifically marshalled to describe trends that are occurring, and the ideological claims about the 'realities' of causation or indeed 'systemic truths'. On one hand, we have the kinds of data series that Picketty has put together to illustrate the topography of inequality occurring over the last 100 years, or the data series compiled by Will Steffan and colleagues that track the 'great acceleration' of forms of environmental degradation alongside indicators of economic growth over the last 200 years. These data are compiled with full documentation of sources, modes of estimation and data gaps, and we are invited into the process by which their plausibility is established. How data is interpreted in terms of primary and secondary causes, systemic dynamics and future trends is influenced by a complex array of factors that render the resultant 'theories' forms of discursive intervention in world-making. Of course the data has been collected and categorized according to certain theories as well, so there is a some circularity to this movement between the extra-discursive and discursive. It is important to be aware of how we are performing the world through the analyses we create and adhere to. I am always keen to ask of any theory—what is its implications for action? Does it expand the openings for intervention or close them down? Is it a strong theory that lines everything up? Or is it a humble theory that accepts uncertainty and yet still brings to light some interesting connections or a framing that can be worked with?

SS: Economic discourse and popular narratives about 'the economy' are currently pressing, but as you have mentioned, so too are the narratives provided by mainstream economics rooted in the neoclassical tradition. How do you think we can deal with economics today? While I understand that it is often preferable, and necessary, to step away and change the object of critique – to focus on experiments, social movements and possibilities that in fact engender this idea of diverse economies – contemporary power dynamics still put those practicing mainstream (or in some cases mainstream-friendly heterodox ideas) in positions with considerably more power, authority, and political influence. And this has a real impact on our lives. For those fighting in the trenches against this way of thinking, what strategies do you have in order to open up the transformative capacities of economic thought?

KG: I think I may have somewhat answered this question in my previous response, but I will go a little further into method and motivation. To open up the transformative capacities of economic thought, it is important to open up the transformative capacities of the researcher and thinker. One must become a subject of transformation and not an enforcer of inherited rules and values. First, it is helpful to cultivate the capacity to observe closely and read against the grain. Here the practice of 'reading for difference' has been very important to our project of building ethically oriented community economies. This allows us to 'start where you are' with what is at hand to build other worlds. Reading for difference brings to light multiple 'more than capitalist' economic relations. Once identified they can be theorized within their complex constituting assemblages. Here the interdependence of economic relations with all other aspects of life is foregrounded and openings for tinkering and intervening can be theorized. The kind of economic thought that will support this work is anti-essentialist and open to a variety of dynamic forces. Its charter must be to create new narratives of economy that point to a different way of living in the world together (with other humans and earth others).

Section two: taking back the economy

SS: Your more recent book, *Take Back the Economy*, is co-authored with Jenny Cameron and Stephen Healy. I find the approach that you take in this book quite interesting, and radically different from the theoretically dense work in *The End of Capitalism*. I think some of the ideas from the section called "Take Back Finance" could be helpful to our discussion of crisis. In a book which deals with a rather radical refiguring of economic life, by reframing the economy, taking back work, thinking about the way we live differently, taking back business, the market and property, in many ways, I think this section on finance is the most ambitious. You say in this chapter: "The global financial crisis [GFC] is an ongoing event in which the gamblers began to go bust at the same time. International investors from Iceland to India exchanged their savings for fractions of thousands of US mortgages, only to have their fortunes dashed as the subprime mortgage market crashed. [...] Now in its fifth year, the GFC is not going away. A lucky few have made a killing. But many institutions in the corporate and public finance sectors have been badly damaged or destroyed. Communities and nations are suffering, and the life chances of current and future generations have been put at risk" (161).

As a 'way out' or a moment to 'take back' the economy, many alternatives are discussed, including the *Caja Laboral* in Spain (part of the Mondragon cooperative), the Kerala region of India, and the Norwegian Government Petroleum Fund. All three are surviving with varying degrees of prosperity amidst their own conditions of contradiction. These contradictions are often used by others as a way of criticizing these alternatives, or of reasserting capitalism's power to colonize or appropriate new forms of economic behaviour. So if we look at microfinance, for example, we can find a lot of work criticizing it as being something easily co-opted by larger forms of capitalist finance. But I imagine you would not agree with such a conceptualization. So how did these particular examples, which are born of and fraught with contradiction, allow us to think the economy and capitalism otherwise? Or, in other words, is there something about the contradiction that helps us think economic activities outside of capitalism?

KG: I'd like to say that the book is in the format that it is, so that a popular audience could possibly read it. Many non-academics have read this book, I know. There are two things behind this. One thing that we talked about in *A Postcapitalist Politics*, which is the book that came out ten years after *The End of Capitalism*, was a kind of ethics of thinking. How do we think about the world? And what are the kinds of stances one can take as someone who's interested and concerned about futures, for instance? And we juxtaposed this very critical stance, a stance which has been associated with critical scholarship, with what we call a reparative stance.

A reparative stance is more curious, more open, more exploratory. And we argued that the critical sensibility sees everything in terms of what it's not achieving, or how it's falling down on this particular issue, or 'that might be good, but only for these people and not for the rest.' So the way that we've been taught in academic training to home in on contradictions, on the problems, that's what 'good scholarship' is. You have to always have a skeptical relationship with that which is being argued. We said instead: 'Well, it's actually one of our problems, that we're not using our thinking powers to make connections, to think about how people might have taken one step forward, but could take another if they started thinking about x or y.'

This is an ethics of thinking that actually works with the world that tries to offer a more reparative and less judgmental kind of stance. So we really argued strongly for that in the *Post Capitalist Politics* and tried to present our action research mobilizing that kind of approach. And in a way, in *Take Back the Economy*, we've taken that on again, that kind of approach to the world. The idea was to write a book specifically that would have a popular audience, that would reframe things like work and business and finance and property as something that you actually had a relationship with, but that that relationship could be brought back to something quite simple, like how do we actually survive well?

Why are we working? Why do we spend our lives working to earn money in order to live? And are there other ways of living and combining the different kinds of labor, including caring labor and volunteering, and unpaid as well as wage labor, you know? Are there ways of relating to property other than private property?

So we tried to reframe economies in terms of things that matter to people – you know, surviving well. How do we encounter others that are producing goods and services at a distance? Those in the Global South producing our smartphones? How do we relate to these distant others? How do we relate to Earth Others where resources are being extracted and we're not replenishing and maintaining environments? Asking these ethical questions is a way of reframing markets and transactions. How do we think about business as a context in which wealth is generated? And how is that wealth distributed? What are the different ways that we can enact business so that there is more surplus distribution to those who produce it and those communities that support those that produce it, and so on?

So the idea was to take all the theoretical insights that we've developed and put them into a kind of everyday language and everyday issues and concerns, and then think through what it means. The other side of the book is to document examples of where something is being done that's interesting in terms of building more ethical economies. The examples that are being cited are not presented as utopian solutions, but rather as places where people are undergoing some kind of experimentation with interacting with each other in a more ethical way. And clearly, people can critique those examples because 'well, it might be ethical to the Basque people to have worker cooperatives where everyone can enjoy them, and if there's a technological change, those people will be supported with a wage while a new kind of technology is being introduced. But what about the people on the other side of the country that aren't part of that?' So there are ways in which the critical sensibility likes to come back and say: 'Yeah, that project is good. But you haven't thought about why,' or 'This person, or this group, isn't a part of it.' So what we tried to do in those examples is show who is part of the ethical community that's being constructed, who is being included in this ethical negotiation. And clearly, some people are not being included. What is it that's happening, and what are the ways in which these experiments are trying to expand to include those who were previously outside? And I think, for example, in the case of Mondragon, we can look at the many ways in which that is happening. But what's important there, is that there's a form of democratic ownership and cooperation, and development of cooperative subjects that is very interesting and quite different from what's happening in lots of places in the world.

In the terms of Kerala,[2] what we have is a society, a province that over many, many, many years, not just since the communists got the power in the 1950s, has placed a strong emphasis on women's education, on literacy. So investment has come into these kinds of non-economic processes and it's had an incredible effect in terms of social justice. Of course, you know, it has also produced an educated population who emigrate because they think they can get more money elsewhere.

So there are a lot of criticisms of careless economic development because of the ways in which its economic growth is not mirroring its social justice growth. But I'm interested in exploring why we're so focused on growth, in a society where we've got the great acceleration producing these environmental problems, where growth has to be re-thought.

The Norway case is an interesting one of a sovereign wealth fund.[3] Of course, it's based on fossil fuels, so it's very flawed, but it's an attempt to take a finite resource, socialize it to some extent, and put that into renewable investments, into renewable resources. So what's interesting there is that transition from, yes, something that's creating the problem, to a society deciding to set up a wealth fund. You know, in Australia we've been mining coal for centuries and we're still the largest coal exporter. Have we ever set up a sovereign wealth fund that's trying to do something with that non-renewable resource, to generate a future? No. Norway has done that. We've got something we can learn from that.

So my feeling is that all of these cases are experiments. We can try and identify what they're doing that's of an interesting nature in terms of building ethical economies. We shouldn't expect that they are fully doing everything that we'd like to see, but we can use our powers of analysis to try and see what kind of assemblages are being marshalled here, what kind of effects they're producing, where might they be strengthened, and where we can start to join in that conversation that is traveling along with these experiments, not being 'duped' by them.

But when we bring up criticism, we are not doing it in a way to pull them down or to show 'well, there's nothing that can be done,' which I think is some of the effect of the more critical scholarship on these well-known examples. But of course, the book includes many other examples that are less well-known and that are much smaller or even larger but aren't as well written-up. And they are offered as forms of inspiration for different kinds of strategies. They are all written up to try to highlight the strategy we think is interesting in terms of building what we call a more ethically oriented economy.

SS: The focus on experimentation is certainly very powerful. To add to this, then, I'd like to address the question of 'community' in this piece. How do you conceptualize the notion of community, which seems to me to be central to creating resistance to crisis, to suffering, to many of the challenges we face?

KG: Well, community is a very difficult concept because different societies attach different meanings to the term. And in the Anglo world, it has often been linked to this very cloying sense of people who share a particular identity or a place, and therefore have some bond that's almost unquestioned. And, you know, many people have pointed out that the term is very central to fascism, for instance, just as it's used in all sorts of different political strategies. But where we employ the term, we try to reframe it again and build on the work of Jean Luc Nancy, a French social theorist, who really just starts with the basic point that we are all born into a social world, we're all born into a community of beings that are sharing a planet, are sharing a common world.

And part of living in that world is to construct relationships that will support us. So, for us, the notion of community is that it is a process. It's a process of living together and of living well. And the notion of a community for us, recently, has been extended, of course, to include the Earth Others that we are also in a community with. So it's not necessarily just a human community. It's all the others with whom we are interdependent in order to live. Now, that can be a global community – the paper that we've written most recently (Gibson-Graham *et al.* 2016) is about the attempts we have taken as a world community – as beings in common on this planet – to try and manage and take responsibility for our atmospheric commons and the failures of that and the attempts and successes of that.

Community helps us bring the sense of an economy back to the notion that it is really how we negotiate our interdependence with each other, with Earth others, with our future, with future others, and so on. And so, really, it's trying to make these terms into process, economy into process, community into process, class into process.

As with any language, it works in some contexts more easily than others. And in the francophone world, I'm not sure about Quebec, but certainly in France, the term community is associated with a very particular kind of politics and it doesn't work well in translations. In other contexts, it's linked to different kinds of words. And these are the challenges for people who are translating *Take Back the Economy* have in trying to link it and define it in a way that people can feel it is not raising all those other worries they have, you know, about community equals this or certain kinds of collectivity or a certain kind of sameness, that is, ethnic sameness and so on. But it's one of those issues around the politics of language that has to be continually re-examined. For us, it's a way of putting forward a particular vision. And clearly, other people have got other ways of naming other economies, whether it's the social economy, the solidarity economy, the *buen vivir* economy. There are many different terms at the moment that appear to be getting at a similar kind of thing.

SS: One of the things that I noticed when I was reading this book was that it was refreshingly free of jargon, of overly economistic language, which is really wonderful. And I noticed that there is also a certain kind of implicit feminism, especially in the discussion of the nature of work. But there's no explicitly feminist discourse in this book. Is this a strategic decision that you made?

KG: Well, yes, as you said, the book is very much in everyday language, so it isn't pushing particular discourses or theories, and yet it is informed by very particular discourses and theories. I would say that feminism is very much in there. I think a kind of ecological sensibility or an environment humanities kind of perspective or discourse is informing the book. There is also an attempt to employ a post-development or post-colonial approach. I don't think that it is well developed, but that sensibility is behind the ways in which things are presented and examples are drawn, and so on. So it's not explicit because we wanted to create a new common sense.

That's partly what the book is about. It's trying to say that gender equality is part of the new common sense. Of course, gender equality is being challenged in a lot of places but in a way it is common sense. And so let's not draw the attention of the reader to a new political strategy so much as show that the values of gender equality are already here. And trying to talk about these things in ways that make them seem common-sensical is a strategy of helping people, to start to identify and feel affected by other species and other ecologies, helping people already be affected by things like work–life balance, and daycare, and so on.

SS: Going back to the idea of community, what is your understanding of the relationship between community and class? How can we understand community as a process and as a way of negotiating, even creating, a particular economic vision, while at the same time relating this to the language of class which is prevalent in Marxist language or political-economy analysis?

KG: One of our first theoretical moves away from a kind of mainstream political economy was to move to what we called an anti-essentialist analysis of class. So we wanted to separate out class from, or really pare class down to, being just a process of production, appropriation and distribution of surplus in many different forms. What this does is separate class as a process from the more static notions of status or power that are often conflated with class, or put into this notion of the middle class, and the working class or the elite class and the ruling class and all these kinds of things. So, the language of class is very inflected by many different kinds of analysis really, and, I think, that because of this it has lost its use in many ways.

There are ways in which I think class theory in this sense is not helping us to understand the realities of many people's lives because the kind of consumption and status relationships and class can be mitigated by the fact that you are still in a very precarious position of being exploited in a workplace, or could be losing your job, and so on. So, I think if we pared back class to being a series of process relationships around the production, appropriation and distribution of surplus over which are laid many other issues of ability such as consumption practices, power practices, political practices, and so on, we can start to unpack some of the processes that are actually going on.

Why is it that Trump is being supported across the board in terms of certain types of very wealthy people, and certain kinds of very poor people? And yet in the old kind of vision of class you had working class interests and ruling class or middle-class interests that were clearly defined or aligned? These things are all breaking down now. So when we look at class as a process, I think it opens up a lot of different issues. People can occupy multiple class positions. What does that mean for relating to women who are working in the home and working in workplaces and working in their communities all in different kinds of relationships of social reproduction, production, and distribution and so on?

So, how that relates to community is, I think, a really interesting thing because if we go back to saying community is how we negotiate to be in common, its politics are that it is a negotiation between different kinds of class processes. Between, for example, the kinds of ways that we might try and share labor and households in a gender equitable way to produce a kind of communist household, you might say, rather than a feudal one where women are being exploited by the husband. How does that intersect with working in a workplace where you might be in a managerial position where you're being asked to work sixteen hours a day in the derivative sector, for instance, in order to be a part of the process that's actually making decisions about the distribution of profits and being rewarded for the role in that process even though you're not an owner in any kind of way. So, I think it's complexifying to look at these things as a set of processes. I think it can potentially lead to new kinds of political alliances that have been prohibited up until now.

Notes

1. This refers to a question posed from the floor during the colloquium by Marcelo Vieta (see his article earlier in this special issue).
2. See Chapter 6 of *Take Back the Economy*: "The southern Indian state of Kerala presents an amazing example of long-term investment in improving well being for all. Kerala is a state of thirty-three million people with a mixed population that is 60 percent Hindu, 20 percent Muslim, and 20 percent Christian. Although it is poor by standard measures of per capita cash income, the population is rich by other measures. [...] Since the state of Kerala was formed in 1956, state governments, many of them communist led, have prioritized land reform, food security, health and education. [...] Since the late 1950s a much higher proportion of state government expenditure has consistently been spent on education in Kerala than in all the other Indian states" (2013, pp. 168–169).
3. "In 1990 a sovereign wealth fund, the Government Petroleum Fund, was established to receive oil and gas revenues. In 2006, it was split in two, with the Government Pension Fund Global receiving 95 percent of the petroleum revenues. Currently this fund has holdings of US $513 billion and is the second largest investment fund owned by a government. Clear principles of transparency are followed to ensure that the people of Norway are informed about their investment. Importantly, no more than 4 percent of the fund can be spent in the annual budget. The rest is invested overseas and managed so that it can be drawn on in the future" (p. 171).

Disclosure statement

No potential conflict of interest was reported by the authors.

References

Gibson-Graham, J.K., 1996. *The end of capitalism (as we knew it)*. Malden, MA: Blackwell.

Gibson-Graham, J.K., 2006. *A postcapitalist politics*. Minneapolis, MN: University of Minnesota Press.

Gibson-Graham, J.K., Cameron, J., and Healy, S., 2013. *Take back the economy: An ethical guide for transforming our communities*. Minneapolis, MN: University of Minnesota Press.

Gibson-Graham, J.K., Cameron, J., and Healy, S., 2016. Commoning as a post-capitalist politics. *In*: A. Amin and P. Howell, eds. *Releasing the commons*. London and New York: Routledge Press. pp. 192–212.

Laclau, E. and Mouffe, C., 1985. Hegemony and socialist strategy: Towards a radical democratic politics. New York: Verso.

Index

Note: Numbers followed by 'n' refer to notes and those in **bold** refer to tables.

abstract labour 71
aggressive electoral strategy 63
Almeyra, Guillermo 69, 70, 83
American Task Force Argentina (ATFA) 41, 46n11
Antentas, J. M. 58
Argentine: assets 42–3; debt and global debt relations 4; geopolitical contextualization 37; labor movement 6; labour movement 76; military dictatorship 32; ordinary citizens 45; perfect storm 39; post-vulture 45; secondary markets 39
Arrese, A. 14
asalto institucional (institutional assault) 60
asset price Keynesianism 52
Audebrand, L. 73
austerity: authoritarian reactions 98; contemporary 38; European neoliberal 6; neoliberal 75; neoliberal measures 60; neoliberal programme 86n2; programs 1
authoritarianism 7, 64, 75, 102
autogestión 6, 69–71, 75–7, 83–6; cooperation in labour process 80–2; learning language 83–5; self-valorization of living labour 78–80; socialization of surpluses and wealth 82–3
Azzellini, D. 78

bachilleratos populares 82
bailout 2; euroarea funds 60
Bakunin, M. 84
banking policy 19
bankrupt 6, 15–18, **23**, 26, 37, 43, 62, 64, 76, 79
Bauman, Z. 94
Berlant, L. 94–5
Billiet, John 42
bond-holders 4, 32, 38–45, 41
bond payments 38, 42, 44
Bonefeld, W. 72
Bookchin, Murray 62
Brenner, Robert 52
Burgueño, Carlos 41–3

Canada: decision-making 94; Hedging 94; long-term thinking 94; millennials 92–3; precarity 92, 94–5; uncertainty 94
Capape, J. 65n4
capitalism 1, 5–6; economic practice 6; global 100; monopoly 100; political economy 77; predatory 38; speculative 37; vulture 37–8
capitalocentrism 6–7, 70–1, 101
Casino Capitalism (Sinn) 12
casino economy 11, 26n5
Chandler, D. 5
Circles *Podemos* 61
Cline, William 39
clock pendulum **23**
commercial earthquake 11, **21**, 26n5
commercial storm **18**
commodity **23**, 71
complex debt strategy 37
compound pendulum **24**
Conceptual Metaphor Theory 14
concrete labour 72
constant oscillations 21
contagion disease **14**
cooperation/cooperativism 76; in labour process 6, 80–2, 85
Corporate Aftershock: The Public Policy Lessons from the Collapse of Enron (Culp and Niskanen) 12
credit crunch 26n4
credit-driven real estate crisis 52
crisis fatigue 2, 102

debt renegotiation 38, 43
debt repayment 41
Delahaye, B. 84
democratization 54, 65n4
desahucios 52, 58
Digital Phoenix: Why the Information Economy Collapsed and How It Will Rise Again (Abramson) 12–13
dispossession 4, 31–6, 45, 62

economic breakdown 26n4, 75
economic collapse 26n4
economic disease 11
economic insecurity 91
economic recovery strategy 39
economic storms 17–19

empresas recuperadas 6, 70; emergence of Argentina's 74–7
The End of Capitalism (As We Knew It) (Gibson) 7
escapement mechanism 16, 21
Ettlinger, N. 94
European neoliberal austerity 6

Fabian, Ann 1
Fairclough, Norman 2
Faye, Jean-Pierre 2
feedback mechanism **23**
Fernandes, T. 54–5
Fernández Savater, Amador 56
15-M cycle 61, 64
finance overload 2
Financial Alchemy in Crisis (Nesvetailova) 13
financial circulatory system 42
financial collapse 26n4
financial contagion 11, **14**, 26n5
Financial Contagion; The Viral Threat to the Wealth of Nations (Kolb) 13
financial cyclone **18**, 26n5
financial explosion 11, 26n5
financial meltdown 11, **14**
financial melt-down 26n5
financial storm 11, **14**, 26n5
Flesher-Fominaya, Cristina 60
fluctuations 21, **22**
Foley, G. 84
Foreign Sovereign Immunity Act (FSIA) 36, 43
Foreign Sovereign Immunity Law 36
fraudulent internal policies 37
frictionless pendulum 21

Gallego, M. 65n4
gambling **14**, **21**
Gershon, I. 93, 98
Gibson-Graham, J. K. 6, 7
global proliferation 2
Gramsci, A. 84
Griesa ruling 41–2
Guzman, Martin 40

Hall, S. M. 93
hipótesis Podemos 64
Holborow, Marnie 5
holdout creditors 38, 40
House Committee on Financial Services 39
human-faced economic system 73
hyperbolic comets 17

illegitimate regimes 32
impulse-excited mechanism **23**
institutional assault 59–63
International Monetary Fund 31, 36

Jossa, B. 84
Juliá, Santos 65n4

Kornetis, K. 53–4, 57

labour-managed firms 84
Laing, Samuel 9
language politics 7, 98, 99
large-scale privatization 46n4
Lasusa, Mike 46n11
legal scholars 30
Ley Mordaza 70
Llopis, M. A. O. 13
López, A. M. R. 13
Lopez, I. 52
Lozano, Arribas 59

macro-economic policies 49
Marcuse, P. 84
market liberalism 5
Martín, Irene 61
mathematical pendulum 21
McNally, D. 71–4
mental health **14**
mental illness **21**
metaphors of crises: economic storms 17–19; oscillatory movements 19–22; structure 13–17; timeline 11–13; worldviews 22–5
Michalowki, Sabine 37, 38–9
Millar, K. M. 92–5
modernization 36
municipalism 7, 50–1, 59–64
mutual indebtedness **20**

narrating crises 3–5
narrative economy 2
natural disaster 14
Neilson, B. 93
neoliberal adjustments 7
neoliberal austerity 75
neoliberal crisis 74–7
neoliberalism 6
neoliberal reform 5, 58
New South Wales Law Reform Commission 35
non-democratic regimes 38

oscillations **22**; *see also* pendulum
Owen, R. 84

The Panic of 1907: Lessons Learned from the Market's Perfect Storm (Bruner and Carr) *13*
Panic: The Story of Modern Financial Insanity (Lewis) 13
Pateman, C. 84
pendulum: clock **23**; commerce 19–22; compound **24**; cycles **23**; escapement mechanism 16; fluctuations approach **22**; frictionless 21; metaphors storms 4; movement 16; properties 17
Pereyra, Victor Abel 36
periodical comets 17
phallocentrism 101
Plan Argentina Trabaja scheme 86n3

Podemos 7, 59–63, 61, 63; Circles 61; *hipótesis* 64; hypothesis 63; movement-party 50; *Unidos* 63
precarity/precaritization 92, 94–5; economic insecurity 4
pre-Civil War federal republicanism 62
predatory capitalism 38, 46n6
predatory strategy of litigation 45
privatization of pensions 36
Proudhon, P. -J. 84

real estate sector 65n3
recuperation 77–8; economic strategy 42; prefigurations of ERT 72
recurrent crises 18–19, **20**, **21**
Reid, J. 5
remunicipalization 63
resilience 5
Rodriguez, E. 53, 63
Rossiter, N. 93
Rothschild, J. 84

Schön, D. A. 4
Schugurensky, D. 84
secular movement **24**
self-management 6, 57, 73–4, 76, 78–9, 85
self-precarization 93, 95
self-valorization of living labour 6, 71–2, 78–80, 85
Sennett, R. 79
Singer, Paul 32, 43, 46n1
Sitrin, M. 78
socialization 71, 77, 82–3
Spain: asset-price Keynesianism 52; democracy 58; economic and political crises 5, 50; 15-M cycle 6; institutional assault 7; institutional movements 3; language in old institutions 63–4; municipalism 59–63; *Podemos* 59–63; social movements 59
Spanish Criminal Code 60
Stein, G. 65n4
Stiglitz, Joseph 40
The Subprime Virus (Engel and McCoy) 13
sudden storm **18**
supersecular movement **24**

Take Back Finance 106
tariffs 19, 21
temporary exploitation 94
Terkel, S. 92
Thierry, Agustin 2
Thompson, T. P. 75–6
Thorkelson, E. 92
Timmerman, Hector 43
transition itself (CT) 55

unconstitutional regimes 32
Unidos Podemos 63
unionism 76
unnatural prosperity 21

Vara-Miguel, A. 14
Vieta, Marcelo 6
Vigueras, Hernandez 37
Vilarós, T. 54
vulture capitalists 38
vulture funds 4, 30–1
vulture strategy 4, 31, 35, 42

The Wall Street Takeover and the Next Financial Meltdown (Johnson and Kwak) 12
wave of depression 11, **21**, 26n5